A HISTORY
OF THE MISHNAIC LAW
OF APPOINTED TIMES

PART THREE

STUDIES IN JUDAISM IN LATE ANTIQUITY

EDITED BY

JACOB NEUSNER

VOLUME THIRTY-FOUR

A HISTORY
OF THE MISHNAIC LAW
OF APPOINTED TIMES

PART THREE

A HISTORY OF THE MISHNAIC LAW OF APPOINTED TIMES

BY

JACOB NEUSNER

University Professor
The Ungerleider Distinguished Scholar of Judaic Studies
Brown University

PART THREE

SHEQALIM, YOMA, SUKKAH

TRANSLATION AND EXPLANATION

Wipf & Stock
PUBLISHERS
Eugene, Oregon

Wipf and Stock Publishers
199 W 8th Ave, Suite 3
Eugene, OR 97401

A History of the Mishnaic Law of Appointed Times, Part 3
Sheqalim, Yoma, Sukkah: Translation and Explanation
By Neusner, Jacob
Copyright©1982 by Neusner, Jacob
ISBN 13: 978-1-55635-362-8
ISBN 10: 1-55635-362-6
Publication date 3/20/2007
Previously published by E. J. Brill, 1982

In memory of
Rabbi Aaron H. Blumenthal

February 7, 1908　　　　　　　　　　　　　　June 13, 1982

TABLE OF CONTENTS

Preface IX
Abbreviations and Bibliography XVII
Transliterations XXV

SHEQALIM

    I. Introduction to Sheqalim 3
   II. Sheqalim Chapter One 8
  III. Sheqalim Chapter Two 16
  IV. Sheqalim Chapter Three 23
   V. Sheqalim Chapter Four 28
  VI. Sheqalim Chapter Five 37
 VII. Sheqalim Chapter Six 41
VIII. Sheqalim Chapter Seven 48
  IX. Sheqalim Chapter Eight 53

YOMA

    X. Introduction to Yoma 63
  XI. Yoma Chapter One 70
 XII. Yoma Chapter Two 76
XIII. Yoma Chapter Three 81
XIV. Yoma Chapter Four 92
 XV. Yoma Chapter Five 96
XVI. Yoma Chapter Six 105
XVII. Yoma Chapter Seven 112
XVIII. Yoma Chapter Eight 116

SUKKAH

  XIX. Introduction to Sukkah 127
   XX. Sukkah Chapter One 132
  XXI. Sukkah Chapter Two 140
 XXII. Sukkah Chapter Three 148

XXIII. Sukkah Chapter Four 156
XXIV. Sukkah Chapter Five 166

Appendix: Corrections to Jacob Neusner, *Invitation to the Talmud*,
by Richard S. Sarason
Hebrew Union College-Jewish Institute of Religion 176

Index 181

PREFACE

The character of this translation and explanation in detail expresses the purpose of the larger work of which it is part. To present *a history of the Mishnaic law*, I have to give an account of the document itself, first of all to state what I believe Mishnah says, in a rendition, in English, as close to the formal and syntactical character of the Hebrew as English permits. This I do in the translation, which itself is a commentary in its word-choices and patterns and in its version of the division of sentences into stichs, of paragraphs into sentences, and of chapters into paragraphs. (But this last depends, for the convenience of the reader, on the printed text of Ḥanokh Albeck.) The translation makes no important contribution to the explanation of realia or the identification of various places, persons, and things, mentioned in the document. What it does contribute is the first translation of a rabbinic document to take full and faithful account of the rigidly formalized, public and anonymous character of Mishnaic language. I provide complete form-analytical translation of Mishnah and of Tosefta. The *explanation* is rather different from any of its predecessors, so different that it must be called "explanation." For if what have been done in the past are called commentaries, this cannot be represented as a commentary at all.

What I explain is what I believe requires attention. It follows that what I do not say invariably is more important than what I choose to discuss. By radically revising and abbreviating the established exegetical agendum, I believe I have made my richest contribution to the interpretation of Mishnah. This is in two aspects.

First, I have tried to force Mishnah to serve as its own commentary. I do so by relying heavily upon those formal and even substantive traits of the document which serve to provide a clear account of Mishnah's meaning and message. I pay careful attention to matters of form and formulation. We shall see time and again that principally through setting up a contrast, or placing of a phrase for emphasis, or other obvious linguistic and syntactical modes of highlighting its meaning, Mishnah serves as its own first, and therefore best, commentary.

Second, I have revised what I believe to be the definition of those issues appropriate to, and even acceptable for, exegesis of Mishnah in particular, as a singular document of its period. This last point requires some amplification. There are two sides to the problem of explaining what Mishnah means. Both of them are generated by one absolutely false conception, or, more accurately, misleading analogy.

The first problem is the bringing to Mishnah of issues clearly extraneous to its original meaning. This set of comments plainly is needless because the issues are generated by later problems and questions. They are quite naturally addressed to Mishnah, however, by people who assume Mishnah speaks to them and therefore must address issues of importance to them. This ahistorical approach is possibly valid for the generating and unfolding of law. But it is not correct for the interpretation of what Mishnah as a concrete document meant to the particular people who made it up.

The second problem is corollary, namely, the placing of Mishnah's materials into the context of a whole legal system. When Mishnah is read in a larger framework than Mishnah, we are prevented from seeing Mishnah's materials as a coherent corpus on their own. This latter approach to Mishnah is absolutely opposite to our purpose. For I propose to state, and, later, historically to account for the unfolding of, the law of Mishnah *in particular*. If we assume that Mishnah constitutes a single document—and the harmonious internally formal and intellectual traits of Mishnah require that we make that assumption—then we have no choice but to honor the limits of the document when attempting to describe and interpret it.

Until now all commentators to Mishnah have taken only a limited interest in the shape and structure of Mishnah itself. It goes without saying, none has asked a historical-exegetical question ("What does this mean to the person who originally said it *and* who did not know what his successors would want to say about it?") to begin with. The exegetes before me asked a wholly other range of questions. For their problem was a different one. It was dictated by a social and intellectual task quite separate from ours. They addressed themselves not to the exegesis and expression (let alone the world-view) of a given document. Nor could they imagine the notion that the laws in their hands formed discrete units of information. Quite the contrary, they began with what their society gave them: the conception of a completely unitary legal system, expressed to be sure, in discrete documents originating in diverse places and time, but nonetheless all together forming a timeless, seamless conceptual structure. Their task was defined by this rather platonic metaphor, namely, to relate each of the parts to the transcendent whole, and to force the whole to encompass all of the parts. It is not, as I originally thought, the ahistorical (or, anti-historical) and harmonistic purpose of the earlier exegetes which made their Mishnah-commentaries so intellectually prolix, indeed, indifferent and irrelevant to the text under discussion. That is a misunderstanding which it has taken me many years to recognize.

It is, rather, that the earlier exegetes presuppose something much more profound, much less susceptible to articulation. This is, as I said, the construct, "Jewish law," or "*halakhah*." Of this construct, to them Mishnah constitutes an important component. In their mind the correct approach to Mishnah's interpretation is to relate its *halakhah* to other *halakhah*, that is, to "*the* law." This harmonistic, atomistic and yet encompassing approach is natural for people who keep the law and who take for granted their audience wants to know *the* law, even though not all of the law of a given document is practical and practiced. But the point of interest is clear, and it explains to them what is relevant and what is not. Since social context and intellectual framework define what is relevant, their essays—to us, total chaos—to them are orderly and reliable. But the fact remains that in a different world, their language of exegesis is gibberish, just as is ours to them.

When we realize this fact, we understand why it is that the distinctive, documentary character of Mishnah itself has attracted so little interest. Mishnah as such has failed to define the boundaries of appropriate exegesis. The definitive canon awaiting explanation and extension is "the *halakhah*." That is to say, Mishnah is part of that other canon. The canon awaiting interpretation is shaped by Mishnah, only in so far as Mishnah presents its share of legal statements—*the* law. Consequently Mishnah is read not from whole to part, as a sequence of divisions, tractates, and chapters. This I am the first to do, as the formal character of my work makes clear. And this is the right way to approach the document. But by others Mishnah has been and is read essentially as a mass of individual sentences, tens of thousands of bits of legal information, all of them part of, and arrayed against, a larger construct, *the* law, and each of them to be placed into juxtaposition with other bits and pieces of *the* law. So, as I said, the notion of "the *halakhah*" obliterates the character of Mishnah as an autonomous document and at best allows Mishnah the status of an authoritative *source* of law.

The same treatment, of course, is accorded to Tosefta, the two Talmuds, the diverse legal exegetical compilations, Sifra and Sifré, for example, and to much else. The result is that at each point exegetes tend to tell us "everything about everything," so to speak. It is not because they are confused, even though the results are confusing. For despite the fact that their commentaries appear to be not merely allusive, but irrelevant to the text at hand, and even though they are rich in unprovoked questions, artificial dilemmas, and invented solutions, the reason is that the fundamental theory of the document requires precisely those procedures which are followed. If, to take a current and choice example, Saul Lieberman's *Tosefta Ki-Fshutah* ("a comprehensive commentary to the Tosefta") treats Tosefta as an excuse for long disquisitions on diverse philological and legal questions, the obvious reason is that that is precisely how Lieberman thinks the work should be done. And the reason, I believe, is not merely the ahistorical character of the mind-set of the traditionalist, but, as indicated, because of the more profound conviction as to the character of the law and its diverse documentary expressions.

The result of this approach to the study of earlier rabbinic writings to date has been an account of immense philological and legal value. We are able to explain a great deal about the meaning and intention of the sentences of the law, as found (as it happens) in Mishnah and Tosefta (and the rest of rabbinical literature). We can link together diverse conceptions and rules appearing here, there, everywhere; they are formed into a single fabric, even (in the monumental codes of the law) a seamless one. We have what is besought, which is the power to draw upon, and apply to specific circumstances, the whole wisdom and weight of the law. That is to say, the established exegetical program has succeeded in doing precisely what it set out to do. The tasks originally defined by the conception of *"the* law" have been carried out.

The one thing we cannot say on the basis of the available commentaries, both "traditional" and "scientific" (both are wildly inappropriate terms!) is to state clearly what it is that Mishnah (to take our example) wishes to say, in *its* own setting, within the limits of *its* own redactional framework, upon the subjects chosen by *it*, and for purposes defined within the mind of those specific people, its authors, who flourished in one concrete social setting. Reading the document by itself, in its historical context and therefore outside of its atemporal and larger *halakhic* context, requires a different approach. That approach is represented, I firmly believe, in the pages of this book. It is given by this explanation.

So the need for these volumes of translation and explanation is dictated not solely by the concluding, systemic description and interpretation. That was my conception for *Holy Things* and *Women*, and, in retrospect, I think I was altogether too apologetic. Nor is the issue of the work solely the *historical*—primary, original—meaning of the text in the minds of the people who so phrased their ideas and arranged their sentences as to give us these, and not some other, expressions of their ideas. The decisive and determinative issues are simply, What is the Mishnah? What is its shape and structure? What is the agendum of its law? How is that agendum to be delineated and interpreted as a complete and exhaustive account of what Mishnah wishes to say? These questions are answered in this book and its fellows.

The answers I give here are to these questions, not to those many others already dealt with, with greater or less measure of success, in the established and received exegetical tradition. People who want to know what "the tradition" has to say are not apt to open these books and stay on to study them in any event. Other sorts of readers will find their way to these pages. I do not think they will find the methods and suppositions alien or the results unsatisfying. I began this project weighed down by humility before the intellectual achievements of others who have studied these same problems. I conclude it with greater understanding, and not less appreciation, of their work. But at the same time I see much more clearly that, so far as they claim to speak about Mishnah, they have not done what they promised. So far as I claim to present and briefly to explain what it is that Mishnah, in *its* limits, for *its* purposes, to *its* chosen audience, wishes to say, I do what I claim to do.

That fact accounts for the traits of the translation and the character of the explanation—its brevity, severe limitation of the exegetical agendum, and above all, its insistence upon Mishnah's form and formulary expression as definitive of Mishnah's meaning. This is not meant to excuse or apologize. I have worked on Mishnah since 1972, and the last of these books is apt to appear not much before 1984. Twelve years are a long time to devote to a single document, however complex, when one's interest is in only a limited aspect of said document. For, when all is said and done, my real interest remains focused upon the history and structure of nascent rabbinic

Judaism. That means the main work is yet before me, not behind. These twelve years and forty-two books of mine, not to mention many more years of work and many books of my several doctoral students, all are meant only to prepare the way for a different sort of analysis entirely. This is an approach to Mishnah which is at once more historical, more religious-philosophical, and more religious-historical than has even been attempted. I do not know whether it will succeed.

It remains to thank a few among the many to whom much is owed. First of all, I owe thanks to the John Simon Guggenheim Memorial Foundation for awarding to me yet a second Guggenheim Fellowship for 1979-1980 to facilitate completion of my *History of the Mishnaic Law of Appointed Times* and *History of the Mishnaic Law of Damages*. This recognition of the interest of the scholarly world in the results of my work is much appreciated. It also is important to me. At the same time I owe thanks to Brown University for an extraordinary research leave, 1980-1981, awarded in the same connection.

Second, I wish to thank Brown University for paying the costs of typing these manuscripts. Provost Maurice Glicksman and Associate Dean Frank Durand received without complaint a shower of typists' bills. In an age of exceedingly painful budgetary choices, they loyally and generously paid my typists and did so promptly and courteously. This everyday and humble expression of their belief in the worth of my project is just as precious to me as those research fellowships and honorary doctorates which have come my way.

Third, I should be remiss if I did not mention by name the junior colleagues who in my graduate seminar read their work and heard about mine, the graduate students of the period in which this part of the project was coming to completion: Leonard Gordon, Peter Haas, Martin Jaffee, and Alan Peck; and my former colleague, Richard Samuel Sarason, now at Hebrew Union College-Jewish Institute of Religion, Cincinnati. Since the work of all of these as well as of some of my former students is an integral part of this project, they in due course will make their own contributions as well.

Fourth, my colleagues in the Department of Religious Studies have provided a constructive and helpful framework for my teaching and scholarship. I must single out Professors Wendell S. Dietrich and Ernest S. Frerichs with thanks not only for exemplary collegiality but for friendship and love.

Finally, after all these years, I have to mention and take note of the enthusiastic support of my children, Samuel Aaron, Eli Ephraim, Noam Mordecai Menahem, and Margalit Leah Berakhah, who were infants when the work began, and who approach maturity as it ends. I never hoped they would read these books, but I should want them to be proud of knowing that, when I was doing the work, they charmed and cheered my life. 1 could not have done this work without them— nor should I have wanted to. Let a veil of silence be drawn before the next, the best, for only silence can contain all that is felt, all that words cannot say, in homage to Suzanne Richter Neusner.

J.N.

Providence, Rhode Island
May 2, 1979.
5 Iyyar, 5739.
Shalom 'al Yisra'el.

ABBREVIATIONS AND BIBLIOGRAPHY

Abrahams	= I. Abrahams, *Hagigah. Translated into English with Notes, Glossary and Indices* (London, 1948).
Abrahams, *ERE*	= I. Abrahams, "Sabbath," *Encyclopaedia of Religion and Ethics X* (New York, 1928), p. 891-93.
Adler	= L. Adler, *Religion der geheiligten Zeit. Die biblischen Festzeiten und das Judentum* (München, Basel, 1967).
AE	= *Tosafot* R. ʿAqiba Egger. From Mishnah, ed. Romm.
Ah.	= ʾAhilot
Albeck	= Ḥanokh Albeck, *Shishah sidré mishnah. Seder Moed* (Tel Aviv, 1952).
Alexander	= Samuel Alexander, *Space, Time and Deity* (London, 1920).
Andreasen	= N. E. Andreasen, "Festival and Freedom: A Study of an Old Testament Theme," *Interpretation* 1974, 28:281-97.
Andreasen, *Sabbath*	= Niels-Erik A. Andreasen, *The Old Testament Sabbath, a Tradition—Historical Investigation* (Missoula, Mont., 1972).
Ar.	= ʿArakhin
Auerbach	= E. Auerbach, "Die Feste im alten Israel," *Vetus Testamentum* 1948, 8:1-18.
A.Z.	= ʿAbodah Zarah
B.	= Babylonian Talmud
B.B.	= Babaʾ Batraʾ
B.M.	= Babaʾ Meṣiʿaʾ
B.Q.	= Babaʾ Qammaʾ
Barthelemy	= D. Barthelemy and J. T. Milik, "The Oration of Moses," *Qumran Cave I* 1955.
Beckwith	= R. T. Beckwith, "The Day, its divisions and its limits, in biblical thought," *Evangelical Quarterly* 1971, 43:218-27.
Ber.	= Berakhot
Berger	= Isaiah Berger, ed., Analytical Index to *The Jewish Quarterly Review*, 1889-1908 (N.Y., 1966).
Berlin, 1968	= Charles Berlin, *Harvard University Library. Catalogue of Hebrew Books* (Cambridge, 1968) I-VI.
Berlin, 1972	= *Supplement* (Cambridge, 1972) I-III.
Berlin, 1971	= *Widener Library Shelflist, 39. Judaica* (Cambridge 1971).
Bert.	= ʿObadiah of Bertinoro. From Mishnah, ed. Romm.
Bes.	= Beṣah
Bik.	= Bikkurim
Blackman	= Philip Blackman, *Mishnayoth*. Vol. II. *Order Moed. Pointed Hebrew Text, Introductions, Translation, Notes, Supplement, Appendix, Indexes* (London, 1952).
Bouah	= N. Bouah, "Calendriers Traditionnels et Concept de Temps," *Bulletin d'Information et de Liaison des Instituts d'Ethno-Sociologie et de Geographie tropicale*, 1967, 1:9-26.
Brandon	= S. G. F. Brandon, "The Deification of Time," *Studium Generale* 1970, 23:485-497.

Mrs. Lee Haas served as research assistant for this project and located for the bibliography many items which I should otherwise have missed.

Brandon, *History*	= S. G. F. Brandon, *History, Time and Deity* (New York, 1965).
Brandon, *BJRL*	= S. G. F. Brandon, "Time as God and Devil," *Bulletin of the John Rylands Library* 1964, 47:12-31.
Burgelin	= P. Burgelin, "Sur le passage du sacre au profane," *Diogène* 1961, 33:122-131.
C	= H. Loewe, *The Mishnah of the Palestinian Talmud (Hammishnah ʿal pi ketab-yad Cambridge)* (Jerusalem, 1967).
Callahan	= J. F. Callahan, *Four Views of Time in Ancient Philosophy* (Cambridge, Mass., 1948).
Chroust	= Anton-Hermann Chroust, "The Meaning of Time in the Ancient World," *The New Scholasticism* 1947, 21:1-70.
Clark	= C. H. Clark, "Time in Biblical Faith," *South East Asia Journal of Theology* 1959, 1:37-44.
Damages	= Jacob Neusner, *A History of the Mishnaic Law of Damages* (Leiden, 1981f.) I-IV.
Dauenhauer	= Bernard P. Dauenhauer, "Some Aspects of Language and Time in Ritual Worship," *International Journal for Philosophy of Religion* 1975, 6:54-62.
Dederen	= R. Dederen, "On esteeming one day better than another [Rom. 14:5-6]," *Andrews University Seminary Studies* 1971, 9:16-35.
Dem.	= Demaʾi
Deut.	= Deuteronomy
de Vaux	= Roland de Vaux, *Ancient Israel: Its Life and Institutions* (New York, 1961).
Dillmann	= A. Dillmann, *Über das Kalenderwesen der Israeliten vor dem babylonischen Exil* (Berlin, 1881).
Ed.	= ʿEduyot
EG	= *Hiddushé Eliyyahu Migreiditz*. From Mishnah, ed. Romm (Vilna, 1887).
Ehrlich	= E. L. Ehrlich, *Kultsymbolik im Alten Testament und im nachbiblischen Judentum* (Stuttgart, 1959).
Epstein, *Nusaḥ*	= Y. N. H. Epstein, *Mabo lenusaḥ hammishnah* (Tel Aviv, 1954).
Epstein, *Tan.*	= Y. N. H. Epstein, *Meboʾot lesifrut hattanaʾim. Mishnah, tosefta, ummidrashé halakhah*. Ed. E. Ṣ. Melammed (Tel Aviv, 1957).
Erub.	= ʿErubin
"Festivals"	= "Festivals," *Encyclopaedia Judaica* 6 (Jerusalem, 1971) 1237-1246.
Fox	= Matthew Fox, "Demonic *vs.* Sacred Time in American Culture," *Listening* 1976, 11:175-190.
Freedman, *Pes.*	= H. Freedman, *Pesaḥim. Translated into English with Notes, Glossary and Indices* (London, 1948).
Freedman, *Shab.*	= H. Freedman, *Shabbath. Translated into English with Notes, Glossary and Indices* (London, 1948).
Gardner	= Howard Gardner, *The Quest for Mind. Piaget, Levi-Strauss, and the Structuralist Movement* (N.Y., 1973).
Ginsberg	= M. Ginsberg, *Beẓah. Translated into English with Notes, Glossary and Indices* (London, 1948).
Git.	= Giṭṭin
Goldberg	= Abraham Goldberg, *Commentary to The Mishnah. Shabbat.*

	Critically Edited. And Provided with Introduction, Commentary and Notes (Jerusalem, 1976). In Hebrew.
Goody	= Jack Goody, "Time," *International Encyclopedia of the Social Sciences* 16:30-42.
GRA	= Elijah ben Solomon Zalman ("Elijah Gaon" or "Vilna Gaon"), 1720-1797.
Gurvitch	= Georges Gurvitch, *The Spectrum of Social Time* (Dordrecht, 1964).
HA	= Emanuel Hai Riqi. *Hon 'ashir*. In QMH.
Hag.	= Ḥagigah
Hal.	= Ḥallah
Ḥayyot	= Yiṣḥaq Ḥayyot, *Zeraʿ yiṣḥaq*. Ed. H. Y. L. Deutsch (N.Y., 1960).
HD	= *Ḥasdé David*. David Pardo, *Ḥasdé David*. I. Tosefta Zeraʿim Moʿed, Nashim (Livorno. Repr.: 1976).
Hehn	= Johannes Hehn, *Siebenzahl und Sabbat bei den Babyloniern und im Alten Testament* (Leipzig, 1907).
Heidel	= William Heidel, *The Day of Yahweh; a Study of Sacred Days and Ritual Forms in the Ancient Near East* (N.Y., 1929).
Hodgkins	= William Hodgkins, *Sunday: Christian and Social Significance* (London, 1960).
Holy Things	= Jacob Neusner, *A History of the Mishnaic Law of Holy Things* (Leiden, 1979-1980) I-VI.
Hooke	= S. H. Hooke, *The Origin of Early Semitic Ritual* (N.Y., 1938).
Hor.	= Horayot
Hul.	= Ḥullin
ID	= Nathan Lebam. *Imré daʿat*. In QMH.
James	= E. O. James, *Seasonal Feasts and Festivals* (N.Y., 1961).
Jastrow	= Marcus Jastrow, *A Dictionary of the Targumim, the Talmud Babli, and Yerushalmi, and the Midrashic Literature* (1904, Repr.: N.Y., 1950) I-II.
Jenni	= Ernst Jenni, *Die theologische Begründung des Sabbatgebotes im Alten Testament* (Zollikon-Zürich, 1956).
Jung	= Leo Jung, *Yoma. Translated into English with Notes, Glossary and Indices* (London, 1948).
K	= Georg Beer, *Faksimile-Ausgabe des Mishnacodex Kaufmann A 50* (Repr.: Jerusalem, 1968).
Katsh	= Abraham I. Katsh, *Ginze Mishna. One Hundred and Fifty-Nine Fragments from the Cairo Geniza in the Saltykov-Shchedrin Library in Leningrad Appearing for the First Time with an Introduction, Notes and Variants* (Jerusalem, 1970).
Kel.	= Kelim
Ker.	= Keritot
Kil.	= Kila'yim
Kittel	= R. Kittel, *Geschichte des Volkes Israels I* (Leipzig, 1912).
KM	= *Kesef Mishneh*. Joseph Karo. Commentary to Maimonides, *Mishneh Torah*. Published in Venice, 1574-5 Text used: Standard version of Maimonides, *Mishneh Torah*.
Kornfeld	= Walter Kornfeld, "Der Sabbath im Alten Testament," *Der Tag des Herrn* (Vienna, 1958).

Kutsch	= E. Kutsch, "Sabbath," *Die Religion in Geschichte und Gegenwart*, 3rd Ed., edited by Kurt Galling, *et al.* (Tübingen, 1958) V, 1258-60.
Lazarus	= H. M. Lazarus, *Moʿed Katan. Translated into English with Notes, Glossary and Indices* (London, 1948).
Lieberman	= Saul Lieberman, *The Tosefta. According to Codex Vienna, with variants from Codices Erfurt, London, Genizah MSS, and Editio Princeps (Venice, 1521). Together with References to Parallel Passages in Talmudic Literature. And a Brief Commentary. The Order of Moed* (N.Y., 1962).
Lieberman, *TK*	= Saul Lieberman, *Tosefta-Ki-fshutah. A Comprehensive Commentary on the Tosefta*. Part III. Order Moed. I. *Shabbat-Erubin* (N.Y., 1962). IV. II. *Pesahim-Sukkah* (N.Y., 1962). V. *Besah-Hagigah* (N.Y., 1962). In Hebrew.
Levy, *Wörterbuch*	= Jacob Levy, *Wörterbuch über die Talmudim und Midraschim* (1924. Repr.: Darmstadt, 1963) I-IV.
Long	= Burke O. Long, "Recent Field Studies in Oral Literature and their Bearing on OT Criticism," *Vetus Testamentum* 26:187-198. An important step beyond the arguments in *Pharisees* III, pp. 101-180.
Lowy	= S. Lowy, "The Motivation of Fasting in Talmudic Literature," *Journal of Jewish Studies* 1958, 9:19-38.
M	= *Babylonian Talmud Codex Munich* (95) (Repr.: Jerusalem, 1971).
M.	= Mishnah
Ma.	= Maʿaserot
Maimonides, *Comm.*	= Moses b. Maimon, *Mishnah. Seder Moed.* Trans. by Yosef Kappaḥ (second printing, Jerusalem, 1969).
Maimonides, *Seasons*	= Solomon Gandz and Hyman Klein, trans., *The Code of Maimonides. Book Three. The Book of Seasons* (New Haven and London, 1961).
Mak.	= Makkot
Makh.	= Makhshirin
Martin-Achard	= Martin-Achard, Robert, *Essai Biblique sur les Fêtes d'Israël* (Geneva, 1974).
Martineau	= R. A. S. Martineau, "Creation and the Idea of Time," *Hibbert Journal* 1956, 54:275-80.
Maxson	= W. B. Maxson, *Discussion of the original institution, perpetuity, and change of the weekly Sabbath* (Schenectady, 1836).
Me.	= Meʿilah
Meg.	= Megillah
Meinhold	= Johannes Meinhold, *Sabbat und Sonntag* (Leipzig, 1909).
Meinhold, *Woche*	= Johannes Meinhold, *Sabbat und Woche im Alten Testament* (Göttingen, 1905).
Melammed, *Midrash*	= E. Ṣ. Melammed, *Hayyaḥas sheben midrashé halakhah lammishnah velattosefta* (Jerusalem, 1967).
Melammed, *Talmud*	= E. Ṣ. Melammed, *Pirqé mabo lesifrut hattalmud* (Jerusalem, 1973).
Men.	= Menaḥot
Millgram	= Abraham Millgram, *Sabbath, the Day of Delight* (Philadelphia, 1959).
Miq.	= Miqvaʾot
ML	= *Mishneh Lammelekh*. Commentary to Maimonides, *Mishneh Torah*. Judah Rosannes 1657-1727. For source see KM.

Momigliano	= A. D. Momigliano, "Time in Ancient Historiography," *History and Theory: Beiheft* 1966, 6:1-23.
Morgenstern	= J. Morgenstern, "Sabbath," *Interpreter's Dictionary of the Bible*, V. 4 (N.Y., 1962).
M.Q.	= Mo'ed Qaṭan
MS	= *Mele'khet Shelomo*. Shelomo bar Joshua Adeni, 1567-1625. From Mishnah, ed. Romm.
Mueller	= W. Mueller, "Raum und Zeit in Sprachen und Kalendern Nordamerikas und Alteuropas," *Anthropos* 1973, 68 (1/2):156-180.
Muilenburg	= J. Muilenburg, "Biblical View of Time," *Harvard Theological Review* 1961, 54:225-52.
N	= *Mishnah 'im perush HaRambam. Defus Risho'n Napoli* [5]252 [1492] (Jerusalem, 1970).
Naz.	= Nazir
Ned.	= Nedarim
Neg.	= Nega'im
Nid.	= Niddah
Nilsson	= Martin Nilsson, *Primitive Time-Reckoning* (Lund, 1920).
North	= R. North, "The Derivation of Sabbath," *Biblica* 1955, 36:182-201.
Num.	= Numbers
NS	= Ṣevi Gutmacher, *Naḥalat ṣevi*. In QMH.
Oh.	= 'Ohalot
Ohnuki-Tierney	= Emiko Ohnuki-Tierney, "Concepts of Time Among the Ainu of the Northwest Coast of Sakhalin," *American Anthropologist* 1969, 71:488-92.
Or.	= 'Orlah
Otto	= E. Otto, "Zeitvorstellungen und Zeitrechnung im alten Orient." *Studium Generale* 1966, 19:743-751.
Otto	= Rudolf Otto. *The Idea of the Holy: An Inquiry into the non-Rational Factor in the Idea of the Divine and its Relation to the Rational* (N.Y., 1958).
Ozouf	= M. Ozouf, "Space and Time in the Festivals of the French Revolution," *Comparative Studies in Society and History* 1975, 17:372-84.
P	= *Shishah sidré mishnah. Ketab yad Parma DeRossi 138* (Repr.: Jerusalem, 1970).
Pa	= *Mishnah ketab yad Paris. Paris 398-329* (Repr.: Jerusalem, 1973).
Par.	= Parah
Pedersen	= J. Pedersen, *Israel: Its Life and Culture* (London, 1926-47).
Pes.	= Pesaḥim
Pharisees	= J. Neusner, *The Rabbinic Traditions about the Pharisees before 70* (Leiden, 1971) I-III.
Purities	= J. Neusner, *A History of the Mishnaic Law of Purities*, (Leiden, 1974-1977) I-XXII.
Pieper	= J. Pieper, "Über das Phänomen des Festes," *Zeitschrift für Volkenkunde* 1965, 61:248.
Proctor	= Richard Proctor, *The Great Pyramid: Observatory, Tomb, and Temple* (London, 1883).
QA	= *Qorban Aharon*. Aaron Ibn Ḥayyim (d. 1632), *Qorban Aharon, Perush Lassefer Sifra* (Dessau, 1749).

Qehati	= Pinḥas Qehati, *Seder Moed* (Jerusalem, 1976) I-II.
QH	= Moshe Zakhuta, *Qol haramaz*. In QMH.
QMH	= *Qebuṣat meforshé hammishnah* (Jerusalem, 1962).
QS	= Ḥayyim Sofer, *Qol Sofer*. In QMH.
Rabbinowitz	= J. Rabbinowitz, *Taʿanith. Translated into English with Notes, Glossary and Indices* (London, 1948).
Rabad	= Supercommentary to Maimonides, *Code*.
Rabad, *Sifra*	= R. Abraham ben David, Commentary to Sifra. From *Sifra*, ed. Weiss.
Rappaport	= Ṣevi Hirsch Hakkohen Rappaport, *Torat Kohanim*, with the commentaries *ʿEzrat Kohanim* and *Tosefet HaʿEzrah* (Jerusalem, 1972).
Rau	= Catherine Rau, "Theories of Time in Ancient Philosophy," *Philosophical Review* 1953, 62:514-525.
Reicke	= B. Reicke, "Jahresfeier und Zeitenwende im Judentum und Christentum der Antike," *Theologische Quartalschrift* 1970, 150:321-334.
R.H.	= Rosh Hashanah
Rosenthal	= Ludwig A. Rosenthal, *Die Mischna, Aufbau und Quellenscheidung. Erster Theil: Die Ordnung Seraim. Erste Hälfte: Von Berakhot bis Schebiit* (Strassburg, 1903).
Roth	= S. Roth, "Sanctity and Separation," *Tradition* 1974, 14:29-45.
San.	= Sanhedrin
Schiffman	= Lawrence H. Schiffman, *The Halakhah at Qumran* (Leiden, 1975).
Segal	= J. B. Segal, "Hebrew Festivals and the Calendar." *Journal of Semitic Studies* 1961, 6:74-94.
Segal	= M. H. Segal, *Shekalim. Translated into English with Notes, Glossary and Appendices* (London, 1948).
Sens	= Yaʿaqob David Ilan, ed., *Tosafot Shenṣ* (Bené Beraq, 1973).
Shab.	= Shabbat
Shabu.	= Shabuʿot
Shabbat	= *Le Shabbat dans la Conscience Juive: Données et Textes* (Paris, 1973).
Shalev	= Y. Shalev, "Holy day as an experience of Time," *Judaism* 1956, 5:160-66.
Sheb.	= Shebiʿit
Shebu.	= Shebuʿot
Sheq.	= Sheqalim
SifraFink.	= *Sifra or Torat Kohanim. According to Codex Assemani LXVI.* With a Hebrew Introduction by Louis Finkelstein (N.Y., 1956).
SifraHillel	= *Sifra*. With the Commentary of *Hillel b. R. Eliaqim*. Ed. by Shachne Koleditzky (Jerusalem, 1961).
Sifra ed. Weiss	= *Sifra*, ed. Isaac Hirsch Weiss (Repr.: N.Y., 1947).
SifHillel	= *Sifré ... ʿim Perusah ... Rabbenu Hillel bar Eliaqim*. Ed. Shachne Koleditzky (Jerusalem, 1958).
SifHorovitz	= *Siphré d'Be Rab Fasciculus primus: Siphre ad Numeros adjecto Siphre Zutta*. Ed. H. S. Horovitz (Leipzig, 1917).
SifIshShalom	= *Sifré debe Rab. ʿIm Tosafot Meir ʿAyin*. Ed. Meir IshShalom (Friedman). (Vienna, 1864. Repr.: N.Y., 1948).
SifLieberman	= *Siphre Zutta (The Midrash of Lydda). II. The Talmud of Caesarea* (N.Y., 1968).

SifNesiv	= *Sifre... ʿEmeq HaNeṣiv*. Naftali Ṣevi Yehudah Berlin (Jerusalem, 1960).
SifPardo	= *Sefer Sifre debe Rab*. David Pardo (Salonika, 1799. Repr.: Jerusalem, 1970).
SifVolk	= *Sifre... ʿim hagahot... HaGRA veʿim perush Keter Kehunah*. Ṣevi Hirsch Hakkohen Volk. Ed. Yaʿaqob Hakkohen Volk (Jerusalem, 1954).
SifYasq	= *Sifre Zutta leSeder Bamidbar... ʾAmbuhaʾ deSifre*. Yaʿaqob Zeʾeb Yaskobitz (Lodz, 1929. Repr.: Bené Beraq, 1967) I-II.
Simon, *Meg.*	= Maurice Simon, *Megillah. Translated into English with Notes, Glossary and Indices* (London, 1948).
Simon, *R.H.*	= Maurice Simon, *Rosh Hashanah. Translated into English with Notes, Glossary, and Indices* (London, 1948).
Slotki, *Er.*	= Israel W. Slotki, *ʿErubin. Translated into English with Notes, Glossary, and Indices* (London, 1948).
Slotki, *Suk.*	= Israel W. Slotki, *Sukkah. Translated into English with Notes, Glossary, and Indices* (London, 1948).
Söderblom	= N. Söderblom, "Holiness (General and Primitive)," *Encyclopaedia of Religion and Ethics* VI (N.Y., 1938), pp. 731-741.
Sot.	= Soṭah
Solberg	= Winton Udell Solberg, *Redeem the Time: The Puritan Sabbath in Early America* (Cambridge, Mass., 1977).
Suk.	= Sukkah
T.	= Tosefta
T	= *Sidré Mishnah. Neziqin, Qodoshim, Tohorot. Ketab yad Yerushalayim, 1336. Ketab Yad beniqud lefi massoret Teman.* (Repr.: Jerusalem, 1970). Introduction by S. Morag.
Ta.	= Taʿanit
Tem.	= Temurah
Ter.	= Terumot
Thomas	= Northcote Thomas, "The Week in West Africa," *Journal of the Royal Anthropological Institute of Great Britain and Ireland* 1924, 54:183-209.
Toh.	= Ṭohorot
TR	= Saul Lieberman, *Tosefet Rishonim*. II. *Seder Nashim, Neziqin, Qodoshim* (Jerusalem, 1938).
T.Y.	= Tebul Yom
TYB	= *Tifeʾret Yisraʾel Boʿaz*. See TYY.
TYT	= *Tosafot Yom Tob*. Yom Tob Lipmann Heller, 1579-1654. From reprint of Mishnah, ed. Romm.
TYY	= *Tifeʾret Yisraʾel, Yakhin*. Israel ben Gedaliah Lipschütz, 1782-1860. (With supercommentary of Baruch Isaac Lipschütz = TYB.) From reprint of Mishnah, ed. Rom.
Unknown	= *Mishnah. Sedarim Zeraim, Moed, Nashim. Unknown Edition. Printed in Pisaro or Constantinople.* (Jerusalem, 1970).
Uqs.	= ʿUqṣin
V	= *Talmud Babli. Nidpas ʿal yedé Daniel Bomberg bishenat 5282* [= 1522]. *Venezia*. (Venice, 1522. Repr.: Jerusalem, 1971).
Vat 130	= *Manuscripts of the Babylonian Talmud. From the Collection of the Vatican Library.* (Jerusalem, 1972). Series A.
Vat 112	= *Manuscripts of the Babylonian Talmud. From the Collection of the Vatican Library* (Jerusalem, 1974). Series B.

Vidal-Naquet	= P. Vidal-Naquet, "Temps des dieux et temps des hommes. Essai sur quelques aspects de l'experience temporelle chez les Grecs," *Revue de l'histoire des religions* 1960, 157:55-80.
Von Rad	= G. von Rad, *Old Testament Theology* (N.Y., 1962-65).
Webster	= Hutton Webster, *Rest Days, a Sociological Study* (Lincoln, Neb., 1911).
Webster, *Rest*	= Hutton Webster, *Rest Days, a Study in Early Law and Morality* (N.Y., 1916).
Webster	= Hutton Webster, "Sabbath," *Encyclopaedia of Religion and Ethics* X (N.Y., 1928).
Whitehouse	= Owen C. Whitehouse, "Holiness (Semitic)," *Encyclopaedia of Religion and Ethics* VI (N.Y., 1928), pp. 751-59.
Wolff	= H. W. Wolff, "Concept of Time in the Old Testament," *CTM* 1974, 45:35-42.
Women	= Jacob Neusner, *A History of the Mishnaic Law of Women* (Leiden, 1980f.) I-V.
Y.	= Yerushalmi. Palestinian Talmud.
Y.T.	= Yom Ṭob
Yad.	= Yadayim
Yeivin	= Israel Yeivin, *A Collection of Mishnaic Geniza Fragments with Babylonian Vocalization. With Description of the Manuscripts and Indices* (Jerusalem, 1974).
Yeb.	= Yebamot
Z	= M. S. Zuckermandel, *Tosephta. Based on Erfurt and Vienna Codices* (Repr.: Jerusalem, 1963).
Zab.	= Zabim
Zeb.	= Zebaḥim
Zobel	= Moritz Zobel, *Der Sabbat, sein Abbild im jüdischen schrifttum, seine Geschichte und seine heutige Gestalt* (Berlin, 1935).
ZY	= *Zeraʿyiṣḥaq*. By Yiṣḥaq Ḥayyot (Brooklyn, 1960).

TRANSLITERATIONS

א	=	ʾ	מ ם	=	M
ב	=	B	נ ן	=	N
ג	=	G	ס	=	S
ד	=	D	ע	=	ʿ
ה	=	H	פ ף	=	P
ו	=	W	צ ץ	=	Ṣ
ז	=	Z	ק	=	Q
ח	=	Ḥ	ר	=	R
ט	=	Ṭ	שׁ	=	Š
י	=	Y	שׂ	=	Ś
כ ך	=	K	ת	=	T
ל	=	L			

SHEQALIM

CHAPTER ONE

INTRODUCTION TO SHEQALIM

The subject of this tractate is the collection and disposition of the *sheqel*-tax, which is contributed for the altar by all male adult Israelites. Specifically, through the *sheqel*-tax, a poll-tax, each male pays his tiny share of the public and communal offerings and so gains the benefit of the sacrifices owing from the Israelite community as a whole. These are the daily whole-offerings, the additional offerings for the Sabbath and festivals, and the associated drink- and bread-offerings of various kinds. The theory of the tractate, that through paying the *sheqel* the individual joins himself into the salvific exercise effected by the cult, is made explicit only in Tosefta. But it is implicit throughout.

What interests the framers of the tractate is three rather straightforward subjects, first, the collection of the *sheqel*; second, the disposition thereof for the use of the altar; and third, other aspects of the financial administration of the Temple. For a fair proportion of the tractate there is little more than a narrative, composed in part by description of how things are done, and in part of lists, e.g., of Temple authorities, points of collection of funds, and the like. These generate fairly routine problems, for instance, concerning the disposition of a coin found midway between two collection-chests for funds, one for one purpose, one for some other. This rather characteristic kind of Mishnaic exercise, for its part, does not succeed in endowing the tractate with the intellectual vitality manifestly lacking in its narratives and lists. So on the whole the tractate provides mere information.

Scripture's treatment of the theme is scarcely a great deal more interesting than Mishnah's and contributes no important problems for solution. Ex. 30:11-16 is the principal point of interest:

> The Lord said to Moses, "When you take the census of the people of Israel, then each shall give a ransom for himself to the Lord when you number them, that there be no plague among them when you number them. Each who is numbered in the census shall give this: half a *shekel* according to the *shekel* of the sanctuary (the *shekel* is twenty *gerahs*), half a *shekel* as an offering to the Lord. Every one who

is numbered in the census, from twenty years old and upward, shall give the Lord's offering. The rich shall not give more, and the poor shall not give less, than the half *shekel*, when you give the Lord's offering to make atonement for yourselves. And you shall take the atonement money from the people of Israel, and shall appoint it for the service of the tent of meeting; that it may bring the people of Israel to remembrance before the Lord, so as to make atonement for yourselves."

Then, as the following outline makes clear, Mishnah-tractate Sheqalim picks up where Scripture leaves off, providing that information required for a full account of the matter of collecting and spending the *sheqel*-tax.

I. *Collecting the sheqel.* 1:1-2:5

    A. *The imposition of the obligation to pay.* 1:1-7.

1:1-2   On the first of Adar they announce the collection of the *sheqel*-dues and sowing mixed seeds.

1:3-4   On the fifteenth of Adar they set up money-changers' tables in the provinces, and on the twenty-fifth of Adar, in the Temple. At that point the obligation to pay the *sheqel* falls due, and they exact a pledge from all who are obligated to pay it.

1:4   Priests do not pay the *sheqel*.

1:5   If women, slaves, or minors paid the *sheqel*, it is accepted. If gentiles and Samaritans pay it, it is not accepted for that purpose.

1:6-7   The surcharge, to cover the changing of a coin into the coinage used for the Temple, is owing from Levites, Israelites, proselytes, freed slaves, who are subject to the obligation to pay the *sheqel*, but not from priests, women, slaves, or minors, who are not.

    B. *Transporting the sheqel. Sacrilege.* 2:1-5.

2:1   They change *sheqel*s into larger coinage to transport them. They are collected in the provinces. Liability for loss of the *sheqel* in transit.

2:2   If one misappropriates the *sheqel* given to him to pay to the Temple, if this is before the heave-offering of the *sheqel*s is taken up, the fellow is responsible for an act of sacrilege.

2:3-5   He who collects coins and says, "These are for my *sheqel*"—the House of Shammai say, "The surplus is holy and used for a freewill offering." The House of Hillel say, "It is unconsecrated." The disposition of surplus funds given for diverse particular purposes.

II. *The use of the sheqel for Temple offerings for the altar.* 3:1-4:9.

    A. *Taking up sheqels for the public offerings.* 3:1-4.

3:1   At three times in the year they take up the heave-offering of the coins collected in the *sheqel*-chamber.

3:2-3	They take up the heave-offering of the coins of the *sheqel*-chamber with three baskets, each holding three *seahs*.
3:4	He took up the heave-offering of the *sheqel*s and covered the residue, once, a second, and a third time; the third time he did not cover up the residue.

    B. *Disposition of the sheqels for various offerings.* 4:1-9.

4:1-2	What did they do with the heave-offering of the *sheqel*-chamber? They purchase animals for daily whole-offerings and additional-offerings and the required drink-offerings; wheat for the '*omer*, Two Loaves, and Show Bread, and all other offerings of the community. This covers the Red Cow, the red thread, and the like. Disposition of the residue is for the upkeep of the city of Jerusalem.
4:3	With the surplus of the residue they purchase wine, oil, and fine flour.
4:4	With the surplus of the heave-offering of the *sheqel* itself they buy gold plate to decorate the house of the Holy of Holies.
4:5	The surplus of the frankincense is used for paying Temple craftsmen.
4:6	He who sanctifies his property and included were items suitable for use on the altar—dispute.
4:7-8	He who sanctifies his property and in it were cattle suitable for use on the altar—Eliezer: These items are sold, and the proceeds fall, with the rest of the donation, for the upkeep of the Temple building. Joshua: The animals which are suitable for the altar are used for that purpose, and the rest of the donation serves for the upkeep of the buildings.
4:9	Once every thirty days they fix prices the Temple will pay, from the *sheqel*-chamber, for the flour, wine, and oil required for the altar.

III. *The Temple administration and procedures.* 5:1-8:8.

    A. *The administration.* 5:1-2.

5:1	These are they who are appointed, who were in the sanctuary as officers.
5:2	They appoint no fewer than three revenuers and seven supervisors.

    B. *Procedures for sale of drink-offerings.* 5:3-5.

5:3-5	There were four seals in the Temple, inscribed for the drink-offerings owing with various sacrifices. One would purchase the seal and then deliver it to the one in charge of the drink-offerings, who makes the arrangement for the offerings.

    C. *Collecting other funds in the Temple.* 5:6-6:6.

5:6	Two funds in the Temple, one for gifts made in discretion to the poor, the other for utensils.

6   INTRODUCTION TO SHEQALIM

6:1-3   There were thirteen *shofar*-chests in the Temple, for the collection of funds for various purposes, and thirteen acts of prostration.
6:4   There were thirteen tables in the sanctuary.
6:5-6   Thirteen *shofar*-chests in the sanctuary, for new *sheqel*s, old *sheqel*s, bird-offerings, and so on. Six were for freewill-offerings.

    D.   *Disposing of coins and objects found in the Temple and in Jerusalem.* 7:1-8:3.

7:1   Money which is found between the chest for *sheqel*s and that for freewill-offerings, etc. In general: Assign funds found exactly in-between two different chests for the more stringent purpose of the two.
7:2   Money found before cattle-dealers.
7:3   Meat found in the Temple courtyard and its disposition in accord with its presumed status.
7:4-7   Cattle found between Jerusalem and Migdal-Eder.
8:1   Drops of spit found in Jerusalem.
8:2   Utensils found in Jerusalem near an immersion-pool.
8:3   Knife found on the fourteenth of Nisan assumed to be clean. If found on the thirteenth, it is to be immersed.

    E.   *Miscellanies.* 8:4-8.

8:4-7   If the veil of the Temple contracts uncleanness from an Offspring of uncleanness. . ., from a Father of uncleanness. . . .
8:8   Limbs of the daily whole-offering are set down on the lower half of the altar-ramp on the east; those of additional offerings are set down on the lower half of the ramp at the west; those of offerings for New Months are set down on the rim of the altar. Laws of the *sheqel*-dues and of first fruits apply only in the time of the Temple.

This outline of the contents of the tractate shows that the whole is divided into three units of pretty much equal size. The only exegetically difficult materials are at I.A, particularly at M. 1:6-7. But from the viewpoint of interpreting the order of entries, the whole flows with the usual clear logic. We move from a discussion of when one is obligated to pay and how much is to be paid to the transportation of the funds which are collected to the Temple. The logically-required next question is how the funds are used in the Temple, and at the second unit, we see that this matter is fully spelled out. First comes an interest in the procedure of taking up the *sheqels* for use for the public offerings, and, second, the expenditure of the *sheqels* for various offerings, with attention to the disposition of the surplus funds, left over after the heave-offering of the *sheqel* is taken up.

The final unit is somewhat less compelling in the order of its unfolding of the theme of the administration and procedures of the Temple in general. Indeed, each of the three subunits, administration, procedures for sale of drink-offerings, and collecting other funds in the Temple, seems to me independent of the others. C-D clearly belong together, and perhaps there is a connection to be discerned between M. 8:4-7 and M. 8:3 which will account for the character of that entry. (M. 8:4-7 internally form a very tight construction.) But on the whole the final unit does retain a rather miscellaneous character. III.B could be quite comfortable within unit II, for instance. So in the main we must regard the first and second units as the core and center of the tractate, and the final sequence as essentially an appendix of relevant information. So, in all, Sheqalim intends to report on the collection and disposition of the poll-tax for public support of the Temple.

CHAPTER TWO

SHEQALIM CHAPTER ONE

We begin with a fairly straight-forward account of the collection of the half-*sheqels* in the month of Adar, preparatory to the provision of animals for public or communal offerings from the beginning of Nisan and for the year following, M. 1:1-5. This set of materials bears heavy interpolations, at M. 1:1-2, however, since the interest of the opening pericope is not in collection of the half-*sheqel* in particular but in activities in Adar. M. 1:1, glossed by M. 1:2, announces that on the first of Adar the requirement to pay the half-*sheqel* is announced, and on the fifteenth various other preparations for the coming festival-*season* are undertaken. M. 1:3, glossed by M. 1:4, returns then to the matter of the *sheqel*. On the fifteenth of Adar money-changers set up their tables in the countryside and on the twenty-fifth in the sanctuary, for the convenience of the community. At that point the half-*sheqel* is due. Pledges (amounting to payment in kind) are taken from that time forth. M. 1:5 further glosses M. 1:3.

M. 1:6-7 then go on to a separate matter, the surcharge to be paid along with the half-*sheqel*, to cover the Temple's costs in changing the currency or coinage to that which the Temple uses. The payment of the surcharge is required of those who are legally bound to pay the half-*sheqel*, but not of those who contribute it out of good will.

1:1-2

A. On the first day of Adar they make public announcement concerning [payment of] *sheqel*-dues and concerning the sowing of mixed seeds [Lev. 19:19, Deut. 22:9].
B. On the fifteenth day of the month they read the *Megillah* [Scroll of Esther] in walled cities.
C. And they repair the paths, roads, and immersion-pools.
D. And they carry out all public needs.
E. And they mark off the graves.
F. And they go forth [to inspect the fields] on account of mixed seeds.

M. 1:1

A. Said R. Judah, "In olden times [the agents] would uproot them [mixed seeds] and throw them before the [owner].

B. "When transgressors became many, they would uproot them and throw them into the roads.
C. "They [finally] ordained that they should declare ownerless the entire field [in which mixed seeds had been planted]."

M. 1:2

The *sheqel* is due on the first day of Nisan, so there is public notice of one month. Warning also is given about uprooting mixed seeds. From the first of Nisan offerings are purchased from the funds, which now fall due. The rest of the unit speaks of other events of the same season, five tasks to be done on (or after) the fifteenth of Adar, B-F. If, F, it turns out that a farmer has planted mixed seeds in his vineyard, the punishment is as specified by Judah.

A. On the fifteenth day of [Adar] agents of the court go out and repair the paths and roads [M. 1:1C], which were rutted in the rainy season,
B. a month before the festival [of Passover],
C. toward the time [in which] the festival pilgrims come up,
D. so that they should be repaired for the three festivals.

T. 1:1 L p. 200, ls. 1-3

A. On the fifteenth day of [Adar] agents of the court go forth and dig cisterns, wells, and caves.
B. And they repair immersion-pools [M. 1:1C],
C. and water channel[s].
D. Every immersion-pool which contains forty *seah*s of water is suitable for receiving further [drawn] water [if need be].
E. And to [every immersion pool] which does not contain forty *seah*s of water they lead a water-course and so complete its volume to the measure of forty *seah*s,
F. so that it is suitable for receiving further [drawn] water [if need be].

T. 1:2 L p. 200, ls. 3-6

A. On the fifteenth day of [Adar] agents of the court go forth and declare ownerless fields in which mixed seeds have been planted [M. 1:2C].
B. For that which has been declared ownerless by a court is ownerless and exempt from the requirements of tithing.
C. [If] one located mixed seeds planted in a vineyard, one is both permitted [to remove the plants] in regard to prohibitions against stealing and exempt [also] from the requirements of tithing.
D. [If he found them] in a field, he is prohibited in regard to the prohibition against stealing and liable to tithing.

T. 1:3 L p. 200, ls. 7-9

A. On the fifteenth day of [Adar] agents of the court go out and mark off places in which [corpse-]uncleanness is located [M. 1:1E],

B. so that the public will not stumble thereby.

T. 1:4 L pp. 200-201, ls. 9-11

A. They do not mark [as a place in which corpse-uncleanness is located] on a stone or a fence, but they do mark on a fixed rock.

B. They do not leave the marker at the place of uncleanness but at a place of cleanness, near the uncleanness.

C. But he who overshadows it [the uncleanness] is unclean.

D. [If] one found a stone marked off, even though it is not to be kept in that way [A], he who overshadows it is clean.

E. [If] one found two of them, he who overshadows the area between them is unclean.

F. [He who overshadows] the area on top of them is clean.

G. They do not make a marker by reason of the flesh of a corpse or on the bones of a corpse [which do not constitute the greater part of the body of the deceased],

H. for these do not impart uncleanness through overshadowing.

I. They make a marker by reason of the backbone or skull,

J. for these do impart uncleanness through overshadowing.

T. 1:5 L p. 201, ls. 11-16

The roads are repaired at the end of the rainy season and remain passable through the dry season, T. 1:1. Immersion-pools of requisite volume may receive drawn water to make the water therein clearer or more ample; this too is done at the end of the rainy season, T. 1:2. The rest is clear as given. One marks the clean area near a corpse, not the unclean area occupied by the corpse itself.

1:3-4

A. On the fifteenth of that same month [Adar] they set up money-changers' tables in the provinces.

B. On the twenty-fifth [of Adar] they set them up in the Temple.

C. Once they were set up in the Temple, they began to exact pledges [from those who had not paid the tax in specie].

D. From whom do they exact a pledge?

E. Levites, Israelites, proselytes, and freed slaves,

F. but not from women, slaves, and minors.

G. Any minor in whose behalf the father began to pay the *sheqel* does not again cease [to pay].

H. And they do not exact a pledge from priests,

I. for the sake of peace.

M. 1:3

A. Said R. Judah, "Testified Ben Bukhri in Yabneh: 'Any priest who pays the *sheqel* does not sin.'

B. "Said to him Rabban Yoḥanan ben Zakkai, 'Not so. But any priest who does not pay the *sheqel* sins.

C. "'But the priests expound this Scriptural verse for their own benefit: *And every meal offering of the priest shall be wholly burned, it shall not be eaten* (Lev. 6:23).

D. "'Since the *'omer*, Two Loaves, and Show Bread are ours, how [if we contribute] are they to be eaten?'"

M. 1:4

Discussion of the collection of the *sheqel*-tax for the Temple now resumes, A-C, expanded by D-I, and M. 1:3H-I bear in their wake the appendix of M. 1:4. Money-changers serve to change various coins into the *sheqel* required for the Temple tax. In the Temple the money-changers take a pledge from one who has not yet paid his tax and, in exchange, give the required half-*sheqel*. They are therefore essential for the collection of the tax, which serves through the coming year to provide the offerings in the name of the community.

The priests maintain that, by analogy to the priest's meal offering, any offering paid for, whole or in part, by funds deriving from priests must be wholly burned up. If priests give money for, e.g., offerings which Scripture specifically requires to be eaten, M. 1:4D, then the commandment to eat the offerings, such as those listed at D, is contravened by the priests' providing money for the provision of these same offerings. It follows that priests cannot contribute to the *sheqel*-offering. M. 1:3E, H-I, reflect this opinion. Ben Bukhri's view is that if the priest gives the *sheqel*, it constitutes a gift to the community and no longer is his, so Ben Bukhri's theory accords with that of priests.

A. Once they [*tables of money-changers, set up to collect the Temple-tax*] *were set up in the Temple, they began to exact pledges* [*from those who had not yet paid*] [M. 1:4C].

B. They exact pledges from Israelites for their *sheqel*s, so that the public offerings might be made of their [funds].

C. This is like a man who got a sore on his foot, and the doctor had to force it and cut off his flesh so as to heal him. Thus did the Holy One, blessed be he, exact a pledge from Israelites for the payment of their *sheqel*s, so that the public offerings might be made of their [funds].

D. For public offerings appease and effect atonement between Israel and their father in heaven.

E. Likewise we find of the heave-offering of *sheqel*s which the Israelites paid in the wilderness, as it is said, *And you shall take the atonement money from the people of Israel* [*and shall appoint it for the service* *of the tent of meeting; that it may bring the people of Israel to remembrance before the Lord, so as to make atonement for yourselves*] (Ex. 30:16).

T. 1:6 L pp. 201-202, ls. 16-22

T. explains the purpose of the half-*sheqel* tax and of exacting a pledge to cover it.

1:5

A. Even though they have said [M. 1:3F], "They do not exact pledges from women, slaves, or minors," if they paid the *sheqel*, they do accept it from them.

B. A gentile and a Samaritan who paid the *sheqel*—they do not accept it from them.

C. Nor do they accept from them bird offerings for male *Zabs*, bird offerings for female *Zabs*, bird offerings for women who have given birth, sin-offerings, or guilt-offerings.

D. But [offerings brought by reason of] vows and freewill-offerings they accept from them.

E. This is the governing principle: Anything which is vowed or given as a freewill-offering do they accept from them.

F. Anything which is not vowed or given as a freewill-offering do they not accept from them.

G. And so is the matter explained by Ezra, since it is said, *You have nothing to do with us to build a house unto our God* (Ezra 4:3).

M. 1:5

A-B complete the discussion of M. 1:3. B then bears a sizable appendix, C-G, which bears its own amplification at E-F and proof-text at G.

A. They purchase from gentiles [animals for] public offerings through the payment of funds.

B. "And they accept from them [freewill-offerings of] burnt-offerings, peace-offerings, fowl, meal-offerings, wood, incense, and salt," the words of R. Yosé the Galilean.

C. Said to him R. 'Aqiba, "Even if you stay in session and expound your view all day long, [it will not matter]. They accept from them only a burnt-offering or peace-offerings alone."

D. They do not accept from them a freewill-offering for sanctification for the upkeep of the house.

E. But if they sanctified [something for the upkeep of the house], their act of sanctification is valid.

T. 1:7 L p. 202, ls. 22-26

A complements M. 1:5B. B-C do not seem to be represented in M.'s view.

1:6-7

A. And these are liable to the surcharge:
B. Levites, Israelites, proselytes, and freed slaves,
C. but not priests, women, slaves, or minors.
D. He who pays the *sheqel* in behalf of a priest, woman, slave, or minor, is exempt [from the surcharge].
E. And if he paid the *sheqel* for himself and for his fellow, he is liable for a single surcharge [for himself].
F. R. Meir says, "Two surcharges."
G. He who pays a *sela* and takes back a *sheqel* in change is liable to two surcharges.

M. 1:6

A. He who pays a *sheqel* [as a gift] for a poor man, for his neighbor, or for a fellow townsman, is exempt.
B. But if he lent [the money to them], he is liable.
C. Brothers who are partners who are liable to the surcharge are exempt from tithe of cattle.
D. But when they are liable to tithe of cattle, they are exempt from the surcharge.
E. And how much is the surcharge?
F. "A silver *ma'ah* [= 1/24th of a *sela*]," the words of R. Meir.
G. And sages say, "A half [a silver *ma'ah*]."

M. 1:7

The Temple is owed a half-*sheqel*. But there are costs of changing money to be paid. If someone pays over a *sela* worth two *sheqels* and gets a *sheqel* and a half back, there is a loss in the transaction, accounted for by the fee paid to the money-changer. It follows that there is a surcharge owing from those who are required by law to pay the half-*sheqel*, B. But it is not exacted from those who to begin with are not required by law to pay the half-*sheqel*. This point—that those not obligated by law to pay the half-*sheqel*, but who choose to pay it, do not have to pay the surcharge—then is expanded at D. If someone who is liable to the surcharge pays the half-*sheqel* for someone who is not liable, the former does not have to pay the surcharge. The same point is made at E. If someone paid in his own behalf and also paid in behalf of his friend, he pays only for himself. Meir has the theory that the surcharge is required of anyone who owes the half-*sheqel*. Since the friend is liable to the half-*sheqel*, he also should pay the surcharge. In the present case, the man has paid a single coin for the two. Sages' view is that if the man pays a single coin for the two, he nonetheless has to pay the fee for the money-changer, who will break the coin into the two half-*sheqel*s required.

But sages concur, G, that if one pays over a *sela*, which is four *sheqel*s, and takes back a *sheqel* (E), he has to pay the two surcharges. One is for the *sela* which he paid over to the sanctuary, and one is for the *sheqel* which he took back in change.

M. 1:7A-B make a further point. If the half-*sheqel* is paid as a gift, there is no surcharge, just as we noted at M. 1:6D, E. But if one lends the money, then there is no gift, and of course a surcharge is involved. C-D make yet another secondary point. Partners who paid the *sheqel* together—half for each—are liable to the surcharge (M. 1:6E). Our case involves brothers who have inherited the father's estate and divided it. They then enter partnership. They are liable to the surcharge, if they pay the *sheqel* together, like any other partners. Cattle they divided up and then contributed to the partnership does not have to be tithed by these partners. When the estate has not yet been divided, so that the cattle is subject to the tithe as a single herd, belonging to the father's estate, then the brothers do not have to tithe the cattle. They now are not (yet) partners, and, therefore, if the estate pays their half-*sheqel* for each, they do not have to add the surcharge. They are in the status of the sons of a father who pays in behalf of his children.

The amount of the surcharge, in Meir's opinion, is one twelfth of a *sheqel*, one twenty-fourth of a *sela*; Meir then wants a person to pay a half-*sheqel* and a sixth more. Sages want half this quantity, a half-*sheqel* and a twelfth more.

    A. Trustees who paid a *sheqel* in behalf of [adult] orphans—
    B. lo, they are liable to the surcharge.
    C. "He who pays a *sheqel* is liable to a surcharge," the words of R. Meir.
    D. And sages say, "He who pays a *sheqel* is exempt from a surcharge."
    E. He who pays two denars is liable for a surcharge.
    F. "*He who gives a sela and takes back a sheqel in change is liable for two surcharges*," the words of R. Meir [M. 1:6G].
    G. And sages say, "A single surcharge."
    H. How much is the surcharge?
    I. "*A silver ma'ah*, one twenty-fourth of a silver *sela*," the words of R. Meir.
    J. And sages say, "*Half of a ma'ah at four issars*" [M. 1:7G-H].
    K. With these surcharges what do they do?
    L. "They fall to [the fund of] the *sheqel*s," the words of R. Meir.
    M. R. Eleazer says, "For a freewill-offering [when the altar is unoccupied]."

N. R. Simeon Shezuri says, "Golden patches, for the golden foil for the house of the Holy of Holies."

O. Ben 'Azzai says, "The money-changers come and collect them as their fee."

T. 1:8 L pp. 202-203, ls. 26-34

A-B fall into the category of M. 1:7B. The point of C is that the *sheqel* is the half-*sheqel* required in Scripture, so there is no money-changing involved. Meir still requires the surcharge. If one paid two coins, then the money-changer is needed. F-G revise our view of M. 1:6G. T. further complements M. at K-O, an important addition.

CHAPTER THREE

SHEQALIM CHAPTER TWO

The coins paid over for the Temple-tax of the half-*sheqel* become holy. The present chapter deals with some conventional questions raised in connection with such holy things: if they are lost, if they are misappropriated, and if they are not needed. The first is, What do we do if the *sheqel*-coins are lost or stolen *en route* to the Temple? The answer is that there is an oath to be taken by the agents, that they have not misappropriated the funds. To whom do they take it? If the heave-offering of the *sheqels* has been taken up in the Temple, then all the *sheqels* paid for that year, wherever they are located, belong to the Temple, and, it follows, the oath is taken to the Temple revenuers. But if the heave-offering of the *sheqels* has not yet been taken off, the oath is taken to the townsfolk who contributed the money, so M. 2:1, a signal of the interest of Chapter Three. M. 2:2, along these same lines, pursues the issue of sacrilege, that is, inadvertent misappropriation of a coin designated for use in paying the Temple-tax. A fine triplet makes the points that sacrilege does apply, on the one side, and that the *sheqel* may not derive from that which already has been consecrated, on the other. M. 2:3-5, finally, take up the issue of the disposition of surplus funds, set aside for the *sheqel* but not needed for that purpose. This generates a Houses' dispute. The Hillelites regard the funds as secular, the Shammaites want the surplus used for a freewill-offering. The chapter therefore is unified in conception and lays out its problem in a logical and orderly way.

2:1

A. They change *sheqels* into *darics* because of the burden of the journey.

B. Just as there were *shofar*-chests [for receiving the *sheqel* tax] in the Temple, so there were *shofar*-chests in the provinces.

C. Townsfolk who sent their *sheqels*, which were stolen or lost—

D. if the heave-offering already had been taken up, the [townsfolk] take an oath to the Temple revenuers.

E. And if not, they take an oath before the [other] townsfolk, and the [other] townsfolk pay the *sheqel* in their stead.

F. [If the *sheqels*] were found, or the robbers returned them, both these [coins, paid by the other townsfolk] and those [coins, originally put forth] are in the status of *sheqel*s.

G. And they do not go to their credit for the coming year.

M. 2:1

We have three independent items, A, B, and then the important pericope of C-G. Now if the coins are lost, the agents of the court have to take an oath that they have not misappropriated the funds or otherwise mismanaged their work. To whom is this oath owing? If the *sheqel*s are lost, C, and this happened after the act of taking up the heave-offering of the *sheqel*s had taken place, then these *sheqel*s are deemed to have entered into the Temple funds and to have belonged to the Temple. The oath therefore is owing to the revenuers, since the coins, wherever they are located, belong to the Temple. There is no obligation, once the oath is taken, to make restitution. If the act of taking up the heave-offering of the *sheqel*s has not taken place, then the coins—wherever they may be—do not yet belong to the Temple; only the taking of the heave-offering constitutes that act of acquisition which transfers all the coins into Temple property. Then the oath is taken to the townsfolk, to whom the coins still belong. It goes without saying that under all circumstances, the *sheqel*s when they are found, go to the benefit of the Temple.

A. He who designates [a coin for] his *sheqel*, which got lost, and then designated another in its stead,

B. and did not suffice to hand it over [to the Temple revenuer] before the first was found,

C. so that, lo, both of them are now available—

D. this one and that one have the status of *sheqel*s.

E. And the [one separated] first falls to the chest of new [*sheqel*s], the [one separated] second, of old ones.

T. 1:9 L p. 203, ls. 34-36

T.'s problem is parallel to M.'s.

2:2

A. He who hands over his *sheqel* to his fellow to pay the *sheqel* in his behalf, but [his fellow] paid the *sheqel* in his own behalf,

B. if the heave-offering had been taken up, [his fellow] has committed an act of sacrilege.

C. He who pays his *sheqel* from coins which had already been consecrated,

D. if the heave-offering had already been taken up, and an offering [bought from that money] had been offered, he has committed an act of sacrilege.

E. [If he paid the *sheqel*] from coins in the status of second tithe or from coins received in exchange for produce of the Seventh year, he must consume [produce] equivalent to their value.

M. 2:2

Once the appropriation is made, B, the *sheqel* belongs to the sanctuary and cannot be used for private purposes or to meet a personal obligation. C-D go over this same conception. The point of E, concluding this excellent triplet, is that the coins' value must be translated back into produce. That is to say, since the coin used for the *sheqel* was in the status, e.g., of second tithe, the man must take a coin of value equivalent to the *sheqel* and declare the coin to be in the place of the money in the status of second tithe which he had used for his *sheqel*. This then is spent on food in Jerusalem, that is, as would have been the case with the original funds. The same applies to produce of the Seventh Year (M. Sheb. 8:1-5, 9:8).

A. He who designates [a coin] for his *sheqel* but then spent it [for some other purpose]—
B. lo, this person has committed an act of sacrilege.
C. He who spends a coin designated as a *sheqel* by his fellow,
D. lo, this person has committed an act of sacrilege [M. 2:2A-B].
E. [If] he purchased with it [a coin designated for use as his *sheqel*] bird-offerings for male *Zab*s, bird-offerings for female *Zab*s, bird-offerings for women who have given birth—
F. he who brings his sin-offering or his guilt-offering from coins which have been consecrated—
G. he who takes his *sheqel* from his *zuz*-coins already consecrated for the upkeep of the Temple-house—
H. "as soon as he has made a purchase, he has committed an act of sacrilege," the words of R. Simeon.
I. And sages say, "He has committed an act of sacrilege only after the blood [of the animal purchased with the *sheqel*] has been tossed [on the altar, which is the moment at which the offering is effective in securing atonement]."

T. 1:10 L p. 203, ls. 36-40

The point of A-H is in accord with M.'s general view. The issue is at H-I, as explained. This is hardly primary to our tractate.

A. They do not bring meal-offerings, drink-offerings, the meal-offering accompanying a thank-offering, or the bread-offering that accompanies a thank-offering,
B. from produce which has not yet been tithed, heave-offering, first tithe from which heave-offering has not yet been removed, second tithe which has not yet been redeemed for coins, a mixture of common produce and heave-offering, new produce [before the

'omer has been offered], or produce of the Seventh Year [none of which sorts of produce may be eaten by an ordinary Israelite].

C. And if he brought [any of the stated offerings] from any of these, lo, they are invalid.

D. And, it goes without saying, the same rule applies to produce in the status of *'orlah* and from produce deriving from mixed seeds in a vineyard.

T. 1:11 L pp. 203-204, ls. 40-43

The offerings must derive from produce suitable for ordinary use and not already consecrated, in line with M. 2:2.

2:3-5

A. He who saves up [collects] coins and said, "Lo, these are for my *sheqel*"—

B. the House of Shammai say, "The surplus [over what is actually needed for his *sheqel*] goes for a freewill-offering."

C. And the House of Hillel say, "The surplus [over what is actually needed for his *sheqel*] is unconsecrated."

I D. [If he said,] "I shall bring *some* of them for my *sheqel*,"

E. they concur that the surplus is unconsecrated.

II F. [If he said,] "*These* are for the purchase of a sin-offering,

G. they concur that the surplus is for a freewill-offering.

III H. [If he said,] "I shall bring *some* of them for purchase of a sin-offering,"

I. they concur that the surplus is unconsecrated.

M. 2:3

A. Said R. Simeon, "What is the difference between *sheqel*-taxes and the sin-offering?

B. "*Sheqel*-taxes are subject to a prescribed limit, but a sin-offering is not subject to a prescribed limit."

C. R. Judah says, "Also: *Sheqel*-taxes are not subject to a prescribed limit.

D. "For when the Israelites came up from the Exile, they would pay the *sheqel* in *daric*s. Then they went and paid the *sheqel* in *sela*s [double-*sheqel*s]. Then they went and paid the *sheqel* in [*sheqel*]-coins. And they [even] wanted to pay the *sheqel* in *denar*s."

E. Said R. Simeon, "Even so, the charge for everyone was equal. But in the case of a sin-offering, this one may bring a sin-offering worth two, and yet another may bring a sin-offering worth three."

M. 2:4

A. The surplus [of funds designated for use for] a *sheqel*-tax is unconsecrated [M. 2:3C].

B. The surplus of [coins collected to purchase] the tenth of an *ephah*, the surplus of (1) bird-offerings for male *Zab*s, (2) bird-offerings

of female *Zab*s, (3) bird-offerings for women who have given birth, (4) sin-offerings [M. 2:3F], and (5) guilt-offerings—
    C. their surplus is for a freewill-offering.
    D. This is the governing principle: Whatever comes for the purposes of a sin-offering or a guilt-offering—its surplus is for a freewill-offering.
I   E. The surplus of money set aside for a burnt-offering is used for the purchase of another burnt-offering.
II   F. The surplus of money set aside for a meal-offering is used for the purchase of another meal-offering.
III   G. The surplus of money set aside for peace-offerings is used for peace-offerings.
IV   H. The surplus of money set aside for a Passover-offering is used for peace-offerings.
I   I. The surplus of money set aside for the offerings of Nazirs is used for [other] Nazir[s' offerings].
    J. The surplus of money set aside for a [particular] Nazir is used for the purchase of a freewill-offering.
II   K. The surplus of money collected for use of the poor is used by the poor.
    L. The surplus of money collected for a particular poor person is used for that particular person.
III   M. The surplus of money collected for the redemption of captives is used for the redemption of captives.
    N. The surplus of money collected for the redemption of a particular captive is used for that particular captive.
IV   O. The surplus of money collected for burying the dead is used for the dead.
    P. The surplus of money collected for a particular deceased person is used for his heirs.
    Q. R. Meir says, "The surplus of money collected for a particular deceased person is left over until Elijah comes."
    R. R. Nathan says, "[With] surplus of money collected for a particular deceased person they build a sepulchre on his grave."
    M. 2:5

M. 2:3, with its gloss at M. 2:4 and the thematic restatement of its (Hillelite) views included at the elegant construction of M. 2:5, takes up the question of the disposition of coins set aside for particular cultic purposes. M. 2:3 is interesting in that its triplet, D-I, restates and explains the basic dispute, A. If someone specifies that *some* of the coins will be used for his *sheqel*, obviously there is no reason to regard as consecrated all of them—but only those needed, hence, the surplus. If he specifies, moreover, that all of the coins will be used for a sin-offering, then all are holy, and the surplus cannot be as unconsecrated. To be sure, another sin-offering is not possible.

It must serve for a particular sin. So the unneeded funds go for a freewill-offering. Likewise, the specification of H does not yield a dispute. The point at issue in A-C then is clear.

The exposition of the Hillelite view now (M. 2:4) requires an explanation of why in their view the rule for the *sheqel* differs from that for the sin-offering. Simeon provides that explanation, and it is a good one. If a person says, "These are for my *sheqel*," he can be referring *only* to a fixed part of the entire collection of coins, since, everyone knows, there is a limit to what he will need. Hence his primary intention cannot be to consecrate all the coins, but only those he in fact will require. The surplus never was subject to his intention. Judah objects to this view, but Simeon's reply is a sound one: the *sheqel* is not a variable tax.

M. 2:5, finally, takes up other matters. Its two sets of four entries, M. 2:5E-H, I-P, make their point clearly. The distinctions of the pairs of I-Jff. exhibit M.'s usual clarity of expression through laying down self-evident contrasts. So M. must be permitted to provide its own exegesis.

A. The surplus of wine [designated for the drink-offering] is used for wine [for the drink-offering].
B. The surplus of oil is used for oil.
C. The surplus of salt is used for salt.
D. The surplus of wood is used for wood.
E. The surplus of frankincense is used for frankincense.
F. The surplus of frankincense in dishes used for frankincense for the Show bread is used for that same purpose.
G. *The surplus of funds set aside [for offerings needed by] Nazirites [who cannot afford the offerings] is used for Nazirites* [M. 2:5I].
H. The surplus of funds collected for offerings for purification of people afflicted with *saraʿat* is used for that same purpose.
I. If one said, "[The funds are] for this particular Nazirite," "... for this particular person afflicted with *saraʿat*," the surplus goes for a freewill-offering [M. 2:5J].
J. *The surplus of funds collected for use of the poor is used by the poor.*
K. *The surplus of funds collected for the redemption of captives is used for the redemption of captives* [M. 2:5K, M].
L. But if one said, "It is for this particular poor person," "... for this particular captive," the surplus is for him.
M. *The surplus of funds collected for burying the dead is used for the dead.*
N. *The surplus of funds collected for [burying this] particular deceased person is used for his heirs.*
O. *R. Meir says, "The surplus of money collected for a particular deceased person is left until Elijah comes."*

P. R. Nathan says, "[*With*] *the surplus of funds collected for that particular dead person they build a sepulchre on his grave* [M. 2:50-R],

Q. "or they sprinkle perfume before his bier."

R. They do not collect for a given garment [and give the poor man some other] garment.

S. And they do not collect funds for this particular captive and use them for some other captive.

T. But they do not interfere with the charity-collectors on that account.

T. 1:12 L p. 204, ls. 43-50

T. complements, then cites and glosses M., a set of self-explanatory materials.

CHAPTER FOUR

SHEQALIM CHAPTER THREE

The chapter presents a narrative of the procedure for "taking up the heave-offering of the chamber," that is, setting apart those *sheqel*s which will be used for the coming season's public offerings. The procedure is done three times, before each of the pilgrim-festivals. The narrative is fairly standard, with some sizable interpolations of precedent and homily.

3:1

A. At three times in the year do they take up the heave-offering of the [coins collected in the] [*sheqel*-] chamber:

B. half a month before Passover, half a month before 'Aṣeret [Pentecost], and half a month before the Festival [of Sukkot].

C. "And these are the 'threshing floors' [the times at which the obligation to tithe becomes operative] for tithing cattle," the words of R. 'Aqiba.

D. Ben 'Azzai says, "On the twenty-ninth of Adar, on the first of Sivan, and on the twenty-ninth of Ab."

E. R. Eleazar and R. Simeon say, "On the first of Nisan, on the first of Sivan, and on the twenty-ninth of Elul."

F. On what account did they rule, "On the twenty-ninth of Elul," instead of saying, "on the first of Tishré"?

G. Because it is a festival day, and it is not possible to give tithe on a festival day.

H. Therefore they set it a day earlier, on the twenty-ninth of Elul.

M. 3:1 (C-H = M. Bekh. 9:5)

The heave-offering of the chamber of *sheqel*s, A, is the point at which the *sheqel*s to be used for the coming season are taken up for the purchase of the public offerings. This is done before the festivals, at which point demands on the Temple treasury are greatest. 'Aqiba glosses by observing that at this same time cattle born during the preceding period become liable to the process of tithing. At this point they are tithed, and those which are left over from the procedure of the tithe of cattle become available for sale and use on the coming festival. The other authorities do not differ about B, but about C. Ben Azzai sets variable dates, two weeks before Passover, less than a week before Pentecost, and a month and a half before Tabernacles.

Ben 'Azzai deems animals born in Elul to be tithed as a separate group, M. Bekh. 9:5. Eleazar and Simeon allow two weeks for Passover, less than a week before Pentecost, and two weeks before Tabernacles. F-H gloss E. For further discussion see *Holy Things* III, pp. 229-232.

3:2-3

A. With three baskets, each holding three *seah*s, they take up the heave-offering of the [coins collected in the] [*sheqel-*]chamber.

B. And written on them are the Hebrew letters, *alef, bet, gimel*.

C. R. Ishmael says, "Written on them were the Greek letters, *Alpha, Beta, Gamla*."

D. He who takes up the heave-offering went in wearing neither a sleeved cloak, nor shoes, sandals, phylacteries, or an amulet—

E. lest [in the coming year] he lose all his money and people say [about him], "Because of a transgression against the [*sheqel-*] chamber did he lose his money."

F. Or lest he get rich, and people say about him, "From the heave-offering of the [*sheqel-*] chamber did he get rich."

G. For a person must give no cause for suspicion to other people just as he must give no cause for suspicion to the Omnipresent,

H. as it is said, *And be guiltless towards the Lord and towards Israel* (Num. 32:22).

I. And so it says, *So shall you find favor and good understanding in the sight of God and humanity* (Prov. 3:4).

M. 3:2

A. A member of the household of Rabban Gamaliel would go in and take his *sheqel* between his finger-tips and thrown it in front of the one who takes up the heave-offering [of the *sheqel*s, so as to make sure his coin would be used for the purchase of the public sacrifices].

B. And the one who takes up the heave-offering intentionally pushes it into the basket.

C. The one who takes up the heave-offering does not do so until he says to them, "Shall I take up the heave-offering?" And they say to him, "Take up heave-offering, take up heave-offering, take up heave-offering," three times.

M. 3:3

The procedure for appropriating the funds is described in standard narrative style. The glosses, M. 3:2G-I, 3:3A-B, do not spoil the flow.

A. What is meant by *half a month before Passover, before Aseret* [*Pentecost*], *before the Festival* [*of Tabernacles*] [M. 3:1B]?

B. R. Yosé b. R. Judah says, "It is no less than fifteen days before the festival."

C. Why do they write on the baskets [used for taking up the heave-offering of the *sheqel*-funds] *alef, bet, gimmel* [M. 3:2B]?

D. Because they begin to take out the needed funds from the first basket. When the first is completely empty, they take out the necessary funds from the second. When the second is completely empty, they take out the necessary funds from the third.

E. When all three of them are completely empty, the time has come for taking up heave-offering [of the *sheqel*s once more, that is, before Pentecost or before Tabernacles, at which time it is possible to take up the heave-offering of the *sheqel*s again].

F. They take up a heave-offering of *sheqel*s from what is newly contributed, but if not, they take up a heave-offering of *sheqel*s from what is old [left over after the heave-offering is taken].

T. 2:1 L p. 205, ls. 1-5

T. glosses M.

A. When one went in to take up the heave-offering of the [*sheqel*-]chamber, they would search him when he went in and when he came out.

B. And they continue chatting with him from the time that he goes in until the time that he comes out,

C. "to fulfill the requirement of the following: *And be guiltless towards the Lord and towards Israel* (Num. 32:22).

D. "And, *And you shall do what is right and good in the sight of the Lord* (Deut. 6:18)," the words of R. 'Aqiba.

E. R. Ishmael says, "Also that which is right in the sight of Heaven.

F. "For it says, *So shall you find favor and good understanding in the sight of God and humanity* (Prov. 3:4)."

G. The sages inclined to accept the opinion of R. Ishmael,

H. for it is said, [*So shall you purge the guilt of innocent blood from your midst,*] *when you do what is right in the sight of the Lord* (Deut. 21:9).

I. Now there is no "goodness" here [in the law concerning the Canaanite cities, which must be utterly destroyed, sparing not even the righteous in them].

J. And it says, *The Mighty One, God, the Lord! The Mighty One, God, the Lord! He knows, and let Israel itself know!* [*if it was in rebellion or in breach of faith toward the Lord, spare us not today*] (Joshua 22:22).

T. 2:2 L pp. 205-206, ls. 5-13

T. complements M. 3:2E-F, G-I.

3:4

A. He took up [heave-offering] the first time and covered [the residue] with covers.

B. [He took up the heave-offering] a second time and covered [the residue] with covers.

C. But the third time he did not cover [it up].

D. [He covered the first two times], lest he forget and take up heave-offering from those *sheqels* from which heave-offering already had been taken.

E. He took up the heave-offering the first time in behalf of the Land of Israel, the second time in behalf of cities surrounding it, and the third time in behalf of Babylonia, Media, and the more distant communities.

M. 3:4

The narrative continues, with D glossing A, B.

A. He took up the heave-offering [of *sheqels*] the first time and said, "Lo, this is from the Land of Israel in behalf of the whole people of Israel" [M. 3:4E].

B. *Then he covered it with coverings*,

C. because the people of Syria would come and contribute the *sheqel* to [that same fund, and he did not wish to mix in their *sheqels* with the ones designated from the Land of Israel].

D. Then he took up the heave-offering the second time and said, "Lo, this is from the lands of Ammon and Moab and from the cities surrounded by a wall in the Land of Israel."

E. Then he covered it up with coverings,

F. because the people of Babylonia would come and contribute the *sheqel* to [that same fund].

T. 2:3 L p. 206, ls. 13-16

A. He took up the heave-offering from the third basket and said, "Lo, this is from Babylonia and Media and from places distant from the Land of Israel,

B. "in behalf of all Israelites."

C. But he did not cover it up.

D. This was the richest fund of all of them, for in it were golden *istras* and golden *darics*.

E. He removed the covers and what was left was mixed together.

F. But they did not mix them together with [the *sheqels*] of the preceding year,

G. lest they have to take up the heave-offering once more and turn out to take the heave-offering needed for this year from last year's money.

T. 2:4 L p. 206, ls. 16-20

T. 2:3-4 complement M. 3:4.

A. "They do take up heave-offering on the account of that which is subject to a pledge, that which already has been collected [but which got lost *en route* to the Temple], and that which is going to be collected in the future," the words of R. Meir.

B. R. Yosé says, "They take up heave-offering for that which is subject to a pledge and for that which has already been collected [but which got lost *en route* to the Temple], but not for what is going to be collected in the future."

C. R. Simeon b. Eleazar says, "They would do so only in the [third and] last act of taking up the heave-offering of the *sheqels*.

D. "For it is possible that a resident of the Land of Israel will have need [and will not be able to pay on time, but will pay afterward], and it will turn out that he pays the *sheqel* with the Babylonians."

E. The laws of sacrilege apply to them throughout their year [in which they are used for the purchase of public offerings].

F. Once their year has passed, the laws of sacrilege do not apply to them.

G. [Then] these and those fall to the fund for the upkeep of the Temple-house [but not for the purchase of offerings for the altar].

T. 2:5 L pp. 206-207, ls. 21-25

Meir's view is that the appropriation affects even *sheqels* not in the possession of the Temple. Yosé concurs in part, and Simeon specifies that point at which the appropriation is deemed to affect *sheqels* not now in the chamber. T. supplements M. in a rather general way.

CHAPTER FIVE

SHEQALIM CHAPTER FOUR

The basic structure of the first unit of the chapter, M. 4:1-5, is a four-part account of the disposition of Temple-income, each part beginning with a reference to a Temple-fund or asset and the question: "What did they do with it?" Thus M. 4:1 asks about the purpose of the heave-offering of the chamber, M. 4:3, the surplus funds left over there, and, finally, any surplus left over of the heave-offering of *sheqel*s itself. M. 4:5 supplements what is originally a cogent triplet, asking what is done with the surplus of the frankincense, a special problem, as I shall explain. The main point is that the heave-offering of the *sheqel*s is used for the purchase of public offerings, the surplus of the residue is used for wine, oil, and flour; the surplus of the heave-offering is used for gold plate for the buildings or for other utensils used therein, a matter subject to dispute.

The next set, M. 4:6-8, has to do with the disposition of objects consecrated to the Temple. The disposition of surplus, M. 4:5, is served by what is an appendix. The principal point of interest is a dispute between Eliezer and Joshua on whether cattle consecrated to the Temple are sold for the benefit of the altar, as Joshua maintains, or are sold for the benefit of the fund for the upkeep of the Temple-house, which is the case with other sorts of consecrated objects in general, as Eliezer holds. M. 4:9, finally, states that once in thirty days they fix the prices to be paid by the *sheqel*-chamber for the goods and services—e.g., wine, oil, flour—required for the public offerings, a useful appendix to the principal construction. There are some textual problems in T. to 4:9, which will not detain us.

4:1-2

I A. As to the heave-offering [of the *sheqel*-chamber]: What did they do with it?

B. They purchase with it [animals for] daily whole-offerings, additional offerings, and their drink-offerings,

C. [wheat for] the *'omer*, the Two Loaves, and the Show Bread,

D. and all [other] offerings made in behalf of the community.

E. Those who guard the aftergrowths of the Seventh Year receive their salary from the heave-offering of the [*sheqel*-]chamber.

F. R. Yosé says, "Also: He who wishes to volunteer [may serve as] an unpaid guardian [of the aftergrowths]."

G. They said to him, "You too rule that they [the *'omer*, Two Loaves, and Show Bread] derive only from public funds."

M. 4:1

A. The red cow [Num. 19:1ff.], the goat which is sent out, and the red thread [Lev. 16:5] derive from funds of the heave-offering of the [*sheqel*-]chamber.

B. The [cost of building] a causeway for the red cow, the causeway for the scapegoat which is sent forth, the thread between its horns, the [cost of the upkeep of the] water channel, the wall of the city and its turrets, and all needs of the city [of Jerusalem] derive from the residue [of funds of the *sheqel*-]chamber [coins not taken up with the heave-offering thereof].

C. Abba Saul says, "The ramp of the red cow—the high priests make it at their own expense."

M. 4:2

The essay on the disposition of the funds deriving from the Temple-tax names four ways in which the money is used: M. 4:1B-D, E, M. 4:2A, a triplet, then M. 4:2B. The first three come from funds deriving from the appropriation, or the taking up of the heave-offering; the fourth then is from the funds left over. The main point, of course, is M. 4:1B-D: Offerings made in behalf of all the people must derive from funds contributed by them all. E-G is a secondary development of M. 4:1C.

The point of E is that, in the Seventh Year, when no crops may be sown, it is necessary to watch over the aftergrowth of wheat, so that there will be grain for the preparation of the *'omer*, the Two Loaves, and the Show Bread (C). Since in ordinary years the wheat itself is purchased with the heave-offering of the *sheqel*-chamber, in the Seventh Year the wheat is secured through an appropriation from that same budget. Guards are hired to see that neither human beings nor animals eat the specified fields' aftergrowth, which then is kept for use in the cult. Yosé's position is rejected, G, because if a person guards without pay, then the produce of the field guarded by him automatically becomes his possession, and this, M. 4:1C makes clear, is not possible. An individual cannot supply what the entire community must give.

M. 4:2A completes the trilogy. M. 4:2B then specifies how excess funds are used, after the three acts of taking up the heave-offering have left over in the chamber sizable sums of money. The city and its needs are met from public funds.

A. Women who would weave the hangings,
B. *the House of Garmu [which] would prepare the Show Bread,*
C. *the House of Abtinas [which] would prepare the incense* [M. 5:1M, N]—
D. [all] take their salary from the heave-offering of the [*sheqel-*]chamber.
E. The golden altar and utensils used for service, the clothing of the priests, the clothing of the high priest, the cedar-wood and hyssop and crimson thread [M. 4:2A], come from [funds of] the residue of the [*sheqel-*]chamber.
F. The ramp for the red cow—
G. *Abba Saul says, "The high priests make it at their own expense"* [M. 4:2C].
H. [If] the first [high priest] built it and did not make use of it and died, even though he did not make use of it, his fellow [and successor] is not to make use of it.
I. But he tears it down and builds another in its stead.
J. And more than sixty pieces of gold have to be spent on it.
K. "The ox which is offered on account of the community's inadvertent transgression of any and all commandments and the goats offered in atonement for idolatry to begin with are purchased from a collection for that purpose," the words of R. Judah.
L. R. Simeon says, "They derive from funds of the heave-offering of the *sheqel*-chamber."

T. 2:6 L pp. 207-208, ls. 25-34

T. 2:6A-D specify others who receive their salary from the *sheqel*-chamber. The remainder complements T. mainly by adding further, relevant facts, and an appropriate dispute, L-M. Simeon's view is not included in M.

4:3

II A. As to the surplus of the residue of the [*sheqel-*]chamber: What did they do with it?
B. They purchase with it wine, oil, and fine flour.
C. "And the profit [of the resale] belongs to the Temple," the words of R. Ishmael.
D. R. 'Aqiba says, "They do not make money in what belongs to the Temple or in what belongs to the poor."

M. 4:3

A-B continue the established construction: The gloss, C-D, concerns profits deriving from the resale of wine, oil, or flour to those requiring these things. 'Aqiba does not concur that there should be a profit at all.

A. Public supervisors of the poor who had money left over after making their distribution to the poor should not purchase with it produce on consignment,
B. because of the possibility of loss to the poor.
C. But they purchase [produce] with it from the lowest to the highest price.

T. 2:8 (continued) L p. 208, ls. 36-38

T. takes the side of 'Aqiba on the use of charity-funds. If there is a surplus, the supervisors may not use the money to purchase produce on consignment (that is, a bargain in which the seller sees to the sale in exchange for half of the profits), since there is a possibility of loss of funds. Only the most secure investments may be undertaken, and, in the present case, C, this means having the produce in hand, not relying upon an agent to sell it and return the profits.

4:4

III A. The surplus of the heave-offering [itself] [of the *sheqel*]: What do they do with it?
B. [They buy] golden plate for decorating the house of the Holy of Holies.
C. R. Ishmael says, "The surplus of the profits [on wine, oil, and flour sold to people bringing private offerings (M. 4:3C)] goes for [purchase of animals for sacrifice] for 'dessert' [the unused time of the altar],
D. "and the surplus of the heave-offering [of the *sheqel*s] is for purchase of utensils for service."
E. R. 'Aqiba says, "The surplus of the heave-offering [of the *sheqel*s] goes for 'dessert', and the surplus of the drink-offerings is for purchase of utensils for service."
F. R. Hananiah, Prefect of the Priests, says, "The surplus of the drink-offerings goes for 'dessert,' and the surplus of the heave-offering [of the *sheqel*s] is for the purchase of utensils for service."
G. But neither one [E, F] concurred in the matter of profits [both maintaining that profits are not permissible]. M. 4:4

The dispute is between B, D, E, and F. E-F of course are neatly balanced. Both are out of phase with C-D, as G explains, and all differ from B. The "dessert" is the time at which the altar is not used for prescribed offerings, public and private. Burnt-offerings are made then, to keep the altar occupied all day long.

D. What is the dessert [unused time] of the altar?
E. For: they purchase burnt-offerings and keep the altar in use [by offering them up].

T. 2:8 (continued) L p. 208, ls, 38-39

T. glosses M.

4:5

A. The surplus of the frankincense: What did they do with it?
B. They set aside from it the wages of the craftsmen.
C. And [after] they declare it unconsecrated in exchange for the wages of the craftsmen,
D. they hand it over to the craftsmen as their salary.
E. And they go and buy it back from them [with money raised up] from a fresh heave-offering [of the *sheqel*s].
F. If the new [heave-offering] came in due time, they buy it back [with money] from the new heave-offering [of the *sheqel*s], but if not, [they buy it back with money] from the old.

M. 4:5

Frankincense is prepared for the whole year in advance. Enough is readied to serve for the solar year of 365 days. But the lunar calendar, followed in the cult, has only 354. Eleven *mina*s of frankincense are annually left over, except in a leap year. Since public offerings from the first of Nisan onwards derive from the heave-offering of the new *sheqel* (M. 3:9), there will be an annual surplus of elevent days' worth of frankincense, A-B, for the stated purpose, wages for Temple employees. Now this cannot be paid directly to the craftsmen. First, it is to be deconsecrated, C, and then handed over to the workers, D. The frankincense then is bought back out of the new funds, the *sheqel*s taken up after the first of Nisan, so it can be used for the new cycle, which begins in Nisan. F then glosses E.

A. As to all public offerings offered on the first of Nisan—
B. [If] the new [heave-offering of the *sheqel*s] came in due time, they are offered from [funds deriving from] the new [heave-offering of the *sheqel*s].
C. And if not, they are offered from [funds deriving from] last year [M. 4:5F].
D. [If] people volunteered the funds on their own, they are valid,
E. on condition that they give the funds to the community [for public use].

T. 2:7 L p. 208, ls. 34-36

A-C restate the principle of M. 4:5F.

4:6

A. He who sanctifies his property, and included in it were items suitable for use for public offerings—
B. "they are to be given to the craftsmen for their salary," the words of R. 'Aqiba.
C. Said to him Ben 'Azzai, "That [method, of M. 4:5] is not correct [in this case].

D. "But: They set apart from it the wages of the craftsmen.
E. "And they render it deconsecrated in exchange for the money due to the craftsmen.
F. "And they pay it over to the craftsmen as their salary.
G. "And then they go and buy it back from them out of the new heave-offering [of the *sheqel*s]."

M. 4:6

In 'Aqiba's conception, the items suitable for the altar, e.g., wine, flour, spices, are paid over to the craftsmen, B, then bought back, G. Ben 'Azzai specifies a slightly more complicated procedure. Labor cannot be exchanged directly for something holy. The items suitable for the altar are set apart in the amount equivalent to what is owing the craftsmen. Then money due to the craftsmen is exchanged for the items. The flour, wine, oil, or spice then is paid over to the craftsmen, who sell it back to the Temple. In this way the item is acquired by the heave-offering of the *sheqel*s of the current year. It now may serve as a public offering. No longer is the individual who gave over the wine, oil, flour, and the like, responsible for a public offering, since the object has been acquired by public funds.

F. *He who consecrates his property, and included in it were items suitable for use for public offerings—*
"*they are to be given to the craftsmen for their salary,*" *the words of R. 'Aqiba.*
G. *Said to him Ben 'Azzai, "That is not the correct method* [M. Sheq. 4:6A-C].
H. "But: A worker who performs work in the sanctuary, whether for a *maneh* or for two hundred *zuz* may not say, 'Give me this cow for a *maneh*,' or '. . . this cloak for fifty *zuz*.'
I. "For that which is consecrated is not rendered unconsecrated in exchange for an act of labor, but only in exchange for coins alone.

T. 2:8 (concluded) L p. 208, ls. 39-43

A. "What they do they do?
B. "*They set apart from it the wages of the craftsmen and render it deconsecrated in exchange for the money due to the craftsmen.*
C. "*Then they pay it over to the craftsmen as their salary, and go and buy it back out of the heave-offering of the [sheqel-]chamber*" [M. 4:6D-G].

T. 2:9 L pp. 208-209, ls. 43-45

What T. contributes is T. 2:8I, the reasoning of Ben 'Azzai. I have introduced T. 2:8I into my explanation of M.

4:7-8

A. He who sanctifies his property and in it were cattle suitable for use on the altar,

B. males and females—

C. R. Eliezer says, "The males are to be sold for those who require burnt-offerings,

"and the females are sold for those who require peace-offerings.

D. "And proceeds received for them fall with the value of the rest of the donation for the upkeep of the Temple-house."

E. R. Joshua says, "The males themselves are offered up as burnt offerings, "and the females are to be sold for those who require peace-offerings, "and let one bring burnt-offerings with their proceeds.

F. "And the rest of the proceeds fall for the upkeep of the Temple-house."

G. R. 'Aqiba says, "I prefer the opinion of R. Eliezer to the opinion of R. Joshua.

H. "For R. Eliezer is consistent, while R. Joshua has made a distinction."

I. Said R. Pappyas, "I heard [a ruling on this subject] in accord with the opinion of each of them:

J. "For: He who sanctifies [his property] on explicit terms follows the opinion of R. Eliezer, and he who sanctifies his property without specification follows the opinion of R. Joshua."

M. 4:7

A. He who sanctifies his property, in which were items suitable [actually] for use on the altar—

B. wine, oil, fowl—

C. R. Eleazar says, "They are to be sold to those who need that item, and let one bring burnt-offerings with the proceeds received for them.

D. "And the rest of the property falls for use in the upkeep of the house."

M. 4:8

At issue is the purpose of the donation. Eliezer's conception is that a dedication of property to the Temple belongs to the fund for the upkeep of the Temple-house. Therefore what can be used for the altar is sold for that purpose, with the proceeds then donated to the fund for the upkeep of the house. Joshua differs. Male cattle themselves are offered up, not converted for use by the Temple-fund for the upkeep of the house. The females likewise are used for the benefit of the altar. (Females cannot serve as burnt-offerings.) 'Aqiba then observes, G-H, that Eliezer treats the entire donation in a consistent way. Everything is for building-maintenance. Joshua treats goods differently from items suitable for the altar. Pappyas proposes that, if a person sanctifies his property and explicitly states that he wants all items treated in the same way—for the upkeep of the house—then, obviously, Eliezer's view is invoked. But if not, then Joshua's is, and what can go right to the altar is sent up there.

At M. 4:8 an Eleazar (and T. sees this one as Eliezer) has the items suitable for the altar sold, and then the proceeds fall to the use of the altar, while the rest of the property goes to the Temple-house fund. So here an Eleazar takes up the position of Joshua.

> A. *He who sanctifies his property, and in it was a beast suitable for use on the altar, male or female—*
> B. *R. Eliezer says, "Males are to be sold for those who require burnt-offerings, and females are to be sold for those who require peace-offerings. And their proceeds fall with the value of the rest of the donation for the upkeep of the house."*
> C. *R. Joshua says, "The males themselves are offered up as burnt-offerings, and the females are to be sold to those who require peace-offerings, and one brings with their proceeds burnt-offerings"* [M. 4:7A-E].
> D. R. Yosé and R. Simeon say, "The opinion of R. Eliezer [at M. 4:8] is the same as the opinion of R. Joshua [at M. 4:7], and the opinion of R. Joshua [at M. 4:7] is the same as the opinion of R. Eliezer [at M. 4:8]."
>
> T. 2:10 L p. 209, ls. 45-50

After citing M. 4:7, D points out the obvious fact that, if we read *Eliezer*, then M. 4:8 shifts the opinions.

4:9

> A. Once every thirty days they fix prices for the [*sheqel-*]chamber.
> B. Whoever undertakes to provide flour at four [*seah*s a *sela*]—
> C. [if] the price stood at [deflated to] three [*sela*s for a *seah*]—
> D. still must provide it at four.
> E. [If he undertook to provide it at] three to a *seah*, and the price stood at [inflated to] four, let him provide it at four.
> F. For the claim of the sanctuary is always paramount.
> G. And if the flour got wormy, the wormy flour is at his expense. And if the wine turned sour, the sour wine is at his expense.
> H. And he does not receive his fee until after the altar has effected acceptance.
>
> M. 4:9

The prices paid by the Temple are set once a month, A. B-F, G-H complete the matter. The Temple pays only when the altar has made use of the wine, flour, or oil, H.

> A. *Once every thirty days they fix prices for the [sheqel-]chamber* [M. 4:9A].

B. [If the supplier] wanted to go back [on his agreed price] during the thirty days, they do not pay attention to him.

T. 2:11 (continued) L p. 209, ls. 50-51

T. explains M. I follow Lieberman's text, as indicated.

A. *Once every thirty days they set prices for the heave-offering of the [sheqel-]chamber* [M. 4:9A].
B. Whoever sold wine, oil, and flour and said, "Pay me my money in the coinage which circulates in my country,"—
C. goes to the revenuer, and the revenuer brings him to the money-changer.
D. If he wants, he says to him, "Pay me off immediately for less right now."
E. This is not prohibited by reason of interest, nor because it is a matter involving the sanctuary.
F. But anyone who sells something to his fellow on condition that he pay him any time in the next twelve months, if he wanted, may say to him, "Pay me for less right now."
G. And this is not prohibited as interest.

T. 2:12 L pp. 209-210, ls. 53-58

A. Once every thirty days they open the *sheqel*-chamber.
B. Whoever sold them wine, oil, or flour, may say to them, "Pay me in the coinage which circulates in my country."
C. They pay no attention to him.
D. But he goes to the revenuer, and the revenuer reaches down and pays him from the coins which come to hand in accord with the required measure [of what is owing].
E. If he wanted, he then brings him over to the money-changer, and the money changer takes [the money] from him and pays him off in the coinage which circulates in his country in accord with the proper measure.
F. For every kind of coin circulates in Jerusalem on this account.

T. 2:13 L p. 210, ls. 58-63

T. 2:12 supplements M. For a picture of the textual problems and their solution, see Lieberman.

CHAPTER SIX

SHEQALIM CHAPTER FIVE

After listing Temple officers, M. 5:1-2, the chapter turns to the purchase of drink-offerings from two of them. One sold seals (receipts), bearing an indication of the sort of drink-offering required. The other received the seals and handed out the drink-offering (M. 5:3-5). There also was a charity-fund, which conducted the affairs of receiving and discretely distributing gifts for the poor (M. 5:6).

5:1

A. These are they who are appointed who were in the sanctuary [as its officers]:
 (1) Yoḥanan b. Pinḥas is in charge of the seals.
 (2) Aḥiah is in charge of the drink-offerings.
 (3) Matthew b. Samuel is in charge of the lots.
 (4) Petaḥiah is in charge of the bird offerings—
(Petaḥiah is the same as Mordecai, and why is he called Petaḥiah? Because he is able to open questions and expound them and knows seventy languages.)
 (5) Ben Aḥiah is in charge of bowel-sickness.
 (6) Neḥuniah digs ditches [for water].
 (7) Gebini is the herald.
 (8) Ben Geber is in charge of closing the gates.
 (9) Ben Bebai is in charge of the knout.
 (10) Ben Arzah is in charge of the cymbals.
 (11) Hugras b. Levi is in charge of the singing.
 (12) The house of Garmu is in charge of making the Show Bread.
 (13) The house of Abtinas is in charge of preparing the incense.
 (14) Eleazar is in charge of the hangings.
 (15) Pinḥas is in charge of the clothing.

M. 5:1

M.'s list of fifteen functionaries is self-explanatory in form and substance.

A. *These are they who were appointed in the sanctuary [as its officers]* [M. Sheq. 5:1A]:
B. Yoḥanan B. Gudegeda is in charge of locking the gates [M. 5:1A8].
C. Ben Totepet is in charge of the keys.
D. Ben Dipai is in charge of the *lulab*.

E. Ben Arza is in charge of the platform [M. 5:1A10].
F. Benjamin is in charge of the ovens.
G. Samuel is in charge of the cakes.
H. Ben Maqlit is in charge of the salt.
I. Ben Pelekh-'Eṣ is in charge of the wood.

T. 2:14 L pp. 210-211, ls. 63-66

T. adds its own names and offices.

5:2

A. They appoint no fewer than three revenuers and seven supervisors.
B. And they do not appoint less than two people to a public position of supervision in property matters,
C. except for Ben Aḥiah who is in charge of the bowel-sickness [M. 5:1A5],
D. and Eleazar who is in charge of hangings [M. 5:1A14].
E. For them did the majority of the congregation accept.

M. 5:2

Aḥiah bought medicine; Eleazar handled funds for the upkeep of the veil. Neither was under supervision of a colleague.

A. *The three revenuers* [M. 5:2A]: What do they do?
B. Through them [people] would redeem [pay off] valuations, declarations of *ḥerem*, acts of consecration, and second tithe.
C. And all the work of consecration was done by them.
D. *The seven supervisors* [M. 5:2A]: What do they do?
E. The seven keys to the courtyard are in their hand.
F. [If] one of them wanted to open up [the courtyard], he could not do so, unless all seven came together.
G. Once all seven of them had come together, the supervisors open the gates, and the revenuers go in and come out.
H. And in order of rank did they go in and come out.
I. Said R. Judah, "Why was the title *amarkal*? Because he is master over all (MR 'L HKL)."
J. They were suitable folk chosen from the priesthood, Levites, or Israelites.
K. He who had a son—the son takes precedence. If he had a brother, the brother takes precedence.
L. Whoever takes precedence in inheritances takes precedence in positions of authority,
M. so long as he follows the custom of his forefathers.

T. 2:15 L p. 211, ls. 66-73

T. explains M. 5:2A.

5:3-5

A. Four seals were in the Temple.

B. And on them was inscribed the following: "Calf," "ram" (male), "kid," "sinner."

C. Ben ʿAzzai says, "There were five, and they were written in Aramaic: "Calf," "ram," "kid," "poor sinner" [Lev. 14:21], and "rich sinner" [Lev. 14:10].

D. "Calf" signifies drink-offerings for [offerings from] the herd, large or small, male or female.

E. "Kid" signifies drink-offerings of the flock, whether large or small, male or female,

F. except for those which accompany rams.

G. "Ram" signifies drink-offerings which come with rams alone.

H. "Sinner" signifies drink offerings which come with the three beasts of those afflicted by *meṣoraʿ*.

M. 5:3

A. He who wanted [to purchase] drink-offerings goes over to Yoḥanan [M. 5:1A1], who is appointed to be in charge of the seals.

B. He pays him the fee and receives a seal from him.

C. He goes over to Aḥiah [M. 5:1A2], who is appointed to be in charge of the drink-offerings.

D. He hands over the seal to him and receives the drink-offerings from him.

E. Then in the evening the two come together, and Aḥiah brings out the seals and receives money for them.

F. If there was an excess [of funds over seals], the excess belongs to the sanctuary.

G. And if there was too little money, Yoḥanan paid out of his own pocket.

H. For the claim of the sanctuary is always paramount.

M. 5:4

A. He who lost his seal—

B. they postpone his [case] until the evening.

C. If they found [money left over] enough to cover his seal, they give it to him.

D. But if not, he got nothing.

E. And the date of that day was written on [the seals], because of deceivers.

M. 5:5

M. provides what is essentially a narrative, based on information already provided. The purpose of the seals was to signify that funds had been paid, in exchange for which drink-offerings were to be provided. Yoḥanan collected the funds, and Aḥiah, who was in charge of purchasing the wine from suppliers, then handed over the necessary drink-offerings. The story is clear as given. Deceivers,

M. 5:5E, might pick up a lost seal and claim it belonged to them on some other day than the day on which it was paid and used.

> A. *Four seals were in the Temple* [M. 5:3A].
> B. [With the seal on which the word] "Sinner" [was imprinted] did one go and get his *log* of oil [with the other drink-offerings].
> C. [With the seal on which the word] "Poor sinner" was imprinted—in accord with the opinion of Ben 'Azzai [M. 5:3C]—did one go and get his *log*.
>
> T. 2:16 (continued) L p. 211, ls. 73-75

T. goes over M.'s ground.

> C. And if they were poured out in the courtyard, they poured out at his expense.
> D. If he has more to bring from his home, lo, this one brings it.
> E. For these were at the service only of one who did not have [any of his own to bring].
>
> T. 2:11 (concluded) L p. 209, ls. 52-53

If the wine is purchased and then is spilled, it must be replaced by the sacrifier. One may bring his own wine; there was no requirement to buy from Yoḥanan and Aḥiah.

5:6

> A. Two chambers were in the Temple, one, the chamber of secret [gifts], the other, the chamber of utensils.
> B. The chamber of secret gifts: Those who fear sin secretly put their contribution into it, and poor folk of good family live off the proceeds [which they receive] in confidence.
> C. The chamber of utensils: Whoever contributes a utensil tosses it into it, and once in thirty days the revenuers open it,
> D. and every utensil which they find there which is useful for the Temple upkeep do they leave [for that purpose].
> E. And as to the rest, they are sold for their value, and the proceeds fall to the chamber for the upkeep of the house.   M. 5:6

M. lays out its ideas with formal precision and is self-explanatory, B, C-E augmenting A.

> D. Just as there was a chamber of secret donations [into which donations for the support of the poor were deposited without fanfare, and from which contributions for the poor were handed out without public announcement] in the sanctuary [M. 5:6B], so there was such a chamber in each and every town,
> E. so that *the poor and good family live off the proceeds* [*which they receive*] *in confidence* [and without public knowledge].
>
> T. 2:16 (concluded) L p. 211, ls. 75-76

T. glosses M.

CHAPTER SEVEN

SHEQALIM CHAPTER SIX

The chapter announces its topic at the outset, M. 6:1A: the Temple had thirteen *shofar*-chests, tables, and acts of prostration, and then systematically provides an exegesis for each of these facts, last to first: M. 6:1-3 for prostrations; M. 6:4 for tables; and M. 6:5-6 for *shofar*-chests. This last item of course is the sole relevant one, since in the *shofar*-chests were received the *sheqel*-taxes, as well as other obligatory and freewill donations to the Temple. T. is somewhat more interesting than M.

6:1-3

A. (1) Thirteen *shofar*-chests, (2) thirteen tables, [and] (3) thirteen acts of prostration were in the sanctuary.
B. The members of the household of Rabban Gamaliel and the members of the household of R. Ḥananiah, Prefect of the Priests, would do fourteen prostrations.
C. And where was the additional one?
D. Toward the wood-shed,
E. for so did they have a tradition from their forebears that there the ark was stored away.

M. 6:1

A. M'ŚH B: A priest was going about his business and saw that a block of the pavement was slightly different from the rest.
B. He came and told his fellow.
C. He did not finish telling [him] before he dropped dead.
D. Then they knew without doubt that there the ark had been stored away.

M. 6:2

A. And where were these thirteen acts of prostration?
B. Four times in the north, four in the south, three in the east, and two in the west,
C. toward the thirteen gates.
D. The gates to the south, counting from the western side: the Upper Gate, Kindling Gate, Gate of the Firstlings, Water Gate.
E. Why is it called Water Gate?
F. For through it they take the flask of water used in the water-offering on the Festival [of Tabernacles].
G. R. Eliezer b. Jacob says, "Through it *the waters trickle forth*

and in time to come they *will issue out from under the threshhold of the house* (Ez. 47:1-5).

H. Opposite them at the north, counting from the west: Jeconiah's Gate, the Gate of the Offering, Women's Gate, Gate of the Song.
I. Why is it called Jeconiah's Gate?
J. Because through it Jeconiah went forth on his way into exile.
K. On the east: Nicanor's Gate.
L. And it had two wickets, one on the right, one on the left
M. And two on the west,
N. which had no names. M. 6:3

M. 6:1B-E, 6:2 are interpolated between M. 6:1A3 and its extensive exposition at M. 6:3. Once we reach that point, the exposition is clear. M. 6:4 takes up A2, and M. 6:5, A1.

A. *Thirteen acts of prostration were in the sanctuary* [M. 6:1A3].
B. R. Judah says, "Toward [each] gate there is an act of prostration, toward each breach there is an act of bending the knee."
C. And all other acts of prostration which took place in the sanctuary which were with regard to an offering were obligatory, were fixed.
D. And in both of these instances there was no act of kneeling, but an act of bowing down and laying forth one's hands alone.

T. 2:17 L pp. 211-212, ls. 76-79

A. R. Eliezer says, "The ark was taken away to exile in Babylonia, since it says, [*Then Isaiah said to Hezekiah, Hear the word of the Lord. Behold, the days are coming, when all that is in your house, and that which your fathers have stored up till this day, shall be carried to Babylonia.*] *No things shall be left, says the Lord* (II Kings 20:16-17).
B. "And 'things' means nothing other than the [ten] 'things' [commandments] which are in it."
C. R. Simeon says, "*Lo, it says, In the spring of the year King Nebuchadnezzar sent and brought him to Babylonia, with the precious vessels of the house of the Lord,* [*and made his brother Zedekiah king of Judah and Jerusalem*] (II Chron. 36:10).
D. "Now what is the meaning of 'the precious vessels of the house of the Lord'? This refers to the ark."
E. R. Judah b. Laqqish says, "The ark was stored away in its proper place, since it says, *And the poles were so long that the ends of the poles were seen from the holy place before the inner sanctuary; but they could not be seen from outside; and they are there to this day* (I Kings 8:8)."

T. 2:18 L p. 212, ls. 79-85

T. 2:17B explains the theory of M. 6:1A3, and this assigns the idea of M. 6:3 to Judah. C-D add to A. Eliezer, T. 2:18, rejects the theory of Gamaliel and M. 6:2, and Simeon agrees with Eliezer.

6:4

A. Thirteen tables were in the sanctuary:
B. eight of marbles in the shambles, on which they rinse the innards [of offerings];
C. two at the west of the ramp, one of marble and one of silver—
D. on the one of marble they lay out the limbs, and on the one of silver, the utensils of service;
E. two in the Porch on the inside, at the entry of the house, one of marble and one of gold—
F. on the one of marble they put the Show Bread when it is brought in, and on the one of gold when it is taken out,
G. for they promote what is holy to a higher status and do not bring it down;
H. one of gold inside, on which the Show Bread is set at all times.

M. 6:4

M. now provides the exegesis of M. 6:1A2. The form of B is carefully followed at the other two stichs, D/C and F/E + H, then G explains why the table of marble is used first, that of gold after. G would be better situated after H. The matter is familiar from M. Men. 11:8.

6:5-6

A. Thirteen *shofar*-chests were in the sanctuary.
B. And written on them were the following [in Aramaic]:
C. (1) "New *sheqels*" and (2) "old *sheqels*,"
D. (3) "bird-offerings," and (4) "young birds for a burnt-offering"; (5) "wood" and (6) "frankincense"; (7) "gold for the Mercy-seat", and on six, "for freewill-offerings."
E. *New sheqels*—those for each year [that is, for the present year].
F. *Old sheqels*—He who did not pay his *sheqel* last year pays his *sheqel* in the coming year.
G. *Bird-offerings*—these are for turtle-doves.
H. *Young birds for a burnt-offering*"—these are for pigeons.
I. "And all of them [of D3, 4] are burnt-offerings," the words of R. Judah.
J. And sages say, "*Bird-offerings*—one is offered as a sin-offering and one as a burnt-offering [as at Qinnim, for a sin-offering].
K. "*Young birds for the whole offering*—all of them are burnt-offerings."

M. 6:5

A. He who says, "Lo, I pledge myself to give wood" should give no less than two pieces;
B. "... frankincense" should give no less than a handful;
C. "... gold" should give no less than a gold *denar*.
D. *And on six of them, for freewill-offerings*—

E. As to the freewill-offering: What did they do with it?
F. They purchase burnt-offerings.
G. The meat is for the Lord, and the hides belong to the priests.
H. This exegesis did Jehoida, the High Priest, expound: *"It is a guilt-offering, he has certainly been guilty before the Lord* (Lev. 5:19)—
I. "This is the governing principle: Whatever is brought because of sin or guilt—with it burnt-offerings are purchased. The meat is for the Lord, and the hides go to the priests.
J. "Thus it turns out two Scriptures are carried out: [*He shall bring*] *his guilt offering to the Lord* (Lev. 5:15), and, *For a guilt-offering for the priest* (Lev. 5:18).
K. "And so it says, *The money for the guilt-offerings and the money for the sin offerings was not brought into the house of the Lord; it was the priests'* (II Kings 12:16)."

M. 6:6

After the list, M. 6:5 A-D, M. systematically explains the disposition of the funds placed in each of the chests. Whoever volunteered or owed the stated donations or offerings would pay for them in this way. Judah, M. 6:5I, maintains that fowl which are given as freewill-offerings are solely prepared as burnt-offerings. Sages, M. 6:5J, rightly note that one who *owes* fowl has his two birds offered as specified. Sages hold that one who offered bird-offerings would deposit funds for them in chest D3. M. 6:6A, B, C go over the ground of M. 6:5 D5, 6, 7. E-F + G-K are slightly out of phase with the established exegetical pattern.

The point of M. 6:6H-K is that money put aside for a sin- or guilt-offering cannot go to priests, since it is used for buying an offering. If money is left over, the priests buy voluntary burnt-offerings, of which they keep the hide. But of the sin- or guilt-offering they do not keep the hide.

A. *Thirteen shofar-chests were in the sanctuary. And written on them were the following words*: "*new sheqels*" *and* "*old sheqels*"; "*bird-offerings*" *and* "*young birds for a burnt-offering*"; "*wood*" *and* "*frankincense*"; "*gold for the Mercy-Seat*"; *and on six,* "*for freewill-offerings.*"
B. "*New sheqels*"—*those for each year* [*that is, for the present year*]; "*Old sheqels*"—*He who did not pay his sheqel last year pays his sheqel in the coming year* [M. 6:5A-F].
C. *And these* [*the old ones*] *fall to the fund of the residue of the sheqel-chamber.*

T. 3:1 L pp. 212-213, ls. 1-4

A. *Bird-offerings* [M. 6:5G]: He who says, "Lo, I pledge myself to give a bird-offering" brings the money for his bird-offering and puts it into the *shofar*-chest.

B. [If] he brought less than was required, they do not accept it from him.

C. [If] he brought more than was required, a priest takes the funds required for his bird-offering and puts them into the *shofar*-chest.

D. And the surplus is not to go to the *shofar*-chest for freewill-offerings.

E. Priests empty them in the normal way and buy with them bird-offerings and offer half of them up as sin-offerings and half of them as burnt-offerings [M. 6:5J].

T. 3:2 L p. 213, ls. 4-6

A. The woman who put the funds for her bird-offering [M. 6:5J] into the *shofar*-chest may eat the meat of animal-sacrifices in the evening.

B. R. Judah says, "There was no *shofar*-chest for bird-offerings,

C. "because of the possibility of confusion.

D. "But he who says, 'Lo, I pledge myself to give two' brings the required funds and puts them into the *shofar*-chest for two.

E. "If he pledged turtle-doves, he brings the money and puts it into the chest for turtle-doves."

T. 3:3 L p. 213, ls. 7-10

T. systematically expands M. Important is the expansion of M. 6:5J-K vs. I at T. 3:3.

A. Wood [M. 6:6A]: He who says, "Lo, I pledge myself to bring wood" brings the price of two sticks of wood and puts it into the *shofar*-chest.

B. Priests take out the money and buy with it wood and offer it up on the altar.

C. They make use of it, and the laws of sacrilege do not apply to it [if it is wasted for private benefit].

D. And if one offered up the wood outside of the Temple courtyard, he is exempt from punishment.

E. But if he said, "Lo, I pledge myself to bring *these* two sticks of wood for use on the altar," he brings two sticks of wood.

F. Priests accept them from him and offer them up on the altar.

G. And they do not make use of them.

H. But the laws of sacrilege apply to them.

I. "And if one offered them up outside of the Temple-courtyard, he is liable," the words of Rabbi.

J. And sages say, "If he offered them up outside of the Temple-courtyard, he is exempt."

K. Both wood one volunteers for the altar and wood one volunteers as an offering go to the chamber which serves as the woodshed.

T. 3:4 L pp. 213-214, ls. 10-16

A. *Frankincense* [M. 6:6B]: He who says, "Lo, I pledge myself to bring frankincense" brings the cost of a handful of frankincense and puts it into the *shofar*-chest.

B. Priests empty it out and buy with it frankincense.
C. And they offer it on the altar.

T. 3:5 L p. 214, ls. 16-18

A. *Gold* [M. 6:6C]: He who says, "Lo, I pledge myself to bring gold" bring the cost of a gold *denar* and puts it into the *shofar*-chest.
B. Priests empty it out and buy with it gold.
C. And they make it into gold plate for the house of the Holy of Holies.

T. 3:6 L p. 214, ls. 18-20

A. *Six chests* [*marked*] *for a freewill-offering* [M. 6:6D]:
B. for the surplus of sin-offerings, guilt-offerings, the surplus of bird-offerings for *Zab*s, bird-offerings for female *Zab*s, bird-offerings for women after childbirth,
C. and the surplus of the offerings of a Nazirite and those of one afflicted with *ṣaraʿat*.

T. 3:7 L p. 214, ls. 20-22

A. He who says, "This *maneh* is for a freewill-offering," "This *sela* is for a freewill-offering," brings it and puts it into the *shofar*-chest for a freewill-offering.
B. Priests empty it out and purchase burnt-offerings with them.
C. The meat is for the Lord, and the hides belong to the priests [M. 6:6H-K].

T. 3:8 L p. 214, ls. 22-24

T. systematically glosses M.'s own glosses of M. 6:5A-D.

A. A proselyte is held back from eating animal-sacrifices until he brings his bird-offering.
B. [If] he brought one bird [of the two], then he may eat animal-sacrifices in the evening.

T. 3:20 L p. 217, ls. 58-59

A. All those who are obligated to bring bird-offerings by the Torah [bring] half of them as sin-offerings and half of them as burnt-offerings,
B. except for the bird-offering of a proselyte.
C. For even though they are obligatory, both of them are offered as a burnt-offering.
D. [If] one wanted to offer his obligatory offering in the form of cattle, he may bring it.
E. [If he brought] burnt-offering of cattle for his atonement offering, he has fulfilled his obligation.
F. [If he brought] the meal-offerings and drink-offerings, he has not carried out his obligation.
G. A bird-offering has been specified only to make things easier for him.

H. If [a proselyte] brought for the offering at the end of his bout with ṣaraʿat, let him bring again for his atonement [as a proselyte].

I. [If one brought his offerings at the end of] his Nazirite vow, let him go and bring one for his atonement offering.

T. 3:21 L pp. 217-218, ls. 58-62

T. 3:21A is relevant to M. 6:5J-K. But the whole is autonomous of M.

CHAPTER EIGHT

SHEQALIM CHAPTER SEVEN

This whole chapter forms an appendix to M. 6:5-6. Once we are told that the Temple has thirteen *shofar*-chests, we ask how we dispose of a coin found not in, but near, one of these chests, and, of much greater urgency to M.'s exegetical logic, a coin found precisely in-between two of the chests. M. 7:1 gives four examples—a triplet and one other—of such a situation, then (as if the meaning were not clear) makes the governing principle explicit. M. 7:2 goes on to dispose of funds found in various locations and at various times in the city of Jerusalem. M. 7:3 deals with meat, and M. 7:4, cattle, which may turn up in or near Jerusalem. There we dispose of the item by reference to its condition; if it conforms to the rules of a given sacrificial procedure, it is then assumed to fall within that category. Since M. 7:4 refers to a beast found within range of Jerusalem, which is assumed to have been consecrated, it also raises the question of who provides the drink-offerings required with the cattle, the finder or the Temple, dealt with at M. 7:5, which bears in its wake yet a secondary development, M. 7:6-7.

7:1

I   A. Money which is found between the chest for *sheqel*s and that for freewill-offerings—

B. [if it is] nearer to the chest for *sheqel*s, it falls to that for *sheqel*s.

C. [If it is] nearer to that for freewill-offerings, it falls to that for freewill-offerings.

D. [If it is] half way in between, it falls to that for freewill-offerings.

II   E. [If it is found] between the chest for wood and the chest for frankincense, [if it is] nearer to the chest for wood, it goes to the chest for wood.

F. [If it is] nearer the chest for frankincense, it goes for the chest for frankincense.

G. [If it is] half way in between, it goes to the chest for frankincense.

III   H. [If it is found] between the chest for bird-offerings and the chest for young birds for whole-offerings,

I. [if it is] nearer the chest for bird-offerings, it goes to the chest for bird-offerings.

J. [If it is] nearer the chest for young birds for whole-offerings, it goes to the chest for young birds for whole-offerings.

K. [If it is] half way in between, it goes to the chest for young birds for whole-offerings.

L. [If it is found] between unconsecrated coins and coins in the status of second tithe,

M. [if it is] nearer the unconsecrated coins, it goes to the purposes of unconsecrated coins.

N. [If it is] nearer to the coins in the status of second tithe, it falls for the purposes of money in the status of second tithe.

O. [If it is] half way in between, it goes to the purposes of money in the status of second tithe.

P. This is the governing principle: They follow the status of that which is nearer, [even if this produces] a lenient ruling.

Q. But if the money is found exactly half way in-between, they impose the more stringent ruling.

M. 7:1

P-Q explain the examples, all in exquisitely perfect form. The relevance of the item is clear. But L-O are out of phase, since the case is domestic, not cultic. The principle is the same.

7:2

A. Money which was found before cattle-dealers—

B. throughout the year, it is deemed money in the status of second tithe.

C. [If it is found] on the Temple mount, it is assumed to be unconsecrated money.

D. [If it is found] in Jerusalem during a pilgrim festival, it is assumed to be money in the status of second tithe.

E. And at all other times of the year, it is deemed to be unconsecrated.

M. 7:2

The contrast of B to D-E suggests that the basic form is a triplet, A-B, D, E, with C interpolated. The point is that money spent on meat is assumed to be second tithe coins brought to Jerusalem for this purpose. Consecrated coins cannot be used to purchase offerings, so C follows. C reverts to A, money found not in the meat-market. Here too, at certain times it is tithe. But the streets are swept daily, so ordinarily found money is deemed unconsecrated.

A. *Money which was found before cattle-dealers at all times is deemed money in the status of second tithe. And [if it is found] on the Temple mount, it is assumed to be unconsecrated money. And [if it is found in Jerusalem] at all other times of the year, it is deemed to be unconsecrated. And at the time of the festival,* all is assumed *to be [second] tithe* [M. 7:2].

B. Said R. Yosé, "This is the opinion of the House of Shammai.

C. "But the House of Hillel say, 'Under all circumstances it is assumed to be in the status of [second] tithe, except for that which is found on the Temple mount on ordinary days of the year,

D. " 'which is assumed to be unconsecrated.' "

T. 3:9 L pp. 214-215, ls. 24-27

T. supplies the authorities of M.

7:3

A. Meat which is found in the courtyard—
I   B. [if it is in] limbs, it is deemed to derive from burnt-offerings [M. Tam. 4:2].
II   C. [If it is in] pieces, it is deemed to derive from sin-offerings.
III   D. [If it is found] in Jerusalem, it is deemed to derive from peace-offerings.

E. In each instance its appearance is allowed to spoil, and it goes out to the place of burning.

F. [If] it is found out in the provinces,

G. [if it is in] limbs, it is deemed to be carrion.

H. [If it is in] pieces, it is permitted.

I. And at the time of a festival, when there is plenty of meat, even limbs are permitted.

M. 7:3

The presumptive status of the meat of unknown origin is determined by its condition. The burnt-offering is cut into limbs, the sin-offering is chopped up for priests' use. Limbs in the provinces may have been carrion thrown to dogs.

A. Pieces of meat which are found in the Temple courtyard strung out on string are permitted.

B. For meat in the status of Holy Things is not strung out on strings.

C. That which is found on the ash-heap in every place is prohibited.

T. 3:10 L p. 215, ls. 27-28

T. complements M. 7:3A and explains A at B; C is obvious.

7:4-7

A. Cattle found between Jerusalem and Migdal 'Eder—and in an equivalent range on all sides of the city—

B. [if] male, they are deemed to be burnt-offerings;
C. [if] female, they are deemed to be peace-offerings.
D. R. Judah says, "That which is suitable for Passover-offerings are Passover-offerings [if they are found] thirty days before that festival."

M. 7:4

A. Aforetimes they would exact pledges from the ones who found [such a beast], until he would bring its drink-offerings.
B. They ended up leaving them and running out.
C. The court ordained that its drink-offerings should derive from public funds.

M. 7:5

A. Said R. Simeon, "Seven rules did the court ordain, and this (1) [foregoing one] is one of them.
B. "(2) A gentile who sent his burnt-offering from overseas and sent drink-offerings with it—they are offered from what he has sent. But if not, they are offered from public funds.
(3) "And so too a proselyte who died and left animals designated for sacrifices, if it has drink-offerings, they are offered from his estate. And if not, they are offered from public funds.
(4) "And it is a condition imposed by the court on a high priest who died, that his meal-offering [Lev. 6:13] should derive from public funds."
C. R. Judah says, "It derives from the funds of the heirs, and it was offered whole."

M. 7:6

A. "[They ordained] (5) concerning salt and wood, that priests should be able to make use of them;
B. "(6) concerning the red cow, that the laws of sacrilege should not apply to its ashes;
C. "(7) concerning invalid bird-offerings, that [others to replace them] should derive from public funds."
D. R. Yosé says, "He who provides the bird-offerings must provide others in place of the invalid ones."

M. 7:7

M. 7:4 concludes the exposition begun at M. 7:1, and M. 7:5-7 form an appendix. Simeon's list, M. 7:6A-B, M. 7:7A-C, bears two interpolations, M. 7:6C, M. 7:7D. The main point is the use of public funds, ordinances 1, 2, 3, 4, 7.

A. A gentile who brought his peace-offerings—
B. [if] he gave them to an Israelite, the Israelite eats them.
C. [If] he gave them to a priest, the priest eats them.
D. A gentile who died and Israelites appropriated his estate,
E. and afterwards it became known that his property had been consecrated—

F. they retrieve [the property] from their possession.

T. 3:11 L p. 215, ls. 28-30

A. Said R. Yosé, "I have heard that he who eats Most Holy Things after the tossing of the blood pays the principal but does not pay the added fifth."

B. R. Ishmael b. R. Yoḥanan b. Beroqah says, "He pays the principal and the added fifth to the priests.

C. "The priests then purchase peace-offerings with the funds and offer them up on the altar."

T. 3:12 L p. 215, ls. 31-33

T. 3:11 is relevant to the theme of M. 7:6B.

CHAPTER NINE

SHEQALIM CHAPTER EIGHT

The exposition of the problem introduced in Chapter Six and expanded in Chapter Seven concludes here: the disposition of objects which are found in Jerusalem and how we decide about their character and effects. M. 8:1 deals with drops of spit, M. 8:2 with utensils, and M. 8:3 with a knife found at or near the time of slaughtering the Passover, a rather neat allusion to the antecedent tractate, reminiscent of M. Erubin Chapter Ten and its clear resonance of M. Shabbat Chapter One.

M. 8:4-7 form a large unit, located here for reasons I cannot understand. M. 8:4 and M. 8:6-7 deal with the distinction between a Father of uncleanness and an Offspring thereof. A veil of the Temple made unclean by the Offspring of uncleanness is immersed in the Temple and put back immediately; one made unclean by a Father is immersed outside and put out to dry until ("to await for") sunset, before being brought in. That rule is supplemented by a totally irrelevant interpolation on the character of the veil. Then, M. 8:6-7, we deal with a triplet of distinctions: (1) meat in the status of Most Holy Things and Lesser Holy Things, (2) the courtyard and the area outside, and (3) a Father of uncleanness and an Offspring of uncleanness. The operative principle governing where these several items are burned is applied variously by the Houses, then Eliezer vs. 'Aqiba. M. 8:8A-C carry forward the concerns of M. 8:4: where we locate certain items which have to be set down for a time during the liturgy. M. 8:8Dff., finally return to the theme of the tractate, the *sheqel*-tax. It does not apply after the destruction of the Temple. In all the chapter is something of a potpourri, and why the large unit, M. 8:4-8D, is inserted I do not know. T., for its part, includes a mass of materials relevant to Yoma, not to Sheqalim. Someone attempting to construct a case against the theory that Mishnah has been subjected to careful redaction along logical-thematic lines (that is, the theory spelled out as *Purities* XXI, pp. 22-112), will find rich supporting evidence in this chapter. To consign the bulk of it to the status of an appendix to the tractate, by contrast, offers little comfort for the contrary view. For it begs the question of why onto this tractate in particular these things are tacked.

8:1

A. "All drops of spit which are found in Jerusalem are assumed to be clean,
B. "except for those [found in] the Upper Market Place," the words of R. Meir.
C. R. Yosé says, "On the ordinary days of the year, those [found] in the middle [of the road] are unclean, and those found on the sides are clean. And at the time of the festival, those [found] in the middle of the road are clean, and those [found] on the sides are unclean,
D. "for, because [at festival time] they [who are unclean] are few in number, they withdraw to the sides of the road."

M. 8:1

The issue of the dispute is clear as given, and Yosé, C, supplies his own exegesis, D. The Upper Market Place had unclean and gentile folk.

8:2

A. "All utensils found in Jerusalem,
B. "on the path down to an immersion-pool, are assumed to be unclean.
C. "[If they are found] on the path up from the immersion pool, they are assumed to be clean.
D. "For the way down is different from the way up," the words of R. Meir.
E. R. Yosé says, "All of them are clean,
F. "except for a basket, shovel, or pick, [which are] particularly used for digging graves."

M. 8:2

Yosé assumes utensils in Jerusalem normally are clean, except those clearly used for grave-digging, F.

8:3

A. A knife found on the fourteenth of Nisan—
B. one slaughters with it forthwith.
C. [If it is found] on the thirteenth, one immerses it again.
D. And as to a chopper, one way or the other, one immerses again.
E. [If] the fourteenth coincided with the Sabbath, one slaughters with it immediately.
F. [If the chopper was found] on the fifteenth of Nisan, one slaughters it with it immediately.
G. [If] it was found tied to a knife, lo, this is in the status of [that] knife.

M. 8:3

The knife found on the fourteenth is assumed clean for use that day. Otherwise it is assumed unclean and undergoes a (second) immersion. After D's contrast to C, the chopper is dealt with. This may be used for slaughtering, so E, F follow. G concludes by linking D + E-F to A-C, a fine piece of redaction.

8:4-7

A. The veil [of the Temple] which contracted uncleanness from an Offspring of uncleanness—
B. they immerse it inside [the courtyard] and bring it in forthwith.
C. And that which was made unclean by a Father of uncleanness—
D. they immerse it outside and spread it out on the Rampart.
E. But if it was new, they spread it out on the roof of the portico,
F. so that people may see how fine is its workmanship.

M. 8:4

A. Rabban Simeon b. Gamaliel says in the name of R. Simeon, Son of the Prefect, "The veil was a handbreadth thick, and was woven on a loom of seventy-two cords,
B. "and each cord was made up of twenty-four threads.
C. "It was forty cubits long, and twenty cubits broad.
D. "It was made by eighty-two young girls [or: it was made up of eighty-two times ten thousand threads].
E. "And they make two a year."
F. "And three hundred priests immerse it."

M. 8:5

A. Meat of Most Holy Things which was made unclean, whether by a Father of uncleanness or by an Offspring of uncleanness,
B. whether inside or outside the Temple courtyard—
C. the House of Shammai say, "All is burned inside,
D. "except for that which was made unclean by a Father of uncleanness, which is burned outside."
E. And the House of Hillel say, "All is burned outside, except for that which is made unclean by an Offspring of uncleanness, which is burned inside."

M. 8:6

A. R. Eliezer says, "That which is made unclean by a Father of uncleanness, whether inside or outside, is to be burned outside.
B. "That which is made unclean by an Offspring of uncleanness, whether inside or outside, is to be burned inside."
C. R. 'Aqiba says, "Where it is made unclean, there it is burned."

M. 8:7

The relevance of this unit to what has gone before is unclear to me. Perhaps M. 8:3's interest in purification-processes is carried forward.

The point of M. 8:4D is that the veil is clean only at sunset. E-F gloss D, and M. 8:5 is a wildly irrelevant interpolation. M. 8:6-7 then follow the distinction of M. 8:4A, C. The distinctions operative for the Houses and Eliezer-'Aqiba are clear as given.

    A. *The veil was forty cubits long and twenty cubits broad* [M. 8:5C].
    B. And it was woven *in blue, purple, and scarlet stuff and fine twined linen, in skilled work* (Ex. 26:31).
    C. There was yet another one, twenty cubits long and ten cubits broad.
    D. And it was woven *in blue, purple, and scarlet stuff, and fine twined linen*, in woven work.
    E. And it was spread out over the entry to the *Hekhal* on the outside.
    F. R. Judah says, "This one which they bring out from the inside was folded over, once into two, and then a second time into four.
    G. "It was spread out over the entry of the *Hekhal* on the outside."
    H. They said to him, "Will an object which served in a state of strict sanctity then go and serve in a state of diminished sanctity?"

    T. 3:13 L pp. 215-216, ls. 34-40

    A. Another matter: Concerning this one it is written, *In skilled work*, and concerning that one it is written, *In woven work*.
    B. R. Nehemiah says, "*Skilled work* refers to one with two surfaces, and woven work refers to one with a single surface [on the fabric].
    C. "But this one, which they take inside, was doubled over once, and the folded in half a second time, thus into quarters.
    D. "And it was kept in the upper room, facing the lower one, as it is said, *And the veil shall separate for you the Holy Place from the most holy* (Ex. 26:33)."

    T. 3:14 L p. 216, ls. 40-44

    A. R. Ḥanina b. Antigonus says, "There were two veils [M. 8:5E], one spread out, and one folded up.
    B. "[If] the one which was spread out was made unclean, they spread out the one which was folded up.
    C. "On the eve of the Day of Atonement they bring in the new one and take out the old one."

    T. 3:15 L p. 216, ls. 44-46

T. complements M. 8:5.

    A. *The meat of Most Holy Things which was made unclean, whether by a Father of uncleanness or by an Offspring of uncleanness, whether inside or outside the Temple courtyard—*
    B. *the House of Shammai say, "All is to be burned inside, except for*

that which was made unclean by a Father of uncleanness, which is burned outside."

C. *And the House of Hillel say, "All is burned outside, except for that which is made unclean by an Offspring of uncleanness, which is burned inside."*

D. *R. Eliezer says, "That which is made unclean by a Father of uncleanness, whether inside or outside, is to be burned outside. And that which is made unclean by an Offspring of uncleanness, whether inside or outside, is to be burned inside"* [M. 8:6-7B].

E. R. Judah says, "R. Eliezer rules in accord with the opinion of the House of Shammai.

F. "R. 'Aqiba rules in accord with the opinion of the House of Hillel" [cf. M. 8:7].

T. 3:16 L pp. 216-217, ls. 46-52

Judah glosses M. 8:6-7.

8:8

I A. Limbs of the daily whole-offering are set down on the altar-ramp, on the lower half, on the east.

II B. And those of the additional offerings are set down on the lower half of the ramp, at the west.

III C. And those of the offerings for the New Months are set down on the rim of the altar, above.

D. [Laws concerning] *sheqel*-dues and first fruits apply only in the time of the Temple.

E. But those concerning tithe of grain, tithe of cattle, and of firstlings apply both in the time of the Temple and not in the time of the Temple.

F. He who [nowadays] declares *sheqel*s and first fruit to be holy—lo, this is deemed holy.

G. R. Simeon says, "He who says, 'First fruit is holy,'—they do not enter the status of Holy Things."

M. 8:8

M. 8:8A-C resume M. 8:4D, E-F. D-F + G belong to the tractate, but not to any of its chapters. D-E and F *vs.* G are clear as given, a complement to E. Ex. 23:19 no longer applies.

A. The limbs of the daily whole offering, concerning which they have said that they put them below [M. 8:8A]—

B. they put them on the lower half of the ramp, on the east.

C. And those which they said they put above—they put them on the upper half of the ramp, to the west.

T. 3:17 L p. 217, ls. 52-54

A. R. Ḥanania b. 'Aqashia says, "Both these and those do they put on the lower half of the ramp.

B. "But: the daily whole offerings are set down on the west, and the additional offerings on the east,
C. *And those of the New Months are set down* under *the rim of the altar, below.*

T. 3:18 L p. 217, ls. 54-56

A. What is the rim of the altar?
B. Between one horn and the next, a place for the passage of the priests and onward.

T. 3:19 L p. 217, ls. 56-57

M. 8:8 accords with T. 3:17.

A. The requirement of a bird-offering for a proselyte applies only in the time of the Temple.
B. And one has to bring it now [set it apart, but not kill it].
C. R. Simeon says, "One does not have to set it apart now,
D. "because of the possibility of disorder" [cf. M. 8:8D-G].

T. 3:22 L p. 218, ls. 62-64

A. On what account did they rule: [The offering of] *sheqels applies only in the time of the Temple* [M. 8:8D]?
B. Because they do not take up heave-offering from what belongs to the previous year [so the *sheqels* put aside nowadays are useless].

T. 3:23 L p. 218, ls. 64-65

A. And on what account did they rule: [The offering of] *first fruits applies only in the time of the Temple* [M. 8:8D]?
B. Because it says, *The first of the first fruits of your ground you shall bring into the house of the Lord your God* (Ex. 23:19).
C. So long as there is a house, there is the requirement to bring the first fruits.
D. When there is no longer a house, there is no longer a requirement to bring the first fruits.

T. 3:24 L p. 218, ls. 65-68

A. A high priest does not enter the courtyard for service unless he was anointed seven days and increases the number of priestly garments to seven.
B. But even though he was not anointed for seven days and did not multiply priestly garments to the number of seven but performed an act of service, his act of service is valid.
C. And likewise, an ordinary priest should not enter the Temple courtyard for an act of service if he has not brought a tenth of an *ephah* of fine flour out of his own pocket.
D. And he offers it up by his own hand.
E. But even though he did not bring a tenth of an *ephah* of fine flour out of his own pocket and did not prepare it by his own hand but performed an act of service, his act of service is valid.

T. 3:25 L p. 218, ls. 68-72

A. A Levite does not enter the Temple courtyard to perform his service unless he has studied for five years,

B. since it says, *This is what pertains to the Levites: from twenty-five years old and upward they shall go in to perform the work in the service of the tent of meeting* (Num. 8:24).

C. And elsewhere it says, *From the age of thirty* (Num. 4:35).

D. Now if it says, "From the age of twenty-five," then how can it say, "from the age of thirty," and if it says, "From the age of thirty," then how can it say, "From the age of twenty-five"?

E. But: All those years which are between the age of twenty-five and the age of thirty he would study. From that time on they would bring him to perform for the Temple service.

F. On this basis have they ruled: Whoever has not given good evidence in his repetition [of traditions] during five years later on will never give any.

G. R. Yosé says, "Three years, since it says, *They were to be educated for three years* (Dan. 1:5)."

T. 3:26 L pp. 218-219, ls. 72-79

A. An elder is not seated in the Hewn-Stone Chamber unless he was made a judge in his own town.

B. Once he was made a judge in his own town, they bring him up and seat him on the Temple mount.

C. From there they bring him up and seat him on the Rampart.

D. From there they bring him up and seat him in the Hewn-Stone Chamber.

T. 3:27 L p. 219, ls. 79-81

T. 3:22-3:24 complements then cites and glosses M. 8:8D-G. I do not see why the rest is located here, except as a bridge to the next tractate's theme. Then the unfolding of the conditions of service goes from priest to Levite to disciple to judge, that is, a normal progression of topics.

YOMA

CHAPTER TEN

INTRODUCTION TO YOMA

What is important to Mishnah's tractate on the Day of Atonement is defined by Scripture. The first seven chapters simply provide a flowing narrative, heavy with interpolated materials to be sure, on the sacrificial rite of the Day of Atonement. The relevant Scriptures are Leviticus 16:1-34. Other allusions to sacrificial rites on the Day of Atonement, specifically, Lev. 23:26-32, Numbers 29:7-11, are taken into account, but only by brief allusion. The Mishnaic narrative, as I shall show, closely follows the lines of Lev. 16:

> The Lord spoke to Moses, after the death of the two sons of Aaron, when they drew near before the Lord and died; and the Lord said to Moses, "Tell Aaron your brother not to come at all times into the holy place within the veil, before the mercy seat which is upon the ark, lest he die; for I will appear in the cloud upon the mercy seat. But thus shall Aaron come into the holy place, with a young bull for a sin offering and a ram for a burnt offering. He shall put on the holy linen coat, and shall have the linen breeches on his body, be girded with the linen girdle, and wear the linen turban; these are the holy garments. He shall bathe his body in water, and then put them on. And he shall take from the congregation of the people of Israel two male goats for a sin offering, and one ram for a burnt offering.
>
> "And Aaron shall offer the bull as a sin offering for himself, and shall make atonement for himself and for his house. Then he shall take the two goats, and set them before the Lord at the door of the tent of meeting; and Aaron shall cast lots upon the two goats, one lot for the Lord and the other lot for Azazel. And Aaron shall present the goat on which the lot fell for the Lord, and offer it as a sin offering; but the goat on which the lot fell for Azazel shall be presented alive before the Lord to make atonement over it, that it may be sent away into the wilderness to Azazel.
>
> "Aaron shall present the bull as a sin offering for himself, and shall make atonement for himself and for his house; he shall kill the bull as a sin offering for himself. And he shall take a censer full of coals of fire from the altar before the Lord, and two handfuls of sweet incense beaten small; and he shall bring it within the veil and put the incense on the fire before the Lord, that the cloud of the incense may cover the mercy seat which is upon the testimony, lest he die; and he shall take some of the blood of the bull, and sprinkle it with his finger

on the front of the mercy seat, and before the mercy seat he shall sprinkle the blood with his finger seven times.

"Then he shall kill the goat of the sin offering which is for the people, and bring its blood within the veil, and do with its blood as he did with the blood of the bull, sprinkling it upon the mercy seat and before the mercy seat; thus he shall make atonement for the holy place, because of the uncleannesses of the people of Israel, and because of their transgressions, all their sins; and so he shall do for the tent of meeting, which abides with them in the midst of their uncleanness. There shall be no man in the tent of meeting when he enters to make atonement in the holy place until he comes out and has made atonement for himself and for his house and for all the assembly of Israel. Then he shall go out to the altar which is before the Lord and make atonement for it, and shall take some of the blood of the bull and of the blood of the goat, and put it on the horns of the altar round about. And he shall sprinkle some of the blood upon it with his finger seven times, and cleanse it and hallow it from the uncleanness of the people of Israel.

"And when he has made an end of atoning for the holy place and the tent of meeting and the altar, he shall present the live goat; and Aaron shall lay both his hands upon the head of the live goat, and confess over him all the iniquities of the people of Israel, and all their transgressions, and all their sins; and he shall put them upon the head of the goat, and send him away into the wilderness by the hand of a man who is in readiness. The goat shall bear all their iniquities upon him to a solitary land; and he shall let the goat go in the wilderness.

"Then Aaron shall come into the tent of meeting, and shall put off the linen garments which he put on when he went into the holy place, and shall leave them there; and he shall bathe his body in water in a holy place, and put on his garments, and come forth, and offer him burnt offering and the burnt offering of the people, and make atonement for himself and for the people. And the fat of the sin offering he shall burn upon the altar. And he who lets the goat go to Azazel shall wash his clothes and bathe his body in water, and afterward he may come into the camp. And the bull for the sin offering and the goat for the sin offering, whose blood was brought in to make atonement in the holy place, shall be carried forth outside the camp; their skin and their flesh and their dung shall be burned with fire. And he who burns them shall wash his clothes and bathe his body in water, and afterward he may come into the camp.

"And it shall be a statute to you for ever that in the seventh month, on the tenth day of the month, you shall afflict yourself, and shall do no work, either the native or the stranger who sojourns among you; for on this day shall atonement be made for you, to cleanse you, from all your sins you shall be clean before the Lord. It is a sabbath of solemn rest to you, and you shall afflict yourselves; it is a statute for ever. And the priest who is anointed and consecrated as priest in his father's place shall make atonement, wearing the holy linen garments; he shall make atonement for the sanctuary, and he shall make atonement for the tent of meeting and for the altar, and he shall make atonement for the priests and for all the people of the assembly. And this shall be an everlasting statute for you, that atonement may be made for the people of Israel once in the year because of all their sins." And Moses did as the Lord commanded him.

The sequence of the Levitical rite thus is laid out at Lev. 16:3-5, which speak of a bull for a sin-offering, a ram for a burnt-offering, and two male goats for a sin-offering and a ram for a burnt-offering, respectively. Scripture has Aaron, the high priest, make an offering for himself, then take care of the two goats; then he offers a bull as a sin-offering for himself, makes an incense-offering, he kills the goat of the sin-offering for the people, and purifies the holy place. After purifying the holy place, Aaron confesses the sins of the people and sends off the scapegoat. He then offers a burnt-offering for himself and for the people and so on. As we shall now see, the narrative of Mishnah restates all of these procedures, adding at the beginning the daily whole-offering, which precedes all of the rites of the Day of Atonement. Indeed, the only way to explain Mishnah's sequence of topics is by reference to the narrative of Scripture.

I. *The conduct of the Temple rite on the Day of Atonement.* 1:1-7:5

    A. *Preparing the high priest for the Day of Atonement.* 1:1-7

1:1   Seven days before the Day of Atonement they set the high priest apart from his house (wife) and also appoint a substitute.

1:2   All seven days he tosses the blood, offers the incense, trims the lamps, and offers up the head and hind leg of the daily whole-offering.

1:3   They hand him over to elders of the court, who read for him the prescribed rite of the Day of Atonement.

1:4   All seven days they give him plenty of food and drink, until the eve of the Day of Atonement at dusk.

1:5   They impose an oath on him to carry out the rite in the correct way.

1:6   They keep him awake all night, by having him expound the relevant Scriptures.

1:7   If he tried to doze, the young priests snap their fingers at him.

    B. *Clearing the ashes off the altar.* 1:8-2:4

1:8   Every day they take up the ashes from the altar at the cock's crow. On the Day of Atonement they do it after midnight.

	By the time the cock crows, the courtyard is filled with masses of Israelites.
2:1-2	Appendix on clearing the ashes from the altar. At first whoever wanted to remove the ashes from the altar did it. Later they cast lots.
2:3-4	Other occasions for casting lots: the second one is for who disposed of the daily whole-offering. The third is for who burns the incense. The fourth is for who brings the offerings up the ramp and puts them on the altar.

C. *The narrative resumes. The daily whole-offering on the Day of Atonement.* 2:5-3:5

2:5-7	The daily whole-offering was offered by nine, ten, eleven or twelve priests, never less, never more.
3:1-2	The supervisor finds out whether the time for slaughtering the morning whole-offering has come.
3:3-4	Five acts of immersion and ten acts of sanctification of the hands and feet does the high priest carry out on the Day of Atonement.
3:4	The first such act of immersion is preparatory to slaughtering the daily whole offering. The offering is carried out.
3:5	The incense offering of the morning.

D. *The narrative continues. The high priest's personal offering for the Day of Atonement.* 3:6-8.

3:6	The high priest sanctifies his hands and feet, immerses, dries off, and changes into the white robes for the rite to come.
3:7	The value of the robes.
3:8	The bullock of the high priest. The high priest confesses his sins while laying hands on the bullock.

E. *The two goats and other offerings on the Day of Atonement.* 3:9-5:7.

3:9	He comes over to the two goats and the box with two lots.
3:10-11	Appendix on certain utensils provided for the cult by donations of individuals and related "historical" materials. [*The simultaneous rites: the scape-goat is killed in the wilderness, and burnt-offering is killed in the Temple in behalf of the people:*]
4:1	He shook the box with the lots and brought up two. The goats then are designated for their respective purposes.
4:2	The high priest tied a crimson thread on the head of the scape-goat and sent if off. He tied a crimson thread on the throat of the goat which was to be slaughtered. He said a confession over the other sacrifice, a bullock, which serves for the sins of the priesthood.
4:3	He slaughtered the sacrifice for the sins of the priesthood, and

	collected its blood, handed it over to someone to stir the blood, and then made an incense offering.
4:4-6	Appendix: Comparison of the preparation of the incense-offering on ordinary days and on the Day of Atonement.
5:1-2	The incense-rite is carried out. This is the one inside the veils, outside of the sight of the people.
5:3	He returns to take up the blood rite of the bullock which he had slaughtered for the sins of the priesthood. He carried out the blood rite.
5:4	Now he slaughters the goat which was to be the sin-offering for the community as a whole, that is, the one not sent out into the wilderness. He receives its blood and flicks it onto the altar. He now carries out the blood-rite for the bullock which he had slaughtered.
5:5	He purifies the golden altar and flicks blood there.
5:6	He tosses blood on top of the altar seven times.
5:7	Analytical unit: the proper order of the rite of the Day of Atonement. Rules applying when the order is not followed.

F. *The Scape-goat and its rule.* 6:1-8

6:1	Analytical unit on the two goats of the Day of Atonement.
6:2-4	The high priest lays hands on the scape-goat and confesses the sins of the people. The goat is led out.
6:5-6	The scape-goat is taken into the wilderness and pushed down into a ravine.
6:7-8	*Meanwhile*: the high priest comes to the bullock and the goat which serve as a sin-offering for the priesthood and the people, respectively. Now he completes the disposition of the carcasses, tearing them open and offering up the innards. He sends out the remaining limbs to the place of burning. The high priest is informed that the goat has reached the wilderness.

G. *The rite is concluded with Torah-reading and prayer.* 7:1-5

7:1	The high priest comes and reads the Torah in the Women's Court. The Scriptural passages selected for that purpose.
7:2	Reference to the location of the high priest. If one can see the priest when he is reading, he cannot see the bullock and goat which are burned. The two rites are done simultaneously.
7:3-4	The high priest changes into golden garments and offered the ram and the ram of the people, Lev. 16:24, and the seven unblemished lambs a year old (Num. 29:8)—that is, he completes the offerings of the day. He offers the incense of the twilight, trims the lamps, and goes home.
7:5	Appendix on the clothing of the high priest.

II. *The laws of the Day of Atonement.* 8:1-9

    A. *Not eating, drinking.* 8:1-7

8:1   On the Day of Atonement it is forbidden to eat, drink, bathe, put on oil, put on a sandal, or have sexual relations.
8:2   Not eating: liability.
8:3   Not eating: inadvertence.
8:4   Not eating: rules for children.
8:5-7   Not eating: rules for pregnant women, sick people. Appendix on saving life in a case of doubt.

    B. *Atonement.* 8:8-9

8:8   Sin-offering and unconditional guilt-offering atone. Death and the Day of Atonement atone when joined with repentence.
8:9   The importance of repentence in the process of atonement.

If we now compare the sequence of the narrative of Scripture to that of Mishnah, we see the following:

16.3   He shall put on the holy linen coat.   M. 3:6-7
16:6   Aaron shall offer the bull as a sin-offering for himself, and shall make atonement for himself and for his house.   M. 3:8
16:7   Then he shall take the two goats and set them before the Lord ... and Aaron shall cast lots upon the two goats, the lot for the Lord and the other lot for Azazel.   M. 3:9, 4:1
16:9   And Aaron shall present the goat on which the lot fell for the Lord and offer it as a sin-offering. But the goat on which the lot fell for Azazel ... is sent away into the wilderness.
16:11   Aaron shall present the bull as a sin-offering for himself and for his house.   M. 4:2-3
16:12   And he shall take a censer full of coals of fire from before the altar and two handfuls of sweet incense and shall bring it within the veil ...   M. 5:1-2
16:14   And he shall take some of the blood of the bull and sprinkle it with his finger on the front of the mercy seat   M. 5:3
16:15   Then he shall kill the goat of the sin-offering which is for the people ...   M. 5:4
16:18   Then he shall go out to the altar which is before the Lord and make atonement for it and shall take some of the blood of the bull and of the blood of the goat and put it on the horns of the altar...   M. 5:5-6
16:20   And when he has made an end of atoning for the holy place and the tent of meeting and the altar, he shall present the live goat. And Aaron shall lay both his hands on the head of the live goat and confess over him all the iniquities of the people of Israel and all their transgressions and sins ... and send him away into the wilderness...   M. 6:2-6

16:23	Then Aaron shall come into the tent of meeting... bathe... and put on his garments and come forth and offer his burnt-offering and the burnt-offering of the people...	M. 6:7-8
16:31	You shall afflict yourselves...	8:1-7

The picture is strikingly clear. The only way to make sense of Mishnah's narrative, its turning this way and that, is to refer to Scripture's picture of the same events. All Mishnah has added to Scripture is the opening unit, the preparation of the high priest for the rite and the daily whole-offering, and, of course, the closing materials on Torah-reading, prayer, and atonement, of which the Priestly Code, obviously, is going to be oblivious. In fact all the framers of Mishnah contribute, at the outset, is the self-evidently required joining of the topic of the daily whole-offering to that of the rite of the Day of Atonement, and, at the end, the homiletical-theological and legal materials on popular observance—as distinct from priestly observance. These latter materials, we shall see, fall completely outside the thematic and narrative framework of the tractate as a whole. But Lev. 16:29-34 present a counterpart. Chapter Eight of Mishnah-tractate Yoma, like Chapter Ten of Mishnah-tractate Pesahim, nonetheless contributes whatever distinctive materials Mishnah has to add to the inherited materials of Scripture. In both cases chapters of this sort call into question the purpose of the framers of the document, who, having nothing much of their own to say and little to contribute even to the elucidation of what Scripture itself has said, nonetheless chose to create a tractate "of their own."

CHAPTER ELEVEN

YOMA CHAPTER ONE

The chapter is composed principally of narrative materials, containing little which is extraneous, on the way in which the high priest spends the week before the Day of Atonement and then the night prior to the service on that day.

1:1-3

A. Seven days before the Day of Atonement they set apart the high priest from his house to the councillors' chamber.
B. And they [also] appoint another priest as his substitute,
C. lest some cause of invalidation should overtake him.
D. R. Judah says, "Also: they appoint another woman as a substitute for his wife,
E. "lest [his wife] die.
F. "Since it says, *And he shall make atonement for himself and for his house* [Lev. 16:6].
G. "*His house*—this refers to his wife."
H. They said to him, "If so, the matter is without limit."

M. 1:1

A. All seven days he tosses the blood, offers up the incense, trims the lamps, and offers up the head and hind leg [of the daily whole offering].
B. But on all other days, if he wanted to offer it up he offers it up.
C. For a high priest offers up a portion at the head and takes a portion at the head [of the other priests].

M. 1:2

A. They handed over to him elders belonging to the court, and they read for him the prescribed rite of the day [of atonement].
B. And they say to him, "My lord, high priest, you read it with your own lips,
C. "lest you have forgotten—or never [even] learned it to begin with."
D. On the eve of the Day of Atonement at dawn they set him up at the eastern gate and bring before him bullocks, rams, and sheep,
E. so that he will be informed and familiar with the service.

M. 1:3

The basic narrative appears to run from M. 1:1A, M. 1:2A, to M. 1:3. Certainly the materials of M. 1:1B-C, D-G *vs.* H, are external to the purpose of the story, and M. 1:2's explanatory materials, B, set up as a rather jarring contrast to A, and C, which explains A, surely do not advance the narrative at all. M. 1:3 introduces a rather sarcastic secondary theme, the high priest's ignorance and dependence upon sages. In this regard, if C is blatant, D-E are remarkable; the high priest then cannot even be relied upon to know the difference between a bullock and a ram.

A. Why do they *set apart the high priest from his house to the councillors' chamber* [M. 1:1A]?
B. R. Judah b. Paterah explained, "Lest his wife turn out to be in doubt as to whether she is menstruating and, if he had sexual relations with her, he will turn out to be unclean for seven days."
C. R. Judah would call it, "The senators' chamber."

T. 1:1 L p. 220, ls. 1-3

A. All chambers in the Temple were exempt from the requirement of having a *mezuzah* on their doorposts, except for the councillors' chamber,
B. for it was the residence of the high priest seven days a year.
C. Said R. Judah, "And was this one the only residence?
D. "But any room which is a residence is liable, and any which is not a residence is exempt."

T. 1:2 L p. 220, ls. 3-6

A. All the chambers in the Temple were deemed to be private domain so far as the Sabbath is concerned and private domain so far as matters of uncleanness are concerned,
B. except for the chamber for wine and oil,
C. which has two entries, one facing the other,
D. and which is private domain so far as the Sabbath is concerned but public domain so far as matters of uncleanness are concerned.
E. Abba Saul would call it, "The chamber of oil."
F. R. Judah says, "Every chamber in the Temple which has two entries facing each other,
G. "for instance, the gates of the courtyard,
H. "constitutes a private domain so far as the Sabbath is concerned, but public domain so far as matters of uncleanness are concerned."

T. 1:3 L pp. 220-221, ls. 6-11

A. Why do they *appoint another priest as his substitute*?
B. *Lest some cause of invalidation should overtake him* [M. 1:1B-C],
C. and [the other] can take his place.
D. R. Hananiah, Prefect of the Priests, says, "For that purpose the prefect was appointed,

E. "[So that] in the case of a priest overtaken by some cause of invalidation, he might serve in his place."

F. "[If the substitute should serve in his place], the high priest returns to the priesthood, and this one who served in his place is subject to all of the religious requirements of the high priesthood," the words of R. Meir.

G. R. Yosé says, "Even though they have said, 'All the religious requirements of the high priesthood apply to him,' he is valid neither as a high priest nor as an ordinary priest."

H. Said R. Yosé, "M'ŚH...B: Joseph b. Elim of Sepphoris served in the place of the high priest for one hour.

I. "And from that time onward he was not valid either as a high priest or as an ordinary priest.

J. "When he went forth [from his high priesthood of one hour], he said to the king, 'The bullock and ram which were offered today, to whom do they belong? Are they mine, or are they the high priest's?'

K. "The king knew what to answer him.

L. "He said to him, 'Now what's going on, Son of Elim! It is not enough for you that you have served in the place of the high priest for one hour before Him who spoke and brought the world into being. But do you also want to take over the high priesthood for yourself?'

M. "At that moment Ben Elim realized that he had been separated [excommunicated] from the priesthood."

T. 1:4 L p. 221, ls. 11-21

A. How does *the high priest take a portion of the head* [*of the other priests*] [M. Yoma 1:2C]?

B. He says, "This sin-offering is mine," "This guilt-offering is mine," "One loaf of the two Two Loaves," "Four or five loaves of the Show Bread [are mine]."

C. Rabbi says, "I say that this one should take half, since it says, *And what is left of the cereal offering shall be for Aaron and for his sons* (Lev. 2:10)—[meaning] that Aaron should be equivalent to his sons [and get half]."

D. Under what circumstances?

E. In the case of Holy Things of the Temple.

F. But in the case of Holy Things of the provinces, all the same are the high priest and the ordinary priest: each gets an equal portion.

T. 1:5 L pp. 221-222, ls. 22-26

A. It is the religious requirement of the high priest to be greater than his brethren in beauty, strength, wealth, wisdom, and good looks.

B. If he is not, how do we know that his brethren should magnify him? Since it says, *And the priest who is higher by reason of his brethren* (Lev. 21:10)—that they should make him great.

C. They said about Pinḥas of Ḥabbata, on whom the lot fell to be high priest, that the revenuers and supervisors came along and found him cutting wood.

D. So they filled up his woodshed with golden *denar*s.
E. R. Ḥanina b. Gamaliel says, "Was he not a stone-cutter? Was he not our father-in-law?
F. "But they found him ploughing, as it says concerning Elisha, *So he departed from there, and found Elisha the son of Shaphat, who was plowing, with twelve yoke of oxen before him, and he was with the twelfth* (I Kings 19:19)."

T. 1:6 L p. 222, ls. 26-33

A. When [unacceptable] kings became many, they ordained appointing priests [at royal behest]—
B. and they appointed high priests every single year.

T. 1:7 L p. 222, ls. 33-34

T.'s systematic glosses of M., as indicated, themselves bear explanatory matter. That is why we have T. 1:2-3, which raises questions unimportant for M. The point of T. 1:7 is to explain why the high priests required instruction from year to year.

1:4-8

A. All seven days they did not hold back food or drink from him.
B. [But] on the eve of the Day of Atonement at dusk they did not let him eat much,
C. for food brings on sleep.

M. 1:4

A. The elders of the court handed him over to the elders of the priesthood,
B. who brought him up to the upper chamber of Abtinas.
C. And they imposed an oath on him and took their leave and went along.
D. [This is what] they said to him, "My lord, high priest: We are agents of the court, and you are our agent and agent of the court.
E. "We abjure you by Him who caused his name to rest upon this house, that you will not vary in any way from all which we have instructed you."
F. He turns aside and weeps.
G. And they turn aside and weep.

M. 1:5

A. If he was a sage, he expounds [the relevant Scriptures].
B. And if not, disciples of sages expound for him.
C. If he was used to reading [Scriptures], he read.
D. And if not, they read for him.
E. And what do they read for him?
F. In Job, Ezra, and Chronicles.
G. Zekhariah b. Qebuṭal says, "Many times I read for him in the book of Daniel."

M. 1:6

A. [If] he tried to doze off, young priests snap their middle fingers before him and say to him, "My lord, high priest: Stand up and drive off [sleep] by walking on the cold stones."
B. And they would keep him busy until the time for the slaughter had come.

M. 1:7

A. Every day they take up the ashes from the altar at the cock's crow or near it,
B. whether before or after it.
C. At the Day of Atonement from midnight, and on festivals at the end of the first watch [they do so].
D. And never did the cock crow before the courtyard was filled with masses of Israelites.

M. 1:8

The high priest is kept from sleeping, so that he will not have a nocturnal emission, which would make him unclean so as to be invalid for performing the rite the next day. The narrative is perfect and bears no needless glosses or interpolations. M. 1:6 seems to me integral, since it explains what happens in the course of the night.

A. Why does *he turn aside and weep* [M. 1:5F]?
B. Because it is necessary to impose an oath on him.
C. And why do *they turn aside and weep* [M. 1:5F]?
D. Because they have to impose an oath on him.
E. And why do they have to impose an oath on him?
F. Because there already was the case of that certain Boethusian, who offered up the incense while he was still outside, and the cloud of incense went forth and frightened the entire house.
G. For the Boethusians maintained that he should burn the incense while he is still outside, as it says, [*And put the incense on the fire before the Lord, that*] *the cloud of the incense may cover* [*the mercy seat which is upon the testimony*] (Lev. 16:13).
H. Sages said to them, "Now has it not also been stated, *And put the incense on the fire before the Lord*?
I. "From this it follows that whoever offers up incense offers up incense only inside.
J. "If so, why is it said, *The cloud of the incense may cover*?
K. "This teaches that he puts into it something which causes smoke to arise.
L. "If therefore he did not put in something which makes smoke to arise, he is liable to the death penalty."
M. Now when this Boethusian went forth, he said to his fathers, "In your entire lives you would expound the Scripture, but you never did the deed properly, until I arose and I went in and did it right."
N. They said to him, "Even though we do expound matters as you say, we do not do things in the way in which we expound them. We obey the words of sages.

"I shall be very much surprised at you if you live for very long."

O. Not three days passed before they put him into his grave.

T. 1:8 L pp. 222-223, ls. 34-44

A. What is the middle finger [which the young priests would snap to keep the high priest awake on the night before the Day of Atonement (M. 1:7A)]?

B. This is the tall finger of the right hand.

C. [They kept him awake by making noise] in speech, not with a wind instrument or a stringed instrument.

D. What did they say [M. 1:7B]? *A song of Ascents. Of Solomon. If the Lord does not build the house, those who build it labor in vain. If the Lord does not watch over the city, the watchman stays awake in vain* (Ps. 127:1).

E. They did not sleep all night.

F. But they kept watch by the high priest, to keep him busy with discourse.

G. So did they behave in the provinces after the destruction of the Temple,

H. as a memorial to the Sanctuary.

I. But in point of fact they sinned.

T. 1:9 L pp. 223-224, ls. 44-48

T. glosses and expands M.

CHAPTER TWELVE

YOMA CHAPTER TWO

The entire chapter forms an appendix to M. 1:8's reference to clearing ashes from the altar. The narrative is interrupted for an account of the normal procedures of clearing the altar and presenting the daily whole-offering. This interest, M. 2:1-4, is itself given an appendix, M. 2:5-7, on the number of priests employed in preparing that and other offerings. None of this advances the story of the Day of Atonement's rites in the Temple.

2:1-2

A. At first whoever wants to take up the ashes from the altar does so.
B. And when they are many [who wanted to do so], they run up the ramp.
C. And whoever gets there before his fellow, within four cubits of the altar, has acquired the right to do so.
D. And if the two came at the same time, the one in charge says to them, "Choose up [by raising a finger]."
E. And what do they put forth?
F. One or two.
G. But they did not put out the thumb in the Temple.

M. 2:1

A. M'SH Š: There were two who got there at the same time, running up the ramp.
B. And one shoved his fellow.
C. And he [the other] fell and broke his foot.
D. When the court saw that the matter was dangerous, they ordained that the right of clearing off the ashes from the altar should be apportioned only by lot.
I E. There were four lots, and this was the first of the four.

M. 2:2

M. 2:1-2 are continuous. M. 2:2A-D explains the origin of M. 2:1, and M. 2:2E links whole to yet more secondary materials which make up the rest of the chapter.

A. How does one cast lots [M. 2:2D]?
B. They enter the hewn-stone chamber and stand round about it in the form of a spiral figure.

C. And the supervisor comes and takes the mitre of one of them.
D. Then they know that from him the lot begins.
E. They did not put forth two by two, but one by one.
F. And individuals among them put out two by two.
G. But they did not count the extra.

T. 1:10 L p. 224, ls. 48-52

A. M'ŚH Š: *There were two who got there at the same time, running up the ramp. One shoved the other* [M. 2:2A-B], within four cubits [of the altar]. The other then took out a knife and stabbed him in the heart.

B. R. Ṣadoq came and stood on the steps of the porch and said,

C. "Hear me, o brethren of the House of Israel! Lo, Scripture says, *If in the land which the Lord your God gives you to possess, any one is found slain, lying in the open country, and it is not known who killed him, then your elders and your judges shall come forth, and they shall measure the distance to the cities which are around him that is slain* (Deut. 21:1-2).

D. "Come and let us measure to find out for what area it is appropriate to bring the calf—for the Sanctuary, or for the courts!"

E. All of them moaned after his speech.

F. And afterward the father of the youngster came to them, saying, "O brethren of ours! I am your atonement. His [my] son is still writhing, so the knife has not yet been made unclean."

G. This teaches you that the uncleanness of a knife is more grievous to Israelites than murder. And so it says, *Moreover Manasseh shed much innocent blood, till he had filled Jerusalem from one end to the other* (II Kings 21:16).

I. On this basis they have said, "Because of the sin of murder the Presence of God was raised up, and the sanctuary was made unclean."

T. 1:12 L pp. 224-225, ls. 55-64

T. 1:10 purports to explain the procedure briefly noted at M. 2:1D-F + G.

2:3-4

II A. The second lot: (1) Who slaughters the animal, (2) who tosses the blood, (3) who clears the ashes off the inner altar, (4) who clears the ashes off the candelabrum, and who brings the limbs up the ramp:

B. (5) the head, (6) right hind-leg, (7) two fore-legs, (8) rump, (9) left hind-leg, (10) breast, (11) neck, (12) two flanks, and (13) innards;

C. the fine flour, the Baked Cakes (Lev. 6:21), and the wine.

D. Thirteen priests acquired the right to participate in the service.

E. Said Ben 'Azzai before R. 'Aqiba in the name of R. Joshua, "In the way in which it walked it was offered."

M. 2:3

III   A.   The third lot: "Those who are new to the burning of the incense, come and draw lots."
IV   B.   The fourth: "Those who are new and those who are experienced—who will bring up the limbs from the ramp to the altar itself?"
M. 2:4

The formal traits of the continuations of M. 2:2E are rather odd, because M. 2:3 and M. 2:4A, B, treat the topic quite separately from one another. In point of fact, M. 2:3A takes up a position on a disputed issue, since M. 2:3E will have had its own list: head, right hind leg, shoulder, throat, two fore-legs, two flanks, rump, left hind leg—different from M. 2:3B. I also cannot make sense of M. 2:3D, which seems to me to ignore C, or my count at A-B is wrong. M. 2:4A makes a place for those who have never had the privilege of burning the incense to have a chance at doing so. M. 2:4B then balances itself against M. 2:4A and refers us back to M. 2:3A, bringing the limbs up the ramp. Now it is time to toss the limbs onto the altar.

A.   R. Judah says, "They did not cast lots for the privilege of carrying the fire-pan,
B.   "but whoever won the right to care for the incense-offering says to the one who is with him, 'You too—for the fire-pan.'"
C.   R. Eliezer b. Jacob says, "There was no lot for carrying the sacrificial fat of the goat.
D.   "But whoever took the limbs up the ramp offers the [fat] up on the altar."
T. 1:11 L p. 224, ls. 52-55

Certainly M. 2:4 concurs, in that it has no lot for the firepan. Eliezer b. Jacob wants the fourth lot for the firepan.

A.   *The superintendent said to them, "Come and cast lots [to determine] who executes the act of slaughter, who tosses the blood, who removes the ashes of the inner altar, who removes the ashes of the candle stick, who carries up the limbs to the ramp, the head, the right hind leg, the two forelegs, the rump, and the left hind leg, the breast, the neck, the two flanks, the innards, the fine flour, the cakes, and the wine* [M. Tam. 3:1A-B]," these are the words of R. Simeon of Mispeh.
B.   R. Yosé says, "The head, the right hind leg, the two forelegs, the breast, the neck, the two flanks, the rump, and the left hind leg."
C.   *Said Ben 'Azzai to R. 'Aqiba in the name of R. Joshua, "In the way in which it walked, it was offered* [M. 2:3E]: the head, the right hind-leg, the breast and throat, the two forelegs, the two flanks, the rump, the left hind leg."
D.   Thirteen acquire rights to it [M. 2:3D].
T. 1:13 (continued) L p. 225, ls. 64-71

T. augments M. 2:3, giving us no fewer than three positions on the same matter.

2:5-7

A. The daily whole offering was offered by nine, ten, eleven, or twelve [priests], no less, no more.
B. How so?
C. It itself was offered by nine [priests].
D. On the Festival [of Tabernacles], in the hand of one [additional priest] was a flask of water—thus ten.
E. At dusk, by eleven: it itself by nine, and two, with two pieces of wood in their hands.
F. And on the Sabbath, by eleven: it itself by nine, and two priests, with two dishes of frankincense for the Show Bread in their hands.
G. And on the Sabbath which coincides with the Feast [of Tabernacles], in the hand of yet another priest was a flask of water.

M. 2:5

A. A ram was offered by eleven: the meat by five, the innards, flour, and wine by two each.

M. 2:6

A. An ox was offered by twenty-four:
B. the head and the right hind-leg—the head by one, and the right hind leg by two;
C. the rump and the left hind-leg—the rump by two, and the left hind leg by two;
D. the breast and the neck—the breast by one, and the neck by three;
E. the two forelegs by two;
F. the two flanks by two;
G. the innards, the fine flour, and the wine by three each.
H. Under what circumstances?
I. In the case of public offerings.
J. But in the case of an individual's offering,
K. if [one priest] wanted to offer it up [all by himself], he offered it up.
L. Flaying and cutting up both these and those [offerings] are subject to the same rules.

M. 2:7

M. 2:3A-D generate a second look at the daily whole offering, with special reference to M. 2:3B, which knows nine priests. Now we expand that same matter, in yet a further appendix.

E. Sometimes thirteen acquire rights to it, sometimes fourteen, sometimes fifteen.
F. *A ram was offered by eleven* [M. 2:6].

G. The lambs offered for the community are offered by eight, for there are no Baked Cakes with them.

H. *An ox is offered by twenty-four:*

I. *the head and the right hind-leg*—two hold the right leg and bring it up to the altar;

J. three hold the dish and offer it up on the altar.

K. *Under what circumstances?*

L. *In the case of public offerings.*

M. But in the case of an individual's offering, whoever wanted to offer it up does so [M. 2:7J-K].

T. 1:13 (concluded) L pp. 225-226, ls. 71-76

E picks up where M. 2:3D leaves off, and T. then slightly restates M.

A. M'SH B: One of the sons of Martha, daughter of Boethus, could take two sides of an ox which cost one thousand *zuz* and walk with them, heel to toe, and bring them up onto the altar.

T. 1:14 L p. 226, ls. 76-78

The strong priest requires no help.

CHAPTER THIRTEEN

YOMA CHAPTER THREE

The narrative, broken off by Chapter Two, resumes here. The principal theme is the slaughter on the Day of Atonement of the animal for every day offerings, that is, the daily whole-offering (M. 3:1-4); then comes the daily incense-offering. Only at that point the rites for the Day of Atonement in particular get underway. They begin with the first of the high priest's five acts of immersion and ten washings ("sanctifications") of the hands and feet. Now, M. 3:8, the bullock prepared by the high priest to atone for himself and his household (Lev. 16:6) is offered, along with the required confession. Then the priest goes eastward, into the courtyard, to cast lots for the scape-goat (M. 3:9). At this point the fact that the lots are made of gold of Ben Gamla's contribution leads the redactor to list four who likewise did praiseworthy things for the Temple, as against four who did not (M. 3:10-11). This sizable interpolation leads to a vast expansion in T. So the tractate's basic narrative is forced to bear a huge burden of interpolations.

3:1-4

A. The supervisor said to them, "Go and see whether the time for slaughtering the sacrifice has come."
B. If it has come, he who sees it says, "It is daylight!"
C. Mattithiah b. Samuel says, "[He says], 'Has the whole east gotten light?'
D. " 'To Hebron?'
E. "And he says, 'Yes.' "

M. 3:1

A. And why were they required to do this?
B. For once the moonlight came up, and they supposed that the eastern horizon was bright, and so they slaughtered the daily whole offering and had to bring it out to the place of burning.
C. They brought the high priest down to the immersion-hut.
D. This governing principle applied in the Temple: Whoever covers his feet [and defecates] requires immersion, and whoever urinates requires sanctification [the washing] of hands and feet.

M. 3:2

A. A person does not enter the courtyard for the service, even if he is clean, unless he immerses.

B. Five acts of immersion, and ten acts of sanctification of the hands and feet, does the high priest carry out on that day.

C. And all of them are in the sanctuary at the *Parvah*-chamber, except for this one alone.

M. 3:3

A. They spread out a linen sheet between him and the crowd.

I B. He took off his clothes, went down, immersed, came up, and dried off.

C. They brought him golden garments, and he put them on, and (1) he sanctified his hands and feet.

D. They brought him the daily whole offering.

E. He cut [the wind-pipe and gullet], and another priest completed the slaughtering on his behalf.

F. He received the blood and tossed it.

G. He went in to offer up the incense-offering of the morning, to trim the lamps, and to offer up the head and limbs, Baked Cakes, and wine.

M. 3:4

The narrative units are M. 3:1A-D, explained by M. 3:2A-B, then M. 3:2C, with interpolated materials at M. 3:2D, 3:3A. M. 3:3B-C, M. 3:4 then complete the narrative, a smooth and uninterrupted account. Roman numerals mark immersions, Arabic ones, washings of hands and feet.

A. Why does one say, "Has the whole east gotten light up to Hebron [M. 3:1C-D]?"

B. Sometimes the rising column of the sun goes up in the usual way, but the rising column of the moon breaks forth over the entire eastern horizon.

C. Abba Yosé b. Ḥanan says, "Daylight has broken forth" [cf. M. 3:1B].

T. 1:15 L p. 226, ls. 79-81

T. cites and explains M.

A. A high priest who goes out of the courtyard to speak with his fellow and went too far out requires immersion [cf. M. 3:3A].

B. They asked Ben Zoma, "What is the reason for this immersion?"

C. He said to them, "If one who goes in from one holy area to another, a place not subject to the punishment of extirpation, requires immersion, he who enters from an ordinary area to a holy place, which *is* subject to punishment of extirpation, surely should require immersion."

D. R. Judah says, "This immersion too was required only because of real dirt.

E. "Sometimes an old source of uncleanness clings to one's hands.
F. "Because one is going to immerse [to clean up], he remembers that he is unclean and goes along."

T. 1:16 L pp. 226-227, ls. 61-86

A. Priests who did not immerse and did not sanctify their hands and feet,
B. and so too a high priest who did not immerse and did not sanctify his hands and feet
C. between one act of service and the next,
D. between putting on one set of garments and putting on the next,
E. and who performed an act of service—their act of service is valid.
F. But priests who did not immerse at all, or who did not sanctify their hands and feet at all,
G. and so too a high priest who did not immerse at all,
H. or did not sanctify his hands and feet at all
I. in the morning [before beginning their acts of service],
J. and who performed an act of service—
K. their act of service is invalid.   T. 1:17 L p. 227, ls. 86-90

A. All the same are a high priest and an ordinary priest who served at dawn without washing hands and feet—they are liable to the death penalty,
B. as it is said, *When they go into the tent of meeting ... they shall wash with water, lest they die. They shall wash their hands and their feet, lest they die* (Ex. 30:20-21).

T. 1:18 L p. 227, ls. 90-92

A. [If] one was standing and making offerings all night long,
B. at dawn he requires sanctification of hands and feet.
C. Rabbi says, "[The reason is that] the passage of the night invalidates the sanctification of hands and feet."
D. R. Eleazar b. Simeon says, "Even if one is occupied in the labor of sacrifice for seven days straight, the passage of night does not invalidate in the case of sanctification of hands and feet."

T. 1:19 L pp. 227-228, ls. 92-95

A. There were five acts of immersion there on that day [the Day of Atonement] [cf. M. 3:3B].
B. *All of them were done in the sanctuary, in the Parvah-chamber, except for the first* [M. 3:3C], which was done in an unconsecrated place, at the Water Gate, and it was at the side of its chamber.
C. R. Judah says, "They heated up iron bars on the eve of the Day of Atonement and tossed them into the cold water,
D. *"to relieve the chill"* [cf. M. 3:5C-D].

T. 1:20 L p. 228, ls. 95-98

T. 1:16 expands on M. 3:3A. The rest then supplements the established theme. T. 1:20 glosses M. 3:3C.

3:5-7

A. The incense-offering of the morning was offered between the tossing of the blood and the offering up of the limbs.
B. That of twilight [was offered up] between the burning of the limbs and the drink-offerings.
C. If the high priest was decrepit or infirm, they heated hot water for him and poured it into the cold water,
D. to relieve the chill.

M. 3:5

A. They brought him to the *Parvah*-chamber, and it was in the sanctuary.
B. They spread out a linen sheet between him and the crowd.
C. (2) He sanctified his hands and feet and took off his clothes.
D. R. Meir says, "He took off his clothes, sanctified his hands and feet."
II E. He went down, immersed, came up, and dried off.
F. They brought him white clothes.
G. He put them on and (3) sanctified his hands and feet.

M. 3:6

M. 3:5A continues M. 3:4G. C-D resume the narrative, preparatory to the second immersion. M. 3:3B is spun out here and at M. 7:3-4.

A. "At dawn he would put on a garment of Pelusium-linen worth twelve *maneh*s, and at dusk, he wore Indian linen worth eight hundred *zuz*," the words of R. Meir.
B. And sages say, "At dawn he would put on a garment worth eighteen *maneh*s, and at dusk, one worth twelve *maneh*s.
C. "In all it was worth thirty *maneh*s."
D. These belong to the public.
E. And if he wanted to spend more, he could do so at his own expense.

M. 3:7

This unit glosses M. 3:6F, but breaks the flow of the narrative and is a needless interpolation.

A. *In all it was worth thirty maneh* [M. 3:7C].
B. These [funds] are taken from the sanctuary.
C. *If he wanted to add, he may do so at his own expense* [M. 3:7E].
D. M'SH B: Ishmael b. Phiabi's mother made for him a tunic worth a hundred *maneh*.
E. And he would stand and make offerings on the altar wearing it.

T. 1:21 L p. 228, ls. 98-101

A. ŠWB M'ŠH B: Eleazar b. Ḥarsom's mother made for him a tunic for twenty thousand, and he would stand and make offerings on the altar while wearing it.
B. But his brethren, the priests, called him down,
C. because [it was so sheer that] he appeared naked while wearing it.

T. 1:22 L p. 228, ls. 101-103

A. A woman who made a white tunic—it is valid,
B. on condition that she give it over for public use.
C. All the same is the rule covering the garments of the high priest and those of the ordinary priest: [funds for] them derive from the heave-offering of the *sheqel*-chamber.

T. 1:23 L p. 228, ls. 103-105

T. cites and augments M.

3:8-9

A. He came over to his bullock.
B. Now his bullock was set between the Porch and the Altar.
C. Its head was to the south and its face to the west.
D. And the priest stands at the east, with his face to the west.
E. And he puts his two hands on it and states the confession.
F. And thus did he say, "O Lord, I have committed iniquity, transgressed, and sinned before you, I and my house. O Lord, forgive the iniquities, transgressions, and sins, which I have done by committing iniquity, transgression, and sin before you, I and my house.
G. "As it is written in the Torah of Moses, your servant, *For on this day shall atonement be made for you to clean you. From all your sins shall you be clean before the Lord* (Lev. 16:30)."
H. And they respond to him, "Blessed is the Name of the glory of his kingdom forever and ever."

M. 3:8

A. He came to the east side of the courtyard, to the north of the altar, with the prefect at his right hand and the head of the father's house at the left.
B. There were two goats.
C. There also was a box with two lots.
D. They used to be a boxwood, but Ben Gamla made them of gold.
E. Consequently he was remembered with honor.

M. 3:9

The first offering for the Day of Atonement is offered, M. 3:8, then the scape-goat comes in view, M. 3:9. M. 4:1 carries the matter forward, after the interpolation generated by M. 3:9D-E.

A. How does he state the confession?
B. "*O Lord, I have committed iniquity, transgressed and sinned before you, I and my house. O Lord forgive the iniquities, transgressions, and sins,*

which I have done in committing iniquity, transgression, and sin before you, I and my house, as it is written in the Torah of Moses, your servant, For on this day shall atonement be made for you to clean you. From all your sins shall you be clean before the Lord* (Lev. 16:30) [M. 3:8F-G].

C. "And the high priest further says, [*And Aaron shall lay both his hands upon the head of the live goat,*] *and confess over him all the iniquities of the people of Israel and all their transgressions, all their sins* (Lev. 16:21)," the words of R. Meir.

D. And sages say, "*Iniquities*—these are those done deliberately. *Their transgressions*—these are acts of rebellion. *Their sins*—these are the misdeeds done inadvertently.

E. "Now after he has confessed the deliberate iniquities and the acts of rebellion, shall he go back and confess their inadvertent misdeeds as well?

F. "But how does he say the confession?

G. "*O Lord, I have committed iniquity, transgressed, and sinned before you...*' And they respond to him, '*Blessed is the name of the glory of his kingdom forever and ever*' [M. 3:8F-H].

H. "For so do we find that it is the way of all those who confess to confess in this way.

I. "David said, *Both we and our fathers have sinned; we have committed iniquity, we have done wickedly* (Ps. 106:6).

J. "Solomon said, *We have sinned, we have transgressed, we have done wickedly* (I Kings 8:47).

K. "Now what is it that Moses said, *Forgiving iniquity, transgression, and sin* (Ex. 34:7)?

L. "But since he was making confession for deliberate violations of the law and acts of rebellion, it is as if they are deeds done inadvertently before him.

M. "And thus did he confess, 'I have sinned, I have transgressed, I have done wickedly before you.'"

T. 2:1 L pp. 229-230, ls. 1:14

T. assigns M. to Meir.

A. *He came to the east side of the courtyard, to the north of the altar* [M. 3:9A].

B. *There were two goats* [M. 3:9B]

C. with their faces toward the people and their backs toward the sanctuary.

D. The high priest's face was toward the sanctuary.

E. Ten times that day he expressed the Divine Name, six in regard to the bullock, three for the goat, and one for the lots.

F. There also was a box with two lots. They used to be of boxwood, but Ben Gamla made them of gold, and consequently he was remembered with honor [M. 3:9B-E].

T. 2:2 (continued) L p. 230, ls. 14-18

T. lightly glosses M.

3:10-11

A. Ben Qatin made twelve stop-cocks for the laver, which had had only two.
B. And he too made a mechanism for the laver, so its water should not be invalidated by being kept overnight.
C. King Monobases had handles made of gold for all the vessels used on the Day of Atonement.
D. Helene, his mother, set a golden candlestick over the door of the sanctuary.
E. She also made a golden tablet, on which was written the pericope of the accused wife.
F. As to Nicanor, miracles were done at his doors.
G. And they remembered him with honor.

M. 3:10

A. But these [were remembered] dishonorably:
B. the members of the household of Garmu did not want to teach others how to make the Show Bread.
C. The members of the household of Abtinas did not want to teach others how to make the incense.
D. Hygras b. Levi knew a lesson of singing but did not want to teach it to anyone else.
E. Ben Qamṣar did not want to teach others how to write.
F. Concerning the first ones listed is stated the following verse: *The memory of the just is blessed* (Prov. 10:7).
G. And concerning these [latter ones] is stated the following verse: *But the name of the wicked shall rot*.

M. 3:11

M. glosses M. 3:9E, with two sets of four, M. 3:10A, C, D, F, M. 3:11B, C, D, E. M. 3:10G is duplicated at M. 3:11F, G.

G. *Ben Qatin made twelve stop-cocks for the laver*, so that twelve priests may sanctify their hands and feet from it at one time.
H. *It had had only two*, so that only two priests could sanctify their hands and feet from it at one time. And he is remembered with honor [M. 3:10A].

T. 2:2 (concluded) L p. 230, ls. 18-20

A. *King Monobases had gold handles made for all the knives used on the Day of Atonement*, and he is remembered with honor [cf. M. 3:10C].
B. *Helene, his mother, set a golden candlestick over the door of the sanctuary. She also made a golden tablet on which was written the pericope of the accused wife* [M. 3:10D-E],
C. so that when the sun rises, sparks of golden light sparkle forth from it, so people know that the sun is rising.

T. 2:3 L p. 230, ls. 20-24

A. All the gates which were there were covered with gold except for Nicanor's gates,
B. for a miracle was done with them.
C. There are those who say it is because their copper is bright.
D. R. Eliezer b. Jacob says, "It was Corinthian bronze and shown like gold [it is as pretty as gold]."
E. Now what is the miracle which was done with them?
F. They say: When Nicanor was bringing them from Alexandria, in Egypt, a gale rose in the sea and threatened to drown them. They took one of them and tossed it into the sea, and they wanted to throw in the other, but Nicanor would not let them. He said to them, "If you throw in the second one, throw me in with it." He was distressed all the way to the wharf at Jaffa. Once they reached the wharf at Jaffa, the other door popped up from underneath the boat.
G. And there are those who say one of the beasts of the sea swallowed it, and when Nicanor came to the wharf at Jaffa, it brought it up and tossed it onto dry land.
H. And concerning it, it is explicitly stated in tradition, *The beams of our house are cedar, our rafters are pine* (Song of Songs 1:17).

T. 2:4 L pp. 230-231, ls. 24-33

A. The members of the household of Garmu were experts in making Show Bread and they did not want to teach others [how to make it] [M. 3:11B].
B. Sages sent and brought experts from Alexandria, in Egypt, who were expert in similar matters, but were not experts in removing it from the oven.
C. The members of the house of Garmu would heat the oven on the outside, ahd it [the loaf of bread] would be removed on the inside.
D. The experts from Alexandria did not do so.
E. And some say this made it get moldy.
F. And when the sages learned of the matter, they said, "The Holy One, blessed be he, created the world only for his own glory, as it is said, *Everyone that is called by my name and whom I have created for my glory* (Is. 43:7)."
G. They sent for them, and they did not come until they doubled their former salary.
H. "They used to take a fee of twelve *maneh*s every day, and they now went and took a fee of twenty four," the words of R. Meir.
I. R. Judah says, "Twenty-four did they take every day, and they now went and took forty eight *maneh*s."
J. Said to them sages, "Now why were you unwilling to teach?"
K. They said, "The members of father's house knew that the Temple is destined for destruction, and they did not want to teach others how to do it, so that they should not be able to do it before an idol in the same way in which they do it before the Omnipresent."

L. And on account of this next matter they are remembered with honor:

M. For a piece of clean bread was never found in the hands of their sons and daughters under any circumstances, so that people might not say about them, "They are nourished from Show Bread."

N. This was meant to carry out the following verse: *You shall be clear before the Lord and before Israel* (Num. 32:22).

T. 2:5 L pp. 231-232, ls. 33-46

A. The members of the house of Abtinas were experts in preparing the incense for producing smoke, [cf. M. 3:11C], and they did not want to teach others how to do so.

B. Sages sent and brought experts from Alexandria, in Egypt, who knew how to concoct spices in much the same way.

C. But they were not experts in making the smoke ascend as well as the others.

D. The smoke coming from the incense made by the house of Abtinas would ascend straight as a stick up to the beams, and afterward it scattered in all directions as it came down.

E. That of the Alexandrians would scatter as it came down forthwith.

F. Now when the sages realized this, they said, "The Omnipresent has created the world only for his own glory, as it is said, *The Lord has made everything for his own purpose* (Prov. 16:4)."

G. Sages sent to them [the members of the house of Abtinas], but they declined to come until the sages doubled their wages.

H. "They had been receiving twelve *maneh*s every day, and now they went and got twenty four," the words of R. Meir.

I. R. Judah says, "They had been getting twenty-four every day. Now they went and got forty-eight *maneh*s."

J. Sages said to them, "Now why were you unwilling to teach [others]?"

K. They said to them, "The members of father's house knew that the Temple is destined for destruction, and they did not want to teach others their art, so that people would not burn incense before an idol in the same way in which they burn incense before the Omnipresent."

L. And in this next matter, they are remembered for good: A woman of their household never went out wearing perfume at any time,

M. And not only so, but when they would marry into their household a woman from some other place, they made an agreement that she not put on perfume,

N. so that people should not say, "Their women are putting on perfume [snitched] from the preparation of the incense for the Temple."

O. Thus they did to carry out the following verse, *And you shall be clear before the Lord and before Israel* (Num. 32:22).

T. 2:6 L pp. 232-233, ls. 46-61

A. Said R. 'Aqiba, "Simeon b. Luga told me, "A certain child of the sons of their sons and I were gathering grass in the field. Then I saw him laugh and cry. I said to him, 'Why did you cry?' He said to me, 'Because of the glory of father's house, which has gone into exile.' I said to him, 'Then why did you laugh?' He said, 'At the end of it all, in time to come, the Holy One, blessed be he, is going to make his descendents rejoice.' I said to him, 'What did you see [to make you think of this]?' He said to me, 'A *smoke-raiser* in front of me [made me laugh].' I said to him, 'Show it to me.' He said to me, 'We are subject to an oath not to show it to anyone at all.' "

B. Said R. Yoḥanan b. Nuri, "One time I was going along the way, and an old man came across me and said to me, 'I am a member of the house of Abtinas. At the beginning, when the house of father was discrete, they would give to one another their scrolls [containing the prescriptions for frankincense]. Now take it, but be careful about it, since it is a scroll containing a recipe for spices.'

C. "And when I came and reported the matter before R. 'Aqiba, he said to me, 'From now on it is forbidden to speak ill of these people again.' "

D. On the basis of this story, Ben 'Azzai said, "Yours will they give you, by your own name will they call you, in your own place will they seat you. There is no forgetfulness before the Omnipresent. No man can touch what is ready for his fellow."

T. 2:7 L pp. 233-234, ls. 61-72

A. Agdis b. Levi knew a certain mode of singing, and he did not want to teach it to others [cf. M. 3:11D].

B. Sages said to him, "Why did you not want to teach it to others?"

C. He said to them, "The members of father's house knew that the Temple was destined for destruction, and they did not want to teach their mode of singing to others, so that they should not sing before an idol in the way in which they say [song] before the Omnipresent."

D. Ben Qamṣar knew [the art] of writing, and did not want to teach anyone else [M. 3:11E].

E. They said to him, "Why do you not want to teach anyone else?"

F. He remained silent.

G. These others found an answer to what [sages] asked, but Ben Qamṣar did not find an answer to what he said.

H. These others sought to increase their own glory and to diminish the glory owing to Heaven.

I. Therefore their own glory was diminished, while the glory of Heaven was increased.

J. And a good name and a good memorial were not theirs ever.

K. *Concerning the first ones, it is said, The memory of the righteous is for a blessing, but concerning these latter ones it is said, But the name of the wicked shall rot* (Prov. 10:7) [M. 3:11F-G].

T. 2:8 L p. 234, ls. 72-80

T. vastly expands on M. 3:10-11.

CHAPTER FOURTEEN

YOMA CHAPTER FOUR

The narrative describes the selection by lot, of the scape-goat and of the goat to serve as a sin-offering, and the preparation of the latter, M. 4:1-3. At the end the high priest takes up the fire-pan and gets some coals for burning incense at the inner altar, M. 4:3D. This detail is given a huge gloss, M. 4:4-6, contrasting the rite of doing so on the Day of Atonement with the rite on all other days of the year.

4:1

A. He shook the box [with the lots] and brought up the two lots.
B. On one was written, "For the Lord," and on one was written, "For Azazel."
C. The Prefect was at his right, and the head of the ministering family [father's house] at his left.
D. If the lot *"for the Lord"* came up in his right hand, the prefect says to him, "My lord, high priest, raise up your right hand."
E. If the one *"for the Lord"* came up in his left hand, the head of the ministering family says to him, "My lord, high priest, raise up your left hand."
F. He put them on the two goats and says, "For the Lord, a sin-offering."
G. R. Ishmael says, "He did not have to say, 'Sin-offering,' but only 'For the Lord.'"
H. And they respond to him, "Blessed is the name of the glory of his kingdom for ever and ever."

M. 4:1

The narrative bears only one gloss, G, which of course represents a dispute, F vs. G. The goat at the priest's right sets the designation indicated by the lot in the right hand.

A. *He shook the box [with the lots] and took up two lots* [M. 4:1A], one in his right hand and one in his left.
B. If it [the one for the Lord] came up in his right hand, all the Israelites were joyful. But if it came up in his left hand, all the Israelites were not joyful.

T. 2:9 L p. 234, ls. 81-82

A. They asked R. 'Aqiba, "What about changing it from the left hand to the right?"

B. He said to them, "Don't give the heretics a chance to ridicule you."

C. R. Judah said in the name of R. Eliezer, "The prefect and the high priest put out their two right hands simultaneously. If it came up in the hand of the high priest, *the prefect says to him, 'My lord, high priest, raise up your right hand.'*

D. "If it came up in the right hand of the prefect, the head of the ministering family [house of the fathers] says to him, 'Prefect, speak in your own behalf.' "

E. *And they put them on the two goats.*

F. *He says, "For the Lord."*

G. And the prefect says, *"For a sin-offering."*

H. R. Ishmael says, *" He did not have to say, 'sin-offering' "* [M. 4:1G].

I. They said to him, "Now has it not already been said, *And he will make [declare] it a sin-offering* (Lev. 16:9)?"

T. 2:10 L p. 235, ls. 83-89

T. supplies M. with a set of secondary questions, then has a different version of M.'s picture of the rite.

4:2-3

A. He tied a crimson thread on the head of the goat which was to be sent forth,

B. and set it up towards the way by which it would be sent out.

C. And on that which was to be slaughtered [he tied a crimson thread] at the place at which the act of slaughter would be made [the throat].

D. And he came to his bullock a second time [M. 3:8A] and put his two hands on it and made the confession.

E. And thus did he say, "O Lord, I have committed iniquity, transgressed, and sinned before you, I and my house and the children of Aaron, your holy people.

"O Lord, forgive, I pray, the iniquities, transgressions, and sins which I have committed, transgressed, and sinned before you, I, my house, and the children of Aaron, your holy people,

F. "as it is written in the Torah of Moses, your servant, *For on this day shall atonement be made for you to cleanse you. From all your sins shall you be clean before the Lord* (Lev. 16:30)."

G. And they responded to him, "Blessed is the name of the glory of his kingdom forever and ever."

M. 4:2

A. He slaughtered it and received its blood in a basin.

B. He handed it over to him who would stir it while standing on the fourth terrace of the sanctuary, so that it would not congeal.

C. He took the fire-pan and went up to the top of the altar.

D. He cleared off coals to either side and scooped up glowing cinders from below.

E. Then he came down and set it down on the fourth terrace of the courtyard.

M. 4:3

The narrative flows smoothly and without a single false move. My translation of B, C, does not capture the match of B's BYT ŠLWḤW and C's BYT ŠHYṬTW. But there is no consistent effort at careful formulation of this sort.

4:4-6

I   A. Every day he would scoop out the cinders with a silver fire-pan and empty them into a golden one.

B. But today he would clear out the coals in a gold one, and in that same one he would bring the cinders in [to the inner sanctuary].

II   C. On other days he would clear out cinders with one holding four *qabs* and empty that into one holding *three*.

D. But today he would clear them out with one holding three *qabs*, and in that same one he would bring the cinders in [to the inner sanctuary].

III   E. R. Yosé says, "Every day he would clear the cinders out in one holding a *seah* and empty it into one holding three *qabs*.

F. "But today he would clear the cinders in one holding three *qabs*, and in that same one he would bring the cinders in."

I   G. Every day it was heavy.

H. But today it was light.

II   I. Every day its handle was short.

J. But today it was long.

III   K. "Every day it was of yellow gold,

L. "But today it was of red gold," the words of R. Menaḥem.

IV   M. Every day one would offer up half a *maneh* of incense at dawn and half at dusk.

N. But today he would add his two handfuls [of incense].

V   O. Every day it was fine.

P. But today it was the finest of the fine.

M. 4:4

I   A. Every day the priests go up on the east side of the ramp and go down on the west.

B. But today the high priest goes up right in the middle of the ramp and goes down right in the middle.

C. R. Judah says, "At all times the high priest goes up in the middle and goes down in the middle."

II   D. Every day the high priest sanctifies his hands and feet from the laver.

E. Today he does it from a golden jug.

F. R. Judah says, "At all times the high priest sanctifies his hands and feet from a golden jug."

M. 4:5

III A. "Every day there were four stacks of wood there.
B. "But today there were five," the words of R. Meir.
C. R. Yosé says, "Every day there were three,
D. "but today there were four."
E. R. Judah says, "Every day there were two.
F. "But today there were three."

M. 4:6

The formal traits are clear as indicated. The whole is an appendix to M. 4:3C. My signification of the formal stichs—two triplets and a five-part entry—may be erroneous.

A. Every day two priests go in, one with the ladle, and one with the fire-pan.
B. Today he [the high priest alone] takes the fire-pan in his right hand and the ladle in his left hand.
C. Under what circumstances?
D. In the case of the incense for the inner altar.
E. But as to the incense of the golden altar, lo, it is deemed equivalent to the rite for the incense of all the other days of the year.
F. *Every day it was heavy, but today it was light. Every day its handle was short, but today it was long* [M. 4:4G-J],
G. so that its arm would assist him.
H. "Every single day it had no cask, but today it had a cask," the words of the Son of the Prefect.
I. "*Every day there were two stacks of wood there, but today three*, one for the large stack of wood, one for the second stack of wood, and one which they add to the incense which is burned inside," the words of R. Judah [M. 4:6E-F].
J. R. Yosé adds one for maintaining the fire.
K. R. Meir adds one for the limbs and the birds which were not wholly consumed the preceding evening.

T. 2:11 L pp. 235-236, ls. 89-97

T. augments, then cites and explains M.

CHAPTER FIFTEEN

YOMA CHAPTER FIVE

The narrative continues with the incense-offering, M. 5:1-2. Then the high priest returns to the blood-rite begun earlier (M. 4:3), and he tosses that blood, M. 5:3. The goat which serves as a sin-offering is slaughtered, and its blood is tossed, M. 5:4. Then the high priest purifies the golden altar, as well as the surface of the altar itself, M. 5:5-6. The account once more is interrupted, now with the conception that, if some of the deeds are done in improper order, the rite is not invalidated, but the deeds have to be done again in the right order, M. 5:7.

5:1-2

A. They brought the ladle and fire-pan out to him.

B. And he took [from the pan] handsful [of incense] and put [the incense] into the ladle—

C. a large one in accord with the large size [of his hand], or a small one in accord with the small size [of his hand],

D. such was the required measure [of the ladle].

E. He took the fire-pan in his right hand and the ladle in his left.

F. He then walked through the Sanctuary, until he came to the space between the two veils which separate the Holy Place from the Most Holy Place,

G. and the space between them was a cubit.

H. R. Yosé says, "There was only a single veil there alone,

I. "since it says, *And the veil shall divide for you between the holy place and the most holy place* (Ex. 26:33)."

J. The outer one was looped up at the south, and the inner one at the north.

K. He walks between them until he reaches the northern side.

L. [When] he has reached the northern side, he turns around toward the south, walks along with the curtain at his left until he has reached the ark.

M. [When] he has reached the ark, he places the fire-pan between the two bars [Ex. 25:12].

N. He piled up the incense on the coals, so that the whole house was filled with smoke.

O. He came out, going along by the way by which he had gone in.

P. And he said a short prayer in the outer area.

Q. He did not prolong his prayer, so as not to frighten the Israelites.   M. 5:1

A. Once the ark was taken away, there remained a stone from the days of the earlier prophets, called Shetiyyah.
B. It was three fingerbreadths high.
C. And on it did he put [the fire-pan].

M. 5:2

The narrative proceeds to a full and nearly perfect account of the incense rite M 5:1H-I are ignored at J.

A. He went in and walked in the Sanctuary until he found himself standing between the golden altar [at his right] and the candelabrum [at his left].
B. The altar was further in than he.
C. The table was set to the north, a third of the way inward, two and a half cubits away from the wall. A candelabrum was opposite it at the south, a third of the way inward, two and a half cubits away from the wall. The altar was right in the middle, extending somewhat outward, toward the two bars of the ark, and extending outward to the east.
D. And all of them were situated from the half way point of the house and inward.
E. *Then he walked through the Sanctuary until he came to the space between the two veils which separate the Holy Place from the Most Holy Place, and the space between them was a cubit* [M. 5:1F-G].
F. This was the place of the *debir* [sanctuary] which Solomon had made.
G. *R. Yosé says, "There was only a single veil there alone, since it says, And the veil shall divide for you between the holy place and the most holy place* (Ex. 26:33)" [M. 5:1H-I].
H. They said to him, "Why does Scripture then say, *Between the Holy Place and the Most Holy Place?*"
I. He said to them, "Between the upper Holy Place and the lower Holy Place.
J. "Another matter: Between Nob, Gibeon, Shilo, and the eternal house."

T. 2:12 L pp. 236-237, ls. 98-107

A. *The outer one was looped up at the south, and the inner one at the north. He walks between them until he reaches the northern side. When he reaches the northern side, he turns around toward the south, walks along with the curtain at his left until he has reached the ark* [M. 5:1J-L].
B. When he reaches the ark, he then pushes the veil aside with his loins.
C. *And he places the fire-pan between the two bars* [Ex. 25:12], *and he piled up the incense on the coals, so that the whole house was filled with smoke. He went out, going along by the way by which he went in. And he said a short prayer in the outer area. He did not prolong his prayer, so as not to frighten the Israelites* [M. 5:1M-Q].

D. M'SH B: A high priest took a long time.

E. They said to him, "Why did you take a long time?"

F. He said to them, "I was praying for you and for the sanctuary of your fathers, that it not be destroyed."

G. They said to him, "No matter, you have no right to change the custom."

T. 2:13 L p. 237, ls. 108-115

T. 2:12A-D supplement M. 5:1F.

A. *A stone was there from the days of the earlier prophets, called Shetiyyah. It was three fingerbreadths high* [M. 5:2A-B].

B. In the beginning the ark was placed on it. When the ark was taken away, on it they would burn the incense before the innermost altar.

C. R. Yosé says, "From it the world was created, as it says, *Out of Zion, the perfection of the world* (Ps. 50:2)."

T. 2:14 L pp. 237-238, ls. 115-118

A. The bottle containing the manna, the flask of the anointing oil, the staff of Aaron, with its almonds and blossoms, and the chest sent as a gift when the Philistines returned the Glory to the God of Israel—all of them are in the house of the Most Holy of Holies.

B. When the ark was stored away, they were stored away with it.

C. The two bars of the ark protruded from the ark until they reached the veil,

D. as it is said, *And the poles were so long that the ends of the poles were seen from the holy place before the inner sanctuary* (II Chron. 5:9).

E. Could they have torn a hole in the veil?

F. Scripture says, *But they could not be seen from outside* (II Chron. 5:9).

G. Could they not be seen on the inside?

H. Scripture says, *The ends of the poles were seen from the holy place before the inner sanctuary.*

I. On this basis: they were very long.

J. The poles were very long and reached the veil and pressed against the veil and were seen on the inside.

K. And concerning them it is stated explicitly in tradition, *My beloved is to me a bag of myrrh, that lies between my breasts* (Song of Songs 1:13).

T. 2:15 L p. 238, ls. 119-126

T. provides relevant information for M. 5:2.

5:3-6

A. He took the blood from the one who had been stirring it [M. 4:3B].

B. He [again] went into the place into which he had entered and again stood on the place on which he had stood.

C. Then he sprinkled some [of the blood], one time upwards and seven times downwards.
D. But he did not intentionally toss it upwards or downwards.
E. But [he did it] like one who cracks a whip.
F. And thus did he count: "One, one and one, one and two, one and three, one and four, one and five, one and six, one and seven."
G. He went out and he set down [the bowl of blood] on the golden stand in the Sanctuary.

M. 5:3

A. They brought him the goat.
B. He slaughtered it and received its blood in a basin.
C. He went into that same place into which he had entered, and stood on that same place on which he had stood.
D. And he sprinkled some [of the blood], one time upwards and seven times downwards.
E. But he did not intentionally sprinkle upwards or downwards.
F. But he [did it] like one who cracks a whip.
G. And thus did he count: "One, one and one, one and two," etc.
H. He went out and he set it on the second stand which was in the Sanctuary.
I. R. Judah says, "There was only one stand there alone.
J. "He took the blood of the bullock and set down the blood of the goat in its place,"
K. and sprinkled some of it on the veil toward the ark outside.
L. [He sprinkled some of the blood] one time upwards and seven times downwards.
M. But he did not intentionally sprinkle upwards or downwards.
N. But he did it like one who cracks a whip.
O. And thus did he count: "One, one and one, one and two," etc.
P. He took the blood of the goat and set down the blood of the bullock, and he sprinkled some of it on the veil toward the ark, on the outside of the veil,
Q. one time upwards and seven times downwards.
R. But he did not intentionally sprinkle upwards or downwards.
S. But he did it like one who cracks a whip.
T. And thus did he count: "One, one and one, one and two," etc.
U. Then he emptied the blood of the bullock into the blood of the goat, and poured the contents of the full basin into the empty one.

M. 5:4

A. *And he went out toward the altar which is before the Lord* (Lev. 16:18).
B. This is the golden altar.
C. He began to purify [the altar] [by sprinkling the blood] in a downward gesture.
D. From what point does he start?

E. From the northeastern corner, then to the northwestern, southwestern, and southeastern ones.

F. At the place at which he begins in the process of purification on the outer altar, at that point does he complete doing the same at the inner altar.

G. R. Eliezer says, "He stood right where he was and purified [the altar by sprinkling the blood of purification]."

H. And at every one he sprinkled the horn from below to above,

I. except for this one which was before him,

J. on which he would sprinkle [the blood] from above to below.

M. 5:5

A. He tossed the blood on the top of the altar seven times.

B. Then did he pour out the residue of the blood onto the western base of the outer altar.

C. And that [the residue of the blood sprinkled on] the outer altar he poured out on the southern base.

D. The two streams of blood then mingled together in the [flow of the] surrounding channel and flowed down into the Qidron brook.

E. They are sold to gardeners for fertilizer.

F. And the law of sacrilege applies to them [until the sale].

M. 5:6

Now the blood-rite is spelled out. The only point of interest is M. 5:4I-J, which give a slightly different account at one detail.

A. *He took the blood from the one who had been stirring it.*

B. *He [again] went into the place into which he had entered [earlier] and again stood on the place on which he had stood* [M. 5:3A-B].

C. *Then he sprinkled some of it* [M. 5:4C] *on the Mercy Seat toward the two bars of the ark,*

D. *one time upwards and seven times downwards. But he did not intentionally sprinkle upwards or downwards. But he did it like one who cracks a whip* [M. 5:3C-E].

E. *And thus did he count, "One, one and one, one and two, one and three, one and four, one and five, one and six, one and seven"* [M. 5:3F].

F. R. Judah said in the name of R. Eliezer, "Thus did he count: 'One, one and one, two and one, three and one, four and one, five and one, six and one, seven and one.'"

G. He went out to his left, along the veil.

H. And he did not touch the veil.

I. But if he touched it, he touched it.

J. Said R. Eleazar b. R. Yosé, "I myself saw it in Rome and there were drops of blood on it. And he told me, 'These are from the drops of blood of the Day of Atonement.'"

T. 2:16 L pp. 238-239, ls. 126-133

T. augments M. with diverse opinions, F-J. H supplements M. 5:4J.

A. He came to circumambulate the altar.
B. *From what point does he start? From the northeastern corner, then to the northwestern, the southwestern, and the southeastern corners* [M. 5:5D-E].
C. *At the place at which he begins the process of purification on the outer altar, at that point does he complete doing the same at the inner altar* [M. 5:5F].
D. And at the place at which he begins preparing the burnt-offering on the outer altar, there he completes the sin-offering on the inner altar.
H. *At every one he sprinkled the horn from below to above, except for the one which was before him, on which he would sprinkle the blood from above to below* [M. 5:5H-J].
I. R. Judah said in the name of R. Eliezer, "He stood right where he was and purified the altar. And at every one he sprinkled the horn from below to above, except for the one diagonally before him, on which he would sprinkle the blood from above to below" [M. 5:5G, H-J].

T. 3:1 L p. 240, ls. 1-8

A. *He tossed the blood on the top of the altar seven times* [M. 5:6A].
B. He did not sprinkle it on the dust or on the coals, but only on the top surface of the altar.
C. And it splattered on the wall.
D. For each act of sprinkling, there was an act of dipping [of the finger].
E. [If] he put the blood on the horn on both sides, it was valid.
F. [If] he put it on the inner side of the horn, it was invalid.
G. [If] he repeated the placing of the blood on the horns, it is invalid.
H. [If] he left out any of the placings, even one, it is invalid.
I. [If] he did the placing of the seven drops before the placing of the four [at the corners], let him go back and place the seven before the placing of the four, before he completes the acts of placing the blood [cf. M. 5:7A-B].
J. He went out and *poured out the residue of the blood on the western base of the outer altar* [M. 5:6B].
K. *And* [*the residue of the blood he had sprinkled on*] *the outer altar he poured out on the southern base* [M. 5:6C].
L. R. Simeon says, "Both these and those did he pour out at the southern base."
M. *The* [*two streams of blood*] *then mingled together in the surrounding channel and flowed down into the Qidron brook. They are sold to gardeners for fertilizer.*
N. *"And the law of sacrilege applies to them"* [M. 5:6D-F], the words of R. Meir and R. Simeon.

O. And sages say, "Sacrilege does not apply to blood."

T. 3:2 L pp. 240-241, ls. 8-17

T. extensively cites and at a few points augments M.

5:7

A. The entire rite of the Day of Atonement stated in accord with its proper order—
B. if he did one part of the rite before its fellow, he has done nothing whatsoever.
C. [If] he took care of the blood of the goat before the blood of the bullock, let him go and sprinkle some of the blood of the goat after he has sprinkled the blood of the bullock.
D. And if before he had completed the acts of placing the blood on the inner altar, the blood was poured out,
E. let him bring other blood and go and sprinkle it to begin with on the inner altar [M. 5:3-4].
F. And so [is the rule] in the case of the sanctuary [M. 5:4], and so in the case of the golden altar [M. 5:5].
G. for each of them constitutes an act of atonement unto itself [and need not be repeated].
H. R. Eleazar and R. Simeon say, "From the place at which he broke off, from there he begins once more."

M. 5:7

M. now reverts to its more familiar, analytical discourse, commenting on the antecedent materials. This explicit allusion, A, to the antecedent narrative must be classed as an external interpolation. C-F illustrate A-B. G. explains C-F, and H takes a still more lenient view of A-B.

A. *The entire rite of the Day of Atonement, stated in accord with its proper order—if one did one part of the rite before its fellow, he has done nothing whatsoever* [M. 5:7A-B],
B. except for taking out the ladle and fire-pan,
C. for if he did one deed before its fellow,
D. what he has done is done.

T. 3:3 L p. 241, ls. 17-19

A. Said R. Judah, "Under what circumstances?
B. "In the case of deeds done inside, while the high priest is wearing white garments.
C. "But as to things done outside, while the high priest is wearing golden garments,
D. "even if he did one deed before its fellow,
E. "or repeated any one of all the rites,
F. "what he has done is done."

T. 3:4 L pp. 241-242, ls. 10-22

A. [If] he put some of the placings of blood inside, and then the blood was poured out,

B. let him bring new blood and begin afresh inside.

C. R. Eleazar and R. Simeon say, "He begins at the place at which he stopped" [cf. M. 5:7H].

D. [If] he completed the placings of blood inside and put some of the placings of blood outside, and then the blood was poured out,

E. let him bring fresh blood and begin at the beginning outside.

F. R. Eleazar and R. Simeon say, "He begins at the place at which he stopped."

T. 3:5 L p. 242, ls. 22-25

A. [If] he finished the placings of blood on the veil outside and placed some of the placings on the altar and then the blood was poured out,

B. let him bring fresh blood and begin as at the beginning, on the altar.

C. R. Eleazar and R. Simeon say, "He begins at the place at which he stopped."

D. [If] he completed the placings of blood on the altar and then the blood was poured out, the placing of the blood onto the foundation does not spoil the rite.

E. "And all of them impart uncleanness to clothing and are burned in the place of ashes," the words of R. Eliezer and R. Simeon.

F. And sages say, "They do not impart uncleanness to clothing and are not burned in the place of the ashes,

G. "except for the very last one, who completes the service [of atonement]."

T. 3:6 L p. 242, ls. 26-31

A. Said R. Yosé, "This is the sign: Whatever is taken from within to be placed without is taken as near as possible to the inner altar.

B. "And whatever is taken from without to be placed within is placed from as near as possible to the inner altar."

C. [If] one put part of the blood of the bullock to be offered inside, outside, and some of the blood of the goat to be placed inside, outside,

D. the ones placed inside have gone to his credit.

E. But the ones placed outside have not gone to his credit.

F. [If] he put part of the placings of blood inside, and then the blood was poured out, let fresh blood be brought, and let him begin, on the altar.

G. If he put part of the placings of blood on the altar, and the blood was poured out, etc. [*sic!*] [cf. M. 5:7D-E].

T. 3:7 L pp. 242-243, ls. 31-36

A. "Even though he has not poured the blood on the foundation [M. 5:6B-C], he has carried out his obligation, as it is said, *And he will complete making atonement* (Lev. 16:20).

B. "If he has made atonement, he has completed [the work]," the words of R. 'Aqiba.

C. R. Judah says, "If he has completed the work, then he has made atonement."

T. 3:8 L p. 243, ls. 36-38

T. 3:3 applies the rule even to the rites done while the high priest is wearing golden garments, outside, and Judah differs, T. 3:4. T. 3:5-6 illustrate the position of Eleazar and Simeon, M. 5:7H. T. 3:6E-G refers to all the bullocks and he-goats of our unit. If the blood is poured out before the individual atonement rite is completed, these beasts must be burned outside the three camps, and the carcasses to be burned impart uncleanness to the garments of those who burn them, Lev. 16:27-28. Eleazar and Simeon invoke this rule for all the animals. Sages apply it only in the case of the beast with the blood of which the atonement rite is completed. Yosé's point, T. 3:7, is that residue of blood of the golden altar, poured out onto the western foundation of the outer altar on the southern side, is taken from the blood sprinkled on the surface of the golden altar, which is sprinkled on the southeastern side, so he takes the blood from that side of the outer altar which is nearest to the inner altar. The dishes of frankincense which are taken from the golden table inside for offering up on the copper altar outside are placed and offered up on the area nearest the inside, on the western side of the outer altar (Lieberman, p. 242, 1:31).

CHAPTER SIXTEEN

YOMA CHAPTER SIX

After an analytical pericope on the law governing the selection and disposition of the two goats of the Day of Atonement, M. 6:1, the narrative resumes at M. 6:2 and proceeds without interruption or extensive interpolation to nearly the end of the chapter, M. 6:7. The narrative covers two themes. The disposition of the scape-goat is spelled out at M. 6:2-6. At the point we return to the high priest, back at the Temple, who now offers up the sacrificial parts of the animals, the blood of which already has been tossed (M. 5:3-6). At the end there is some appended material on how the people in the Temple know the scape-goat has reached its destination. These two themes in fact are meant to be worked out simultaneously, since the two sequences of action take place at the same time; but to M.'s narrator there is no device available to indicate simultaneity.

6:1

A. The two goats of the Day of Atonement—
B. the religious requirement concerning them is that the two of them be equivalent in appearance, height, and value.
C. and that they be purchased simultaneously.
D. But even though they are not equivalent [in these regards], they are valid.
E. [If] one purchased one this day and the other the next, they are valid.
F. [If] one of them died, if before the casting of the lots it died, let [the priest] purchase a mate for the survivor.
G. But if after the casting of the lots it died, let one get another mate and cast lots for them as at the outset.
H. And he says, "If the one belonging to the Lord died, then this one upon which the lot, 'For the Lord' has come up is to stand in its stead.
I. "And if the one which was for Azazel has died, this one upon which the log, 'For Azazel,' has come up will stand in its stead."
J. And the second one is to be put out to pasture until it is blemished, and then it is sold, and the money received for it is to fall to a freewill-offering.
K. For a sin-offering of the community is not left to die.
L. R. Judah says, "It is left to die."

M. And further did R. Judah say, "[If] its blood is poured out, let the one who is to be sent forth be left to die.

N. "[If] the one which is to be sent forth died, let its [the other's] blood be poured out."

M. 6:1

The selection of the goats which serve as sin-offerings on the Day of Atonement is spelled out here. E restates C. F opens a secondary development, loss of one of the goats paired for the rite. There is no problem if this was before the casting of lots. If it was afterward, then a stipulation, H-I, makes it possible to use a mate for the survivor. J is explained by K, and L-N reject that view. Judah further maintains, M-N, that if the one is sacrificed but its blood is spoiled, the survivor—the scape-goat—is not used. This takes to a more extreme position his point at L.

A. The bullock and goat for the Day of Atonement which were lost,

B. and in the place of which one set apart other animals,

C. and which he did not suffice to offer up before the animals first set aside were found—

D. let them be set out to pasture until they suffer a blemish, then be sold,

E. and their proceeds fall for a freewill-offering.

F. *For the sin-offering of the community is not put out to die.*

G. R. Judah says, "*It is put out to die.*"

H. And further did R. Judah state, "*If the blood was poured out, the one which is to be sent forth is left to die.*

I. "*If the one which is to be sent forth died, let its blood be poured out*" [M. 6:1K-N].

T. 3:9 L pp. 243-244, ls. 38-41

T. supplies another examplification, A-D, of M.'s dispute.

A. The religious requirement of the two goats of the Day of Atonement is to be subject to lots.

B. [If] one did not cast lots for it, even so, it is valid.

C. The casting of lots for them is by Aaron, [a high priest], [but] even [if it is done] by an ordinary priest, they are valid.

D. The two goats of the Day of Atonement—before one has cast lots for them, he is permitted to change them [for use] for some other purpose.

E. Once he has cast lots for them, he is not permitted to change them [for use] for some other purpose [cf. M. 6:1F-G].

T. 3:10 L p. 244, ls. 42-45

A. A Passover-offering which is not offered on the first [festival] is to be offered on the second. [If] it was not offered on the second, it is to be offered on the third.

B. Coins not [used for] an offering on the first should be [used for] an offering on the second. [If] they are not used for an offering on the second, they should be [used for] an offering on the third.

C. A festal offering which is not offered on the first should be offered on the second. [If] it is not offered on the second, it should be offered on the third.

D. If it is not offered on the third, it should be offered at some point in the future.

T. 3:11 L p. 244, ls. 45-48

A. Goats set aside for the festival which are not offered on the festival should be offered on the New Month.

B. [If] they are not offered on the New Month, let them be offered on the Day of Atonement.

C. [If] they are not offered on the Day of Atonement, let them be offered on the next festival.

D. For to begin with they were set apart as public offerings only so as to be offered on the outer altar.

E. [If] the goat which is to be sent forth died

F. before the blood of the first [goat] was sprinkled on the altar,

G. even though he has not recited the confession over it,

H. he has fulfilled his obligation,

I. since it says, *He shall bring forth the live goat* (Lev. 16:20).

J. How long is it required to be kept alive?

K. "Until *he finishes making atonement* for the holy" (Lev. 16:20), the words of R. Judah.

L. R. Simeon says, "Until the time of confession."

M. R. Yosé says, "Thus he says, Your people the house of Israel, have sinned, transgressed, and done iniquity [M. 6:2B]."

T. 3:12 L pp. 244-245, ls. 48-56

T. 3:10 augments M. 6:1A-B, F-G. T. 3:12Eff. then expand on the problem of M. 6:1F-G.

6:2-4

A. He comes to the goat which is to be sent forth and lays his two hands on it and makes the confession.

B. And thus did he say, "O Lord, your people, the house of Israel, has committed iniquity, transgressed, and sinned before you. Forgive, O Lord, I pray, the iniquities, transgressions, and sins, which your people, the house of Israel, have committed, transgressed, and sinned before you,

C. "as it is written in the Torah of Moses, your servant, *For on this day shall atonement be made for you to clean you. From all your sins shall you be clean before the Lord* (Lev. 16:30)."

D. And the priests and people standing in the courtyard, when they would hear the Expressed Name [of the Lord] come out of the mouth of the high priest, would kneel and bow down and fall on their faces and say, "Blessed be the name of the glory of his kingdom forever and ever."

M. 6:2

A. He gave [the scapegoat] over to the one who was to lead it out.
B. All are valid to lead it out.
C. But high priests made it a practice of not letting Israelites lead it out.
D. Said R. Yosé, "M'ŚH W: 'Arsela led it out, and he was an Israelite."

M. 6:3

A. They made a ramp for it, on account of the Babylonians,
B. who would pull out its hair and say, "Take and go, take and go."
C. The eminent people of Jerusalem used to accompany him to the first booth.
D. There were ten booths from Jerusalem to the ravine, a distance of nine *ris*—
E. seven and a half to a mile.

M. 6:4

Only M. 6:3B-D's dispute interrupts the narrative.

A. *They made a ramp for it* [M. 6:4A],
B. because of the Alexandrians, *who pull out its hair,*
C. *and say to it, "Take and go, take and go."*
D. *The eminent people of Jerusalem accompany him to the first tabernacle* [M. 6:4B-C].
E. "For there were ten tabernacles within a distance of twelve *miles*," the words of R. Meir.
F. R. Judah says, "There were nine tabernacles in a distance of ten *miles*."
G. R. Yosé says, "There were five tabernacles in a distance of ten *miles*."
H. And they share an *'erub* with one to the other [so that they in the tabernacles may accompany the man] [M. 6:5B].
I. Said R. Yosé son of R. Judah, "I can arrange them in two tabernacles [only]."

T. 3:13 L p. 245, ls. 56-60

T. cites and glosses M.

6:5-6

A. At each booth they say to him, "Lo, here is food, here is water."
B. And they accompany him from one booth to the next,
C. except for [the man in] the last [tabernacle] among them,

D. who does not go along with him to the ravine.
E. But he stands from a distance and observes what he does.

M. 6:5

A. Now what did he do?
B. He divided the crimson thread.
C. Half of it he tied to a rock, and half of it he tied between its horns.
D. He then pushed it over backward, and it rolled down the ravine.
E. And it did not reach half way down the mountain before it broke into pieces.
F. He came and sat himself down under the last tabernacle until it got dark.
G. At what time does the one who takes the goat impart uncleanness to garments [Lev. 16:26]? Once he has gone forth from the wall of Jerusalem.
H. R. Simeon says, "Once he has pushed it into the ravine."

M. 6:6

Apart from M. 6:6G-H, the narrative flows smoothly, and its points are clear. The dispute at G-H is familiar; its principle recurs at M. 6:7E-G.

A. They asked R. Eliezer, "Lo, if the goat which is to be sent fell sick, what is the law as to carrying it?"
B. He said to them, "Can he carry others?"
C. "[If] the one who sends it fell sick, what is the law as to sending it with someone else?"
D. He said to them, "Thus may you and I be in peace."
E. "[If] he pushed it down and it did not die, what is the law as to going down after it and killing it?"
F. He said to them, "Thus be the fate of the enemies of the Omnipresent."
G. And sages say, "[If] it fell ill, he does carry it.
H. "[If] the one who sends it fell ill, one does send it with someone else.
I. "[If] one pushed it down and it did not die, one should go down after it and kill it."

T. 3:14 L pp. 245-246, ls. 61-65

Eliezer's answers are meant to be negative, as shown at G-I.

6:7-8

A. [Meanwhile, the high priest] came to the bullock and goat which are to be burned.
B. He tore them open and removed their innards.
C. He put them onto a dish and offered them up on the altar.
D. He then twisted [the limbs of the beasts] on poles, and they carried them out to the place of burning.

E. And when do they impart uncleanness to clothing [who carry out the limbs of the goat and bullock]?

F. Once they have gone past the wall of the courtyard.

G. R. Simeon says, "Once the fire has taken hold of the greater part of [the beasts' carcasses]."

M. 6:7

A. They said to the high priest, "The goat has reached the wilderness."

B. Now how did they know that the goat had come to the wilderness?

C. They made sentinel-posts, and waved flags, so they might know that the goat had reached the wilderness.

D. Said R. Judah, "Now did they not have a more impressive sign than that? From Jerusalem to Bet Hiddudo is three *miles*. They can walk a *mile*, come back a *mile*, and wait sufficient time to walk a *mile*, and so they will know that the goat has reached the wilderness."

E. R. Ishmael says, "Now did they not have another sign? There was a crimson thread tied to the door of the sanctuary. When the goat had reached the wilderness, the thread would turn white,

F. "as it says, *Though your sins be as scarlet, they shall be as white as snow*" (Is. 1:18).

M. 6:8

The narrator returns to the high priest, who is still back at the Temple (M. 6:3). These beasts were killed and then blood was tossed (M. 5:3-6). Now we disposed of them. M. 6:7E-G are an intrusion. It seems to me that the narrative ends at M. 6:8A, then resumes at M. 7:1A. E-F surely indicate the principal source of the information of the narrative, which is Scripture, not memory of the cult.

A. "The goat which is sent forth, even though it does not impart uncleanness to clothing, imparts uncleanness to food," the words of R. Meir.

B. Sages say, "It does not impart uncleanness to food or drink,

C. "because it is alive,

D. "and what is alive does not impart uncleanness to food or drink."

E. At what point does it impart uncleanness to clothes?

F. "Once it has gone beyond the wall of Jerusalem," the words of R. Meir.

G. R. Judah says, "When it has reached the ravine."

H. R. Simeon says, "From the time of its being pushed into the ravine" [cf. M. 6:6G-H].

T. 3:15 L p. 246, ls. 65-69

A. "Bullocks which are to be burned and goats which are to be burned, even though they do not impart uncleanness to clothing, impart uncleanness to food and drink," the words of R. Meir.

B. And sages say, "The [red] cow and cows which are to be burned impart uncleanness to food and drink. But the goat which is to be sent forth does not impart uncleanness to food and drink,

C. "because it is alive, and a living being does not impart uncleanness to food and drink."

D. At what point does it impart uncleanness to clothing?

E. "Once they have gone beyond the wall of the courtyard," the words of R. Meir.

F. R. Judah says, "Once one has thrown them into the fire."

G. *"R. Simeon says, "Once the fire has caught hold of the greater part of them"* [M. 6:7G].

T. 3:16 L p. 246, ls. 69-74

A. Where do they burn them?

B. In the great house of ashes, outside of Jerusalem, north of Jerusalem, beyond the three camps.

C. Rows of priests were set up around the fire

D. because of the pressure of the crowd,

E. so that [the crowd] should not push to see and fall into the fire.

F. All the same are the one who burns and the one who helps out at the time of the burning—

G. they impart uncleanness.

H. But the ones who arrange the wood on the pyre and who kindle the fire with a torch do not impart uncleanness to [their] clothing.

T. 3:17 L p. 247, ls. 75-79

M. 6:6G concurs with Meir, T. 3:15F. T. extensively complements M., linking M.'s discrete disputes of Simeon.

CHAPTER SEVENTEEN

YOMA CHAPTER SEVEN

The rite is now concluded with Scripture-reading and prayer, M. 7:1 + 2, and the final offerings of the day, M. 7:3-4 + 5.

7:1

A. The high priest came to read [in the Women's court].
B. If he wanted to read while wearing linen garments, he reads [wearing them].
C. If not, he reads wearing his own white vestment.
D. The beadle of the community takes the scroll of the Torah and gives it to the head of the community, and the head of the community gives it to the prefect [of the priests], and the prefect gives it to the high priest.
E. The high priest rises and receives it and reads *After the death* (Lev. 16), and *Howbeit on the tenth day* (Lev. 23:26-32).
F. Then he rolls up the Torah and holds it to his heart and says, "More than what I have read out before you is written here."
G. *And on the tenth* (Num. 29:7-11) which is in the Book of Numbers he reads by heart.
H. Then he says eight blessings over it: ". . . for the Torah, . . . for the Temple service, . . . for the confession, . . . for the forgiveness of sin, . . . for the sanctuary (by itself), for Israel (by themselves), . . . and for the priests (by themselves), and for the rest of the Prayer."

M. 7:1

The narrative is smooth and uninterrupted.

A. *Eight blessings does he say over them* on that day [M. 7:1H]:
B. *For the Torah,* just as they say a blessing over the Torah in the Synagogue;
C. *for the Temple service, for the confession, for the forgiveness of sin,*
D. in their usual order,
E. *for the sanctuary,* a blessing *by itself;*
F. *for Israel,* a blessing *by itself;*
G. *for the priests,* a blessing *by itself;*
H. *and the remainder of the prayer*—a supplication:
I. a prayer, "for your people Israel need salvation from you."
J. And he seals the prayer with, ". . . who hears prayer."
K. All of the people read from their own scroll,
L. to show their worthiness in public.

T. 3:18 L p. 247, ls. 80-85

T. glosses M. as indicated.

7:2

A. He who can see the high priest when he is reading cannot see the bullock and goat which are burned.

B. And he who can see the bullock and goat when they are burned cannot see the high priest when he is reading.

C. But this is not because he is not permitted to do so, but because it was quite a distance.

D. And the rites concerning both of them were done simultaneously.

M. 7:2

M. links M. 7:1 and M. 6:7. The point is at D, just as I pointed out above in regard to the killing of the two goats.

7:3-4

A. If [the high priest] reads [the Scriptures] wearing linen garments, he (4) sanctified his hands and feet, took them off, descended, (III) immersed, came up, and dried off.

B. They brought him the golden garments.

C. He put them on and (5) sanctified his hands and feet.

D. "Then he went out and prepared his ram and the ram of the people [Lev. 16:24], and the seven unblemished lambs a year old [Num. 29:8]," the words of R. Eliezer.

E. R. 'Aqiba says, "They were offered with the daily whole offering made at dawn.

F. "And the bullock, burnt-offering, and goat offered outside (Num. 29:11) were offered with the daily whole offering made at dusk."

M. 7:3

A. He (6) sanctified his hands and feet and took off his clothes and went down and (IV) immersed and came up and dried off.

B. They brought him white garments, and he put them on, and (7) sanctified his hands and feet.

C. He went in to bring out the ladle and firepan.

D. He (8) sanctified his hands and feet, took off his clothes, went down and (V) immersed, came up and dried off.

E. They brought him golden garments and he put them on. He (9) sanctified his hands and feet, and entered in to offer up the incense made at dusk, to trim the lamps.

F. Then he (10) sanctified his hands and feet, and took off his clothes.

G. They brought him his own clothing and he put it on.

H. Then they accompany him all the way home.

I. And they celebrate a festival for all his friends when he has come forth whole from the sanctuary.

M. 7:4

The rest of the promised hand-washings and immersions, M. 3:3B, now are supplied. The narrative bears the interpolated dispute, M. 7:3D *vs.* E-F, as to the time at which the specified offerings are prepared at this time. Then the work is done.

A. R. Eliezer says, "Thus is the order of the offerings [which] they offered up:
B. "The bullock which is a whole offering, and the goat which is prepared outside were offered with the whole offering of the morning.
C. "and afterward the bullock and goat which are prepared inside,
D. "and afterward the ram of the people,
E. "and afterward seven unblemished rams" [cf. M. 7:3D].
F. R. 'Aqiba says, "The bullock which is a whole offering and the seven unblemished rams were afterward with the whole offering of the morning,
G. "as it is said, *Beside the burnt offering in the morning, which is for a continual burnt offering* (Num. 28:23).
H. "And afterward the bullock and goat which are prepared inside,
I. "and afterward the goat which is prepared outside,
J. "as it is said, *Beside the sin-offering of atonement and the continual burnt offering and its meal offering and drink offering* (Num. 29:11).
K. "And afterward the ram of the people" [cf. M. 7:3E-F].
L. R. Judah says in the name of R. Eliezer, "One is offered with the daily whole offering of the morning and six are offered with the daily whole offering of dusk."

T. 3:19 L pp. 247-248, ls. 85-93

T. restates M.'s dispute.

A. *They celebrate a festival for his friends,*
B. *when he has come forth whole [from the sanctuary]* [M. 7:4I].
C. M'SH B: Simeon b. Qimḥit went forth to speak with an Arab king, and spit spurt out of [the king's] mouth and fell on his [Simeon's] clothes. His brother went in and served in his stead as high priest. The mother of these men witnessed two high priests [who were her sons serving] on the same day.

T. 3:20 L p. 248, ls. 93-96

T. cites and augments M. with an example of what can happen.

7:5

A. The high priest serves in eight garments, and an ordinary priest in four:

B. tunic, underpants, head-covering, and girdle.
C. The high priest in addition wears the breastplate, apron, upper garment, and frontlet.
D. By these did they receive inquiries for the Urim and Thummim.
E. And they received inquiry only from the king, the court, or from someone in the service of the public.

M. 7:5

The repeated references at M. 7:3-4 to the garments seems to me to explain the inclusion of this otherwise irrelevant appendix.

CHAPTER EIGHTEEN

YOMA CHAPTER EIGHT

The sole rule of the tractate is that on the Day of Atonement one is not to eat, drink, anoint, make use of sandals, bathe, and the like, M. 8:1A. The rule about not eating is exegetically expanded in the normal analytical way at M. 8:2-6, with an appendix extended from M. 8:6 to M. 8:7. M. 8:8 and M. 8:9 conclude with some theological sayings on the importance of repentence in attaining atonement for sin. These are irrelevant to both the narrative and the law of the tractate.

8:1

A. On the Day of Atonement it is forbidden to (1) eat, (2) drink, (3) bathe, (4) put on any sort of oil, (5) put on a sandal, (6) or engage in sexual relations.

B. But a king and a bride wash their faces.

C. "And a woman who has given birth may put on her sandal," the words of R. Eliezer.

D. And sages prohibit.

M. 8:1

B glosses A3, and C *vs.* D gloss A5.

A. A man should not put on an iron studded shoe and walk about his house,

B. even from one bed to another.

C. But Rabban Simeon b. Gamaliel permits.

D. And so did Rabban Simeon b. Gamaliel say, "If one's hands were dirty with mud or excrement, he may rinse them off in water, so that they will not dirty his clothes."

E. [If] he was going to receive his father, master, [or] disciple, he crosses over the sea or river in the normal way,

F. even up to his neck,

G. and need not scruple [as to bathing].

H. Male and female *Zab*s immerse in their normal way on the night [prior to] the Day of Atonement.

I. Menstruating women and women who have given birth immerse in their normal way on the night [prior to] the Day of Atonement.

J. R. Yosé b. R. Judah says, "From the twilight onward, one should not immerse until it gets dark."

K. R. Yosé says, "Priests immerse in the normal way at dusk, so that they may eat food in the status of heave-offering in the evening."

T. 4:5 (continued) L pp. 250-251, ls. 21-30

A-B augment M. 8:1A5, D-K, M. 8:1A3.

8:2

A. He who eats a large date's bulk [of food], inclusive of its pit—
B. he who drinks the equivalent in liquids to a mouthful—
C. is liable.
D. All sorts of foods join together to form the volume of the date's bulk,
E. and all sorts of liquids join together to form the volume of a mouthful.
F. He who eats and he who drinks—
G. [these prohibited volumes] do not join together [to impose liability for eating or for drinking, respectively].

M. 8:2

D-E expand A-C, and F-G qualify D-E. The whole, of course, serves to augment M. 8:1A1, 2.

8:3

A. [If] one ate and drank in a single act of inadvertence, he is liable only for a single sin-offering.
B. [If] he ate and did a prohibited act of labor, he is liable for two sin-offerings.
C. [If] he ate foods which are not suitable for eating,
D. or drank liquids which are not suitable for drinking—
E. [if] he drank brine or fish-brine—
F. he is exempt.

M. 8:3

The point of A-B is clear in the contrast between the two protases. C-D + F, bearing the illustration of E, invoke a familiar conception.

A. *He who eats* on the Day of Atonement [*food*] *in the volume of a large dried date's bulk, inclusive of its pit* [M. 8:2A]—
B. that produced in the Land of Israel—
C. is liable.
D. R. Simeon b. Eleazar says, "Even of the volume of the fig produced in Namarin."
E. [If] he ate leaves of reeds, vines, dates, carobs, or anything not suitable for eating, he is exempt.
F. [If he ate] lettuce leaves, vetches' leaves, onion sprouts, vegetable foliage, or anything which is suitable for eating, he is liable [cf. M. 8:3C-F].

G. [If] he ate, went and ate again, went and ate again, if the interval elapsed from the start of the first act of eating to the conclusion of the last act of eating is sufficient to eat a half-loaf of bread, [the food eaten in the several acts of eating] joins together [to impose liability].

H. And if not, it does not join together.

I. [If] he drank, went and drank again, if the interval elapsed from the start of the first act of drinking to the conclusion of the last act of drinking is sufficient to drink a quarter-*log* [of liquid], [the liquid drunk in the several acts of drinking] joins together [to impose liability].

J. And if not, it does not join together [M. 8:3A].

K. Just as eating [is culpable] in an olive's-bulk [of food], so is drinking [culpable] in an olive's bulk [of liquid].

L. *He who drinks brine or fish-brine is exempt* [M. 8:3E-F].

M. R. Eleazar says, "He who drinks a mouthful of liquid is liable."

T. 4:3 L pp. 249-250, ls. 7-16

After citing M. 8:2A, T. 4:3E-F make the same point as M. 8:3C-F. G-J augment M. 8:3A.

8:4

A. As to children, they do not impose a fast on them on the Day of Atonement.

B. But they educate them a year or two in advance, so that they will be used to doing the religious duties.

M. 8:4

M. continues its discourse on M. 8:1A1.

A. *On the Day of Atonement it is forbidden to eat, drink, bathe, anoint, put on sandals, [and] have sexual relations* [M. 8:1A].

B. [It is not permitted to put on] even felt shoes.

C. Minors are permitted to do all of them except putting on sandals,

D. [the exception being] for appearance's sake.

T. 4:1 L p. 249, ls. 1-3

A. Children nearing puberty—

B. *they educate them a year or two in advance,*

C. *so that they will be used to doing their religious duties* [M. 8:4B].

D. R. 'Aqiba would conclude [the prayer] in the study house for the children,

E. so their parents may feed them.

F. M'SH B: Shammai the Elder did not want to feed his son. They decreed that he feed him with his own hands.

T. 4:2 L p. 249, ls. 3-6

T. cites and illustrates M., joining the rule of M. 8:1 to the special interest of M. 8:4.

8:5-7

A. A pregnant woman who smelled food [and grew faint]—they feed her until her spirits are restored.
B. A sick person—they feed him on the instruction of experts.
C. If there are no experts available, they feed him on his own instructions,
D. until he says, "Enough."

M. 8:5

A. He who is seized by ravenous hunger—they feed him, even unclean things, until his eyes are enlightened.
B. He who was bitten by a crazy dog—they do not feed him a piece of its liver's lobe.
C. And R. Mattiah b. Harash permits doing so.
D. Further did R. Mattiah b. Harash say, "He who has a pain in his throat—they drop medicine into his mouth on the Sabbath,
E. "because it is a matter of doubt as to danger to life.
F. "And any matter of doubt as to danger to life overrides the prohibitions of the Sabbath."

M. 8:6

A. He upon whom a building fell down—
B. it is a matter of doubt whether or not he is there,
C. it is a matter of doubt whether [if he is there], he is alive or dead,
D. it is a matter of doubt whether [if he is there and alive] he is a gentile or an Israelite—
E. they clear away the ruin from above him.
F. [If] they found him alive, they remove the [remaining] ruins from above him.
G. But if they found him dead, they leave him be [until after the Sabbath].

M. 8:7

The exposition of M. 8:1A1 concludes at M. 8:5-6C. M. 8:6D-F, 8:7 then form an appendix.

A. *He who was seized by ravenous hunger*—they feed him [that which violates the law in] the least [possible measure] [M. 8:6A].
B. How so?
C. [If] there were before him untithed produce and produce of the Seventh Year, they feed him produce of the Seventh Year.
D. [If there were] untithed produce and carrion, they feed him carrion.
E. ... carrion and heave-offering, they feed him heave-offering.
F. ... heave-offering and produce of the Seventh Year, they feed him produce of the Seventh Year—

G. *until his eyes are enlightened* [M. 8:6A].
H. How do they know that he has recovered the light?
I. Sufficient so that he knows the difference between good and bad.
J. R. Judah says, "A pregnant woman who smells [and craves] produce of the Seventh Year—they hand over to her a spindleful.
K. "[If] she smelled and craved food in the status of heave-offering, they hand over to her a spindleful" [cf. M. 8:5A].

T. 4:4 L p. 250, ls. 16-21

T. 4:4 clarifies M.'s rulings and applies them as leniently as possible, e.g., A-F, J-K.

8:8

A. A sin-offering and an unconditional guilt-offering atone.
B. Death and the Day of Atonement atone when joined with repentence.
C. Repentence atones for minor transgressions of positive and negative commandments.
D. And as to serious transgressions, [repentence] suspends the punishment until the Day of Atonement comes along and atones.

M. 8:8

The concluding unit now turns toward the effectiveness of the Day.

L. The sin-offering and unconditional guilt-offering effect atonement for what is written in their connection.
M. *Death and the Day of Atonement effect atonement along with repentence.*
N. *Repentence effects atonement for minor transgressions, of positive and negative commandments* [M. 8:8B-C], except for a violation of the commandment not to take [the name of the Lord in vain].
O. And what are major transgressions? [Those punishable by] extirpation or by death at the hands of an earthly court, and not taking [the name of the Lord in vain] counts with them.
P. R. Judah says, "For everything from not taking [the name of the Lord in vain] and beneath, repentence effects atonement.
Q. "For everything from not taking [the name of the Lord in vain] and above, inclusive of not taking [the name of the Lord in vain], repentence suspends the punishment, and the Day of Atonement effects atonement."

T. 4:5 (concluded) L p. 251, ls. 30-35

A. R. Ishmael says, "There are four kinds of atonement.
B. "[If] one has violated a positive commandment but repented, he hardly moves from his place before they forgive him,
C. "since it is said, *Return, backsliding children. I will heal your backsliding* (Jer. 3:22).

T. 4:6 L pp. 251-252, ls. 35-37

A. "[If] he has violated a negative commandment but repented, repentence suspends the punishment, and the Day of Atonement effects atonement,

B. "since it is said, *For that day will effect atonement for you* (Lev. 16:30).

T. 4:7 L p. 252, ls. 37-39

A. "[If] he has violated [a rule for which the punishment is] extirpation or death at the hands of an earthly court, but repented, repentence and the Day of Atonement suspend [the punishment], and suffering on other days of the year wipe away [the sin],

B. "since it says, *Then will I visit their transgression with a rod* (Ps. 89:32).

C. "But he through whom the Name of Heaven is profaned deliberately but who repented—repentence does not have power to suspend [the punishment], nor the Day of Atonement to atone,

D. "but repentance and the Day of Atonement atone for a third, suffering atones for a third, and death wipes away the sin, with suffering.

E. "And on such a matter it is said, *Surely this iniquity shall not be purged from you until you die* (Is. 22:14)."

T. 4:8 L p. 252, ls. 39-45

T. 4:5L-Q cite and complement M. 8:8.

8:9

A. He who says, "I shall sin and repent, sin and repent"—

B. they give him no chance to do repentence.

C. ... "I will sin and the Day of Atonement will atone,"—the Day of Atonement does not atone.

D. For transgressions done between man and the Omnipresent, the Day of Atonement atones.

E. For transgressions between man and man, the Day of Atonement atones, only if the man will regain the good will of his friend.

F. This exegesis did R. Eleazar b. ʿAzariah state: "*From all your sins shall you be clean before the Lord* (Lev. 16:30)—for transgressions between man and the Omnipresent does the Day of Atonement atone. For transgressions between man and his fellow, the Day of Atonement atones, only if the man will regain the good will of his friend."

G. Said R. ʿAqiba, "Happy are you, O Israel. Before whom are you made clean, and who makes you clean? It is your Father who is in heaven,

H. "as it says, *And I will sprinkle clean water on you, and you will be clean* (Ez. 36:25).

I. "And it says, *O Lord, the hope [miqweh = immersion-pool] of Israel* (Jer. 17:13)—Just as the immersion-pool cleans the unclean, so the Holy One, blessed be he, cleans Israel."

M. 8:9

F repeats the point of D-E, and G concludes with a further homily.

    A. The sin-offering, guilt-offering, death and the Day of Atonement all effect atonement only along with repentence,
    B. since it says, *But on the tenth day of the seventh month [is a Day of Atonement]* (Lev. 23:27).
    C. If [the sinner] repents, atonement is effected for him, and if not, it is not effected for him.
    D. R. Eleazar says, "*Forgiving* [*iniquity, transgression, and sin*] (Ex. 34:7)—He forgives iniquity to penitents but he does not forgive iniquity to those who do not repent."
    E. R. Judah says, "Death and the Day of Atonement effect atonement along with repentence.
    F. "Repentance effects atonement with death.
    G. "And the day of death—lo, it is tantamount to an act of repentance."

                      T. 4:9 L pp. 252-253, ls. 45-49

T. develops a view parallel to M. 8:9A-C.

    A. Whoever bestows merit on the community—they never suffice him to commit a transgression,
    B. lest his disciples inherit the world [to come], while he descends to Sheol,
    C. as it said, *For you will not leave my soul in hell* (Ps. 16:10).

                      T. 4:10 L p. 253, ls. 49-52

    A. Whoever brings sin on the community—they never suffice him to effect repentence,
    B. lest his disciples descend to Sheol, while he inherits the world [to come],
    C. as it is said, *A man who does violence to any person shall flee to the pit, let no man stay him* (Prov. 28:17).

                      T. 4:11 L p. 253, ls. 52-54

    A. They bring about merit in behalf of a meritorious person,
    B. to assign to him passages worthy of being told about him [e.g., the story of the daughters of Zelophahad],
    C. and demerit in behalf of a disreputable person,
    D. to assign to him passages worthy of being told about him.
    E. They make public hypocrites' [evil deeds] on account of the desecration of the divine name,
    F. as it is said, *When a righteous man turns from his righteousness and commits iniquity and I lay a stumbling block before him, he shall die* (Ezek. 3:20)—
    G. to make public [his hypocrisy].

                      T. 4:12 L p. 253, ls. 54-58

    A. R. Yosé says, "[If] a man sins two or three times, they forgive him. [But on the] fourth, they do not forgive him,

B. "as it says, *Forgiving iniquity, transgression, and sin, but he will by no means clear the guilty* (Ex. 34:7).

C. "Up to this point he clears [him]. From this point forward he will not clear [him],

D. "since it says, *For three transgressions [of Israel—but for four, I will not turn away the punishment]* (Amos. 2:6).

E. "And it says, [*He will deliver his soul from going into the pit*]. *All these things does God do two or three times for a man* [Job 33:28-29].

F. "And it says, *Withdraw your foot from your neighbor's house, lest he be weary of you* (Prov. 25:17)."

T. 4:13 L pp. 253-254, ls. 59-63

A. The religious duty of saying the confession [applies] at the eve of the Day of Atonement at dusk.

B. But sages have said, "A man should say the confession before eating and drinking,

C. "lest he be distracted while eating and drinking."

D. And even though he has said the confession before eating and drinking, he has to say the confession after eating and drinking,

E. lest some untoward matter have affected the meal.

F. And even though he has said the confession after eating and drinking, he has to say the confession in the evening [prayer].

G. And even though he has said the confession in the evening [prayer], he has to say the confession in the morning [prayer].

H. And even though he has said the confession in the morning [prayer], he has to say the confession in the additional prayer.

I. And even though he has said the confession in the additional prayer, he has to say the confession in the afternoon prayer.

J. And even though he has said the confession in the afternoon prayer, he has to say the confession in the prayer for the closing of the gates—

K. lest some untoward matter have affected any part of the entire day [of Atonement].

L. At what point in the service does he say the [confessions]?

M. After the Prayer.

N. The one who passes before the ark says it in the fourth [benediction].

O. R. Meir says, "He prays seven [benedictions] and concludes the confession [with a blessing]."

P. And sages say, "He prays seven [benedictions].

Q. "And if he wanted to conclude the confession with a blessing, he does so."

R. "And he has to specify each individual sin," the words of R. Judah b. Peterah,

S. "as it is said, *O Lord, these people have sinned a great sin [and have made a god of gold]* (Ex. 32:31)."

T. R. 'Aqiba says, "It is not necessary.

U. "If so, Why does it say, *And made a god of gold*?

V. "But: Thus did the Omnipresent say, 'Who made you make a god of gold? It is I, who gave you plenty of gold.'"

T. 4:14 L pp. 254-255, ls. 63-76

A. Matters concerning which one has said confession on the preceding Day of Atonement one does not have to include in the confession on the coming Day of Atonement,
B. unless he did those same transgressions [in the intervening year].
C. [If] he committed those transgressions, he must include them in the confession.
D. [If] he did not commit the transgressions but he [nonetheless] included them in his confession—
E. concerning such a person the following is said: *As a dog returns to his vomit, so a fool returns to his folly* (Prov. 26:11).
F. R. Eliezer b. Jacob says, "Lo, such a person is praiseworthy,
G. "since it is said, *For I acknowledge my transgressions* (Ps. 51:3)."

T. 4:15 L p. 255, ls. 77-81

A. R. Eleazar b. R. Simeon says, "A strict rule applies to the goat which does not apply to the Day of Atonement,
B. "and to the Day of Atonement which does not apply to the goat:
C. "for the Day of Atonement effects atonement [even if] no goat [is offered].
D. "But the goat effects atonement only along with the Day of Atonement.

T. 4:16 L p. 255, ls. 81-83

A. "A more strict rule applies to the goat:
B. "For the goat['s sacrifice takes effect] immediately,
C. "but the Day of Atonement [takes effect only] at dusk."

T. 4:17 L p. 255, ls. 83-84

T. concludes with its own independent homiletical materials. The bulk of the *halakhic* units also are autonomous.

SUKKAH

CHAPTER NINETEEN

INTRODUCTION TO SUKKAH

This brief tractate does little more than supply further information about objects and rites defined to begin with by Scripture's commandments for *the Festival*, Mishnah's name for Sukkot, the feast of tabernacles. To be sure, some rites are known to Mishnah which will have surprised the priestly legislators who made up Leviticus and Numbers. But Mishnah has not invented these rites, so far as its language and mode of discourse appear to suggest, but refers to them as data out of Israel's liturgical past. It follows that, like Yoma, Sukkah would be incomprehensible without the frame of Scripture. Like Sheqalim, Sukkah simply tells us what we need to know to do what, to begin with, Scripture requires. In all, the tractate serves as little more than a law-code on rather fundamental facts. The problematic presented by it therefore is not to work out its relationship to Scripture, since it is little more than a conceptually dependent, complementary exegesis of Scripture. It is, rather, to make sense of why anyone would make up such a tractate at all. For in the name of authorities principally of the later second century is given a vast corpus of information which, by rights, should have been available, indeed quite commonplace, for a long time. It follows that, in this presentation of the text with a brief explanation, we cannot confront the really interesting questions presented to us by Sukkah.

Since it is Scripture which lays matters out, we have now to consider the relevant verses:

Leviticus 23:33-43:

> And the Lord said to Moses, "Say to the people of Israel, On the fifteenth day of this seventh month and for seven days is the feast of booths to the Lord. On the first day shall be a holy convocation; you shall do no laborious work. Seven days you shall present offerings by fire to the Lord; on the eighth day you shall hold a holy convocation and present an offering by fire to the Lord; it is a solemn assembly; you shall do no laborious work.
>
> "These are the appointed feasts of the Lord, which you shall proclaim as times of holy convocation, for presenting to the Lord offerings by fire, burnt offerings and cereal offerings, sacrifices and

drink offerings, each of its proper day; besides the sabbaths of the Lord, and besides your gifts, and besides all your votive offerings, and besides all your freewill offerings, which you give to the Lord.

"On the fifteenth day of the seventh month, when you have gathered in the produce of the land, you shall keep the feast of the Lord seven days; on the first day shall be a solemn rest and on the eighth day shall be a solemn rest. And you shall take on the first day the fruit of goodly trees, branches of palm trees, and boughs of leafy trees, and willows of the brook; and you shall rejoice before the Lord your God seven days. You shall keep it as a feast to the Lord seven days in the year; it is a statute for ever throughout your generations; you shall keep it in the seventh month. You shall dwell in booths for seven days; all that are native in Israel shall dwell in booths, that your generations may know that I made the people of Israel dwell in booths when I brought them out of the land of Egypt: I am the Lord your God."

Numbers 29:12-38:

"On the fifteenth day of the seventh month you shall have a holy convocation; you shall do no laborious work, and you shall keep a feast to the Lord seven days; and you shall offer a burnt offering, an offering by fire, a pleasing odor to the Lord, thirteen young bulls, two rams, fourteen male lambs a year old; they shall be without blemish; and their cereal offering of fine flour mixed with oil, three tenths of an ephah for each of the thirteen bulls, two tents for each of the two rams, and a tenth for each of the fourteen lambs; also one male goat for a sin offering, besides the continual burnt offering, its cereal offering and its drink offering.

"On the second day twelve young bulls, two rams, fourteen male lambs a year old without blemish, with the cereal offering and the drink offering for the bulls, for the rams, and for the lambs, by number, according to the ordinance; also one male goat for a sin offering, besides the continual burnt offering and its cereal offering, and their drink offerings.

"On the third day eleven bulls, two rams, fourteen male lambs a year old without blemish, with the cereal offering and the drink offerings for the bulls, for the rams, and for the lambs, by number, according to the ordinance; also one male goat for a sin offering, besides the continual burnt offering and its cereal offering and its drink offering.

"On the fourth day ten bulls, two rams, fourteen male lambs a year old without blemish, with the cereal offering and the drink offerings for the bulls, for the rams, and for the lambs, by number, according to the ordinance; also one male goat for a sin offering, besides the continual burnt offering, its cereal offering and its drink offering.

"On the fifth day nine bulls, two rams, fourteen male lambs a year old without blemish, with the cereal offering and the drink offerings for the bulls, for the rams, and for the lambs, by number, according to the ordinance; also one male goat for a sin offering; besides the continual burnt offerings and its cereal offering and its drink offering.

"On the sixth day eight bulls, two rams, fourteen male lambs a year old without blemish, with the cereal offering and the drink offerings for the bulls, for the rams, and for the lambs, by number, according to the ordinance; also one male goat for a sin offering; besides the continual burnt offering, its cereal offering, and its drink offerings.

"On the seventh day seven bulls, two rams, fourteen male lambs a year old without blemish, with the cereal offering and the drink offerings for the bulls, for the rams, and for the lambs, by number, according to the ordinance; also one male goat for a sin offering; besides the continual burnt offering, its cereal offering, and its drink offering.

"On the eighth day you shall have a solemn assembly: you shall do no laborious work, but you shall offer a burnt offering, an offering by fire, a pleasing odor to the Lord: one bull, one ram, seven male lambs a year old without blemish, and the cereal offering and the drink offerings for the bull, for the ram, and for the lambs, by number, according to the ordinance; also one male goat for a sin offering; besides the continual burnt offering and its cereal offering and its drink offering."

Deuteronomy 16:13-15:

"You shall keep the feast of booths seven days, when you make your ingathering from your threshing floor and your wine press; you shall rejoice in your feast, you and your son and your daughter, your manservant and your maidservant, the Levite, the sojourner, the fatherless, and the widow who are within your towns. For seven days you shall keep the feast to the Lord your God at the place which the Lord will choose; because the Lord your God will bless you in all your produce and in all the work of your hands, so that you will be altogether joyful."

Let us now turn to the layout of the tractate.

I. *The appurtenances of the Festival*: *Sukkah, Lulab.* 1:1-3:15

    A. *The sukkah and its roofing.* 1:1-2:3

1:1   A *sukkah* taller than twenty cubits is invalid. Other points of invalidation.
1:2   He who makes a *sukkah* under a tree is as if he made it in his house.
1:3   A sheet spread over a *sukkah* invalidates it.
1:4   A vine, gourd, or ivy trained over a *sukkah*, and then covered with *sukkah*-roofing, the *sukkah* is invalid.
1:5   Bundles of straw, wood, or brush are not to be used for *sukkah*-roofing.

1:6	They make *sukkah*-roofing with boards, so Judah. Meir prohibits.
1:7	Boards as *sukkah*-roofing, continued.
1:8	Spits or side-pieces of a bed as *sukkah*-roofing.
1:9	He who suspends the sides of the *sukkah*
1:10	If a roof was damaged and one covered the hole with *sukkah*-roofing.
1:11	He who makes his *sukkah* in the shape of a cone (without a roof).
2:1	He who sleeps under a bed in a *sukkah* has not fulfilled his obligation.
2:2	He who props up his *sukkah* with the legs of a bed.
2:3	He who makes his *sukkah* on top of a wagon or a boat.

    B. *The obligation to dwell in the sukkah.* 2:4-9

2:4-6	Those exempt from dwelling in the *sukkah*. Eating in the *sukkah*.
2:7	He who can eat in the *sukkah* but cannot sit there.
2:8	Women, slaves, and minors are exempt from the religious requirements of dwelling in a *sukkah*.
2:9	All seven days a person treats his *sukkah* as his regular dwelling and his house as his sometimes dwelling.

    C. *The lulab and etrog.* 3:1-15

3:1	A stolen or dried up palm branch is invalid.
3:2	A stolen or dried up myrtle branch is invalid.
3:3	A stolen or dried up willow branch is invalid.
3:4	How many myrtle-branches, willow-branches, and palm-branches are required.
3:5-7	A stolen or dried up *etrog* [citron] is invalid. Suitable and unsuitable *etrogs*.
3:8	They bind up the *lulab* (palm-branch, willow-branch, and myrtle-branch) with its own species.
3:9	Waving the *lulab* in the liturgy: At what point in the *Hallel*-psalms.
3:10	Reciting the *Hallel*-psalms.
3:11	Reciting the *Hallel*-psalms.
3:12	Carrying the *lulab* in the Temple and in the provinces.
3:13	Carrying the *lulab* on the Sabbath.
3:14	Special problems relating to the foregoing.
3:15	Special problems relating to the foregoing.

II. *The rites and offerings of the Festival.* 4:1-5:8

    A. *The Festival rites carried out on various days of the Festival.* 4:1-5:4

4:1	The *lulab* and willow-branch are for six or seven days, the *Hallel*-psalms and rejoicing (eating meat) for eight, dwelling in the

	sukkah and the water-libation for seven, flute-playing for five or six days.
4:2	The *lulab* is for seven days: how so?
4:3	The *willow*-branch is for seven days: how so?
4:4	The *lulab* on the Sabbath: how so?
4:5-7	The willow-branch rite: how so?
4:8	The *Hallel*-psalms and rejoicing are for eight days: how so?
4:9-10	The water-libation: how so?
5:1	The playing of the flute: how so?
5:2-4	The celebration of *bet hasho'ebah*.

B. *The offerings.* 5:5-8

5:5	Sounding the *shofar* in the Temple rite. They sound no fewer than twenty-one notes in the Temple and no more than forty-eight.
5:6-8	The priestly-courses and the offerings of animals on the eight days of the Festival.

The plan for the tractate could not be more straight-forward. The framers have taken a special interest in the matter of dwelling in the *sukkah*—that is, a topic subjected to rather slight definition in Scripture itself and particularly relevant to the observance of the festival outside of the Temple. The tractate gives rules for the building of the *sukkah*, with special reference to the roofing which defines its valid state. Logically, the next question is the use of the *sukkah*, that is "dwelling" therein. The requirement to make use of a *lulab* and *etrog* next forms the bridge from the *sukkah* to the liturgy of the festival (I.C. to II). For it is here that the *lulab* and *etrog*, first, are defined and, second, have their use specified. The rites and offerings of the festival form the final point of interest.

As is Mishnah's way, the effort of unit II is to draw together and present as a comprehensive generalization a range of diverse rites, much as is the effort at Mishnah-tractates Zebahim and Menahot. This exercise in organization is successfully effected at II.A. II.B closes the tractate with further information relevant to the cult. The sequence of topics—(1) *sukkah*, (2) *lulab* and *etrog* + *Hallel*-psalms, (3) liturgy of the Festival in general—cannot have been other than what it is, because of the integral relationship, in just this order, of *lulab-etrog-Hallel*-liturgy. It follows that the tractate is tight and logical, leaving no doubt of the highly disciplined character of the program and exegetical and redactional plan of the men who framed it.

CHAPTER TWENTY

SUKKAH CHAPTER ONE

The chapter systematically defines, first the dimensions of the *sukkah*, M. 1:1, second, the requirement that the *sukkah* be located under the firmament and not be under a roof or under the boughs of a tree, M. 1:2-3, and, third, the sort of material which may be used for *sukkah*-roofing, M. 1:4-8. To this point, finally, is added the important fact that the *sukkah*-roofing must be contiguous with the walls of the *sukkah*, M. 1:9-10. There is a brief appendix, formed of materials attributed to Eliezer, M. 1:11, on the acceptable shape of a *sukkah* and on materials used for the *sukkah*-roofing. The program of the chapter is logical and perfect. What can follow, given this complete definition of the character of the *sukkah*, can only be special cases.

1:1

A. A *sukkah* which is taller than twenty cubits is invalid.
B. R. Judah declares it valid.
C. And one which is not ten handbreadths high,
D. one which does not have three walls,
E. or one, the light of which is greater than the shade of which,
F. is invalid.
G. A superannuated *sukkah*—
H. the House of Shammai declare it invalid.
I. And the House of Hillel declare it valid.
J. And what exactly is a superannuated *sukkah*?
K. Any which one made thirty days [or more] before the Festival [of Sukkot].
L. But if one made it for the sake of the Festival,
M. even at the beginning of the year,
N. it is valid.   M. 1:1

There are five issues of invalidation, A, C, D, E, and G. The rules for the minimum and maximum height and other traits are clear as stated. The main point of A-F is that the *sukkah*-roofing must shade the contained space, so that the *sukkah* will have the traits of a dwelling.

A. *A Sukkah which is taller than twenty cubits is invalid.*
B. R. Judah declares it valid [M. 1:1A-B].

C. Said R. Judah, "M'ŚH B: The *sukkah* of Helene was twenty cubits tall, and sages went in and out, when visiting her, and not one of them said a thing."

D. They said to him, "It was because she is a woman, and a woman is not liable to keep the commandment of sitting in a *sukkah*."

E. He said to them, "Now did she not have seven sons who are disciples of sages, and all of them were dwelling in that same *sukkah*!"

T. 1:1 L p. 256, ls. 1-5

A. *A sukkah, the light of which is greater than the shade of which, is invalid* [M. Suk. 1:2E-F].

B. Under what circumstances?

C. [When that is the case for the] upper surface.

D. But if that is the case for the sides, even if the whole of it is full of light, it is valid.

T. 1:2 L p. 256, ls. 5-6

T. cites and glosses M.

A. If one spread *sukkah*-roofing on top of a bed, or on top of a tree, which are [at least] ten handbreadths high,

B. if its shade was greater than its light, it is valid.

C. And if not, it is invalid [M. 1:1E].

T. 1:3 L p. 256, ls. 7-8

A. The *sukkah* made by shepherds, the *sukkah* made by field-workers in the summer, [or] a *sukkah* which is stolen—

B. is invalid.

T. 1:4 (continued) L p. 256, ls. 8-9

T. 1:3 illustrates M. 1:1C, E. T. 1:4 exemplifies the negative of M. 1:1L: a *sukkah* not made with the Festival in mind.

1:2

A. He who makes his *sukkah* under a tree is as if he made it in [his] house.

B. A *sukkah* on top of a *sukkah*—

C. the one on top is valid.

D. And the one on the bottom is invalid.

E. R. Judah says, "If there are no residents in the top one, the bottom one is valid."

M. 1:2

The point is that the roof of the *sukkah* must be exposed to the firmament and not made up, A, in large part by the boughs of the tree. D follows the same principle, now with reference to a *sukkah* covered by another. Judah's view is that, without residents, the upper *sukkah* does not constitute a dwelling, thus excluding A's consideration.

1:3

A. [If] one spread a sheet on top of [a *sukkah*] on account of the hot sun,

B. or underneath [the cover of boughs] on account of droppings [of the branches or leaves of the bough-cover],

C. or [if] he spread [a sheet] over a four-post bed [in a *sukkah*],

D. it is invalid [for dwelling or sleeping and so for fulfilling one's obligation to dwell in the *sukkah*].

E. But he spreads it over the frame of a two-poster bed.

M. 1:3

If a four-poster bed, located in the *sukkah*, is covered over, it is not suitable as a place for sleeping in the *sukkah*, deemed to be like a *sukkah* in a house. But a two-poster covered over has a sloping roof, which does not enter the category of a roof annulling the effects of the *sukkah*-roofing. We note that the apodosis, D, serves a triplet.

B. One may make his fellow into the side of a *sukkah*, so that he may eat, drink, and sleep in the *sukkah* [formed with his fellow as one of the sides].

C. Not only so, but a person may lean a bed on its side and spread a sheet over it,

D. so that the sunshine will not come either onto food or onto a corpse.

E. [For] sages concur with R. Eliezer that they do not set up tents to begin with on the festival day, and it goes without saying, on the Sabbath.

F. And sages say, "They add [to them] on the Sabbath, and, it goes without saying, on the festival."

T. 1:8 (concluded) L p. 258, ls. 20-24

B-D relate to M. at M. 1:3E. On T. 1:8E-F, cf. T. Shab. 12:14, L pp. 54-5, ls. 49-52.

A. M'ŚH B: R. Eliezer was reclining in the *sukkah* of Yoḥanan b. Ila'i' in Caesarion.

B. The sun's rays reached the *sukkah*.

C. He said to him, "What is the law as to spreading a sheet over it?"

D. He said to him, "You have not got a single tribe in Israel which did not produce a prophet."

E. The sun shone half way into the *sukkah*.

F. He said to him, "What is the law as to spreading a sheet over it?"

G. He said to him, "You have not got a single tribe in Israel which did not produce a judge. (The tribes of Judah and Benjamin produced kings on the instruction of prophets)."

H. The sun now shone all the way to the feet of R. Eliezer.
I. [Yoḥanan] took a sheet and spread it over the *sukkah*.
J. And R. Eliezer uncovered his feet and went on his way.

T. 1:9 L p. 258, ls. 24-30

One may not spread a sheet over the *sukkah*, since this nullifies the *sukkah*-roofing. One may not do so on the festival, since it is like building a tent. T. thus illustrates M. 1:3A and also is relevant to T. 1:8E-F, accounting for their inclusion here.

1:4

A. [If] one trained a vine, gourd, or ivy over it and then spread *sukkah*-roofing on [one of these], it is invalid.
B. But if the *sukkah*-roofing exceeded them,
C. or if he cut them [the vines] down,
D. it is valid.
E. This is the general rule:
F. Whatever is susceptible to uncleanness and does not grow from the ground—they do not make a *sukkah*-roofing with it.
G. And whatever is not susceptible to uncleanness, but does grow from the ground [and has been cut off]—they do make a *sukkah*-roofing with it.

M. 1:4

The *sukkah*-roofing must not grow from the ground, F-G, which explains A, C. The consideration of uncleanness is not operative here.

C. If one made a *sukkah*-roofing of ropes or with sheaves of grain, it is valid.

T. 1:4 (concluded) L p. 256, ls. 9

A. [If] one made a *sukkah*-roofing of stalks of flax, it is valid.
B. [If one made a *sukkah*-roofing of] processed stalks of flax, it is invalid.

T. 1:5 L p. 256, ls. 10

A. [If one made a *sukkah*-roofing] of reeds or spears,
B. even though [cf. M. 1:5D] one makes them adhere to one another,
C. [the *sukkah*] is valid.
D. [If] one made a *sukkah*-roofing with sheaves, if the straw was more abundant than the corn, it is valid.
E. And if not, it is invalid.
F. R. Judah says, "[If] one made a *sukkah*-roofing with worn-out garments, it is valid."

T. 1:6 L pp. 256-257, ls. 10-13

The ropes of baste M. 1:4C, illustrate M. 1:4F-G. After processing, T. 1:5B, the stalks are susceptible to uncleanness. The garments of F are insusceptible. The corn is food and susceptible, D.

1:5

A. Bundles of straw, wood, or brush—
B. they do not make a *sukkah*-roofing with them.
C. But any of them which one untied is valid.
D. And all of them are valid [as is] for use for the sides [of the *sukkah*].

M. 1:5

Used when bound up, the bundles look not like roofing but like a storage-area. The bundles in any case may serve as sides or sideposts.

1:6

A. "They make *sukkah*-roofing with boards," the words of R. Judah.
B. And R. Meir prohibits doing so.
C. [If] one put on top of it a board which is four handbreadths broad, it is valid,
D. so long as one not sleep underneath [that particular board].

M. 1:6

Boards are analogous to normal roofing material for a house, B. C-D form a compromise. A single board may be used, but with the stated functional restriction.

1:7

A. A timber-roofing which had no plastering—
B. R. Judah says, "The House of Shammai say, 'One loosens it and removes one [board] between each two.'
C. "And the House of Hillel say, 'One either loosens it or removes one [board] from between each two.'"
D. R. Meir says, "One removes one from between each two, and does not loosen [the others at all]."

M. 1:7

In this secondary development of M. 1:6, Judah now assigns his view, that boards may be used, to both Houses and explains how they make it possible even to use a roof composed of boards. The Shammaites remove every other board and loosen the remaining ones. The Hillelites do either. Now Meir takes up the position of M. 1:6C-D; boards not forming a continuous covering are valid.

A. "*They make a sukkah-roofing with boards,*" the words of R. Judah [M. 1:6A].

B. And sages prohibit,

C. unless there is a space [covered by *sukkah*-roofing] between one and the next equivalent to the breadth of one of the boards [= M. 1:7D].

D. Said R. Judah, "M'SH B: In the time of the danger we used to lean ladders together and make *sukkah*-roofing on top of them out of boards and then sleep under them."

E. They said to him, "There is no proof from what people did in the time of the danger."

F. But all concur that if a board is four handbreadths broad, there must be a distance between one and the next equivalent to the breadth of a board [cf. M. 1:6C, M. 1:7D].

G. [If] one hung up in it nuts, peaches, pomegranates, bunches of grapes, and wreaths of ears of corn, it is valid.

H. [But] one should not eat of any of these, even on the last day of the Festival.

I. But if one made a stipulation concerning them that he would eat of them on the Festival, it is permitted to do so.

T. 1:7 L p. 257, ls. 13-19

A-F augment M. 1:6, 7, as indicated. G-I qualify M. 1:4. These items, G, may be used to decorate the *sukkah*. But if so, that is their designated restricted purpose, and they may not be eaten.

1:8

A. He who makes a roof for his *sukkah* out of spits or with the side-pieces of a bed—

B. if there is a space between them equivalent to their own breadth,

C. [the *sukkah*] is valid.

D. He who hollowed out a space in a haystack to make a *sukkah*-therein—

E. it is no *sukkah*.

M. 1:8

A-C go over the ground of M. 1:7D. The *sukkah* of D-E has not been constructed with the Festival in mind (M. 1:1L-N); or it appears to be a storehouse. In any case, D-E are a misplaced, miscellaneous item.

1:9

A. He who suspends the sides from above to below—

B. if there are three handbreadths above the ground,

C. [the *sukkah*] is invalid.

D. [If he builds the sides] from the ground upward,
E. if [they are] ten handbreadths above the ground,
F. [the *sukkah*] is valid.
G. R. Yosé says, "Just as [the required height] from below to above [when the wall is built up from the ground] is ten handbreadths,

"so [the required height] from above to below [when the wall is suspended from above toward the ground] is ten handbreadths [even though the bottom is not within three handbreadths of the ground]."

H. [If] one sets the *sukkah*-roofing three handbreadths from the walls [of the *sukkah*], [the *sukkah*] is invalid.

M. 1:9

D-F merely restate M. 1:1C, and they are inserted only to pave the way for Yosé's argument, G. He permits the wall to be suspended. H is independent. The *sukkah*-roofing must be close to the wall and not suspended in the center of the ceiling.

1:10

A. A house, [the roof of] which was damaged, and on [the gaps in the roof of which] one put *sukkah*-roofing—
B. if the distance from the wall to the *sukkah*-roofing is four cubits, it is invalid [as a *sukkah*].
C. And so too, [is the rule for] a courtyard which is surrounded by a peristyle.
D. A large *sukkah*, [the roofing of which] they surrounded with some sort of material with which they do not make *sukkah*-roofing—
E. if there was a space of four cubits below it,
F. it is invalid [as a *sukkah*].

M. 1:10

A-B restate the point of M. 1:9H, but with a different measurement in the case in which there is roofing, not empty space, in the gap. At C we have a roof extending more than four cubits from the walls on the sides of the courtyard, and open space in the center. If the center is provided with *sukkah*-roofing up to within four cubits of the existing roof, it is valid. If, D-E, between the walls of the *sukkah* and the valid roofing, there are four cubits of invalid roofing, it is invalid.

A. A large courtyard which is surrounded by pillars—lo, the pillars are tantamount to sides [for a *sukkah*].

T. 1:8 (continued) L pp. 257-258, ls. 19-20

Even though, A, the pillars form a partition between the roof and the *sukkah*-roofing, the *sukkah* is valid, an augmentation of M. 1:10C.

1:11

A. He who makes his *sukkah* in the shape of a cone or who leaned it up against a wall—
B. R. Eliezer declares it invalid,
C. because it has no roof.
D. And sages declare it valid,
E. A large reed-mat,
F. [if] one made it for lying, is susceptible to uncleanness, and [so] they do not make *sukkah*-roofing out of it.
G. [If one made it] for *sukkah*-roofing, they make *sukkah*-roofing out of it, and it is not susceptible to uncleanness.
H. R. Eliezer says, "All the same are a small one and a large one:
I. "[if] one made it for lying, it is susceptible to uncleanness, and they do not make *sukkah*-roofing out of it.
J. "[If one made it for] *sukkah*-roofing, they do make *sukkah*-roofing out of it, and it is not susceptible to uncleanness."

M. 1:11

C. explains the issue of A-D. Complementing M. 1:4F-G, the dispute of E-G *vs.* H-J is on Eliezer's view that one's intention for the mat, not the dimensions of the mat, is definitive of its character. E-G insist not one's plan for using the mat but one's act in making it is definitive.

A. *He who makes his sukkah in the shape of a cone or who leaned it up against a wall* [M. 1:11A]—
B. R. Eliezer concedes that if its roof is a handbreadth in size,
C. or if it was a handbreadth above the ground,
D. it is valid.
E. A reed made mat of wicker or of straw,
F. [if it is] large, they do use it for *sukkah*-roofing.
G. [If it is small], they do not use it for *sukkah*-roofing [M. 1:11E-G].
H. And one made of reeds or of *helaf*—
I. [if it is] large, they use it for *sukkah*-roofing.
J. [If it is] woven, they do not use it for *sukkah*-roofing.
K. R. Ishmael b. R. Yosé said in the name of his father, "Even one which is woven do they use for *sukkah*-roofing."
L. And so did R. Dosa rule in accord with his opinion.

T. 1:10 L p. 258-259, ls. 30-35

T. 1:10A-D complement M. Eliezer accepts any sort of roof-area, rejecting only a *sukkah* lacking any sort of roof. T. 1:10F-J go over the ground of M.'s second dispute.

CHAPTER TWENTY-ONE

SUKKAH CHAPTER TWO

The discussion on the valid and invalid *sukkah* is concluded with some special problems at M. 2:1-3. One is supposed to sleep in a *sukkah*. If one sleeps under a bed in a *sukkah*, one's obligation is not thereby fulfilled. A *sukkah* may be propped up and not able to stand on its own. Judah differs on both points. A *sukkah* which is built on an object not to be used on the festival may not be used on the festival days of Tabernacles, e.g., a *sukkah* built on a tree or a camel, since the tree and camel may not be used on a festival (or a Sabbath), so M. 2:3.

M. 2:4 introduces the remainder of the chapter: exemptions from the obligation to dwell in the *sukkah*, e.g., people who do not have to do so. Similarly, meals eaten at random may be eaten outside of the *sukkah*. M. 2:5 illustrates this latter point. M. 2:6 presents two disputes of Eliezer and sages on how many meals must be eaten in the *sukkah*. M. 2:7 is out of phase. Its problem is a *sukkah* so small that only one's head and the larger part of one's body fit in; the table is in the house. But the reason the matter, subject to dispute by the Houses, is included is the issue of eating meals in such a *sukkah*, which is supplemented in particular. M. 2:8 then presents an important addition to the list of exemptions, and M. 2:9 specifies that the *sukkah* must be the regular place of residence, the everyday house, the random one. If it rains, the obligation no longer pertains.

2:1

A. He who sleeps under a bed in a *sukkah* has not fulfilled his obligation.

B. Said R. Judah, "We had the practice of sleeping under the bed before the elders, and they said nothing at all to us."

C. Said R. Simeon, "M'ŚH B: Ṭabi, Rabban Gamaliel's slave, slept under the bed.

D. "And Rabban Gamaliel said to the elders, 'Do you see Ṭabi, my slave—he is a disciple of a sage, so he knows that slaves are exempt from keeping the commandment of dwelling in the *sukkah*. That is why he is sleeping under the bed.'

E. "Thus we learned that he who sleeps under bed has not fulfilled his obligation."   M. 2:1

A's theory, in line with M. 1:2's, is that the bed constitutes a tent within the *sukkah*. One has thus not slept in the *sukkah*—under its roofing—but under the tent constituted by the bed. The dispute, B, C-E, then consists of contradictory precedents.

2:2

A. He who props his *sukkah* up with the legs of a bed—it is valid.
B. R. Judah says, "If it cannot stand on its own, it is invalid."
C. A *sukkah* [the roofing of which] is loosely put together,
D. but the shade of which is greater than the light,
E. is valid.
F. The [*sukkah*] [the roofing of which] is tightly knit like that of a house,
G. even though the stars cannot be seen from inside it,
H. is valid.

M. 2:2

The dispute is not on use of the legs, A, but of any prop. So long, C-E, F-H, as the roofing conforms to the basic requirement, M. 1:1E, the *sukkah* is valid.

2:3

A. He who makes his *sukkah* on the top of a wagon or a boat—it is valid.
B. And they go up into it on the festival day.
C. [If he made it] at the top of a tree or on a camel, it is valid.
B. But they do not go up into it on the festival day.
E. [If] two [sides of a *sukkah*] are [formed by] a tree, and one is made by man,
F. or two are made by man and one is [formed by] a tree,
G. it is valid.
H. But they do not go up into it on the festival day.
I. [If] three are made by man and one is [formed by] a tree, it is valid.
J. And they do go up into it on the festival day.
K. This is the governing principle: In the case of any [*sukkah*] in which the tree may be removed, and [the *sukkah*] can [still] stand by itself, it is valid.
L. And they go up into it on the festival day.

M. 2:3

The operative principle is that one may not make use of a tree or a camel on the festival day (M. Bes. 5:2). The restrictions then are the same as they are on the Sabbath. The contrast between A-B and C-D is therefore quite clear. E-L then form a secondary, and rather extended, expansion of the same point as is made about C. If the *sukkah* depends upon the tree, then it may not be used on the festival day. If it stands on its own and does not depend on the tree, then it may be used on the festival, as K-L explain. So what we have is a primary statement, in rather trivial terms, and then a secondary development, somewhat overblown, given the obvious point to be made here.

A. [If] one made a *sukkah*-roofing on top of a wagon which is ten handbreadths high—

B. R. Yosé b. R. Judah said in the name of R. Yosé, "He who sleeps under a wagon is like him who sleeps under a bed."

T. 1:11 L p. 259, ls. 35-36

A. [If] one set up four beams and covered them with a *sukkah*-roofing—

B. R. Jacob says, "They regard them in such wise that if one should plane them and there should be a handbreadth by a handbreadth, it is valid.

C. "And if not, it is invalid."

T. 1:12 L p. 259, ls. 37-38

A. And sages say, "[A *sukkah* is valid if] two accord with the requirement of the law, and a third, even a handbreadth in height."

B. R. Simeon says, "The third also must be in accord with the requirement of the law, but the fourth may be even a handbreadth in height."

C. R. Simeon b. Eleazar says in the name of R. Meir, "[If] two sides are made by man and one is formed by a tree, it is valid, and they go up into it on the festival day" [*vs.* M. 2:3E-H].

T. 1:13 L p. 259, ls. 39-41

T. 1:11 places Yosé in opposition to Judah, M. 2:1B. Jacob, T. 1:12, accepts a *sukkah* with minimal walls. Sages, T. 1:13, want at least two sides of valid height. T. 1:13C, places Meir in opposition to M. 2:3F-H.

2:4-6

A. He who makes his *sukkah* among trees, and the trees are its sides—it is valid.

B. Agents engaged in a religious duty are exempt from the requirement of dwelling in a *sukkah*.

C. Sick folk and those who serve them are exempt from the requirement of dwelling in a *sukkah*.

D. [People] eat and drink in a random manner outside of a *sukkah*.

M. 2:4

A. M'ŚH W: They brought Rabban Yoḥanan b. Zakkai some cooked food to taste, and to Rabban Gamaliel two dates and a dipper of water.
B. And they said, "Bring them up to the *sukkah*."
C. And when they gave to R. Ṣadoq food less than an egg's bulk, he took it in a cloth and ate it outside of the *sukkah* and said no blessing after it.

M. 2:5

A. R. Eliezer says, "Fourteen meals is a person obligated to eat in the *sukkah*,
B. "one by day and one by night."
C. And sages say, "There is no fixed requirement, except for the first two nights of the festival alone."
D. And further did R. Eliezer say, "He who has not eaten his meal in the Sukkah on the first night of the festival should make up for it on the last night of the festival."
E. And sages say, "There is no way of making it up.
F. "Concerning such a case it is said, *That which is crooked cannot be made straight, and that which is wanting cannot be reckoned* (Qoh.1:15)."

M. 2:6

The roof of M. 2:4A surely does not rest on the trees. At M. 2:4B, C, D + M. 2:5, M. 2:6A-C, D-F, we turn to the duty of sleeping and eating in the *sukkah*. The exemptions are three, M. 2:4B, C, D. The precedents conflict, M. 2:5A-B *vs.* C. The disputes of Eliezer are clear as stated. We shall notice that M. 2:8 resumes the issue of M. 2:4, and M. 2:9, of M. 2:6.

2:7

A. He whose head and the greater part of whose body are in the *sukkah*, but whose table is in the house—
B. the House of Shammai declare invalid.
C. And the House of Hillel declare valid.
D. Said the House of Hillel to the House of Shammai, "Was not the precedent so, that the elders of the House of Shammai and the elders of the House of Hillel went along to pay a sick-call on R. Yoḥanan b. Haḥorani, and they found him sitting with his head and the greater part of his body in the *sukkah*, and his table in the house, and they said nothing at all to him!"
E. Said the House of Shammai to them, "Is there proof from that story? But in point of fact they did say to him, 'If this is how you act, you have never in your whole life fulfilled the religious requirement of dwelling in a *sukkah*!'"

M. 2:7

The dispute is clear as stated. The Shammaites do not see eating in so small a *sukkah* as noteworthy. The issue continues M. 2:5-6, eating in the *sukkah*.

A. *Agents engaged in a religious duty are exempt from the requirement of dwelling in a sukkah* [M. 2:5B],

B. and [this is the case] even though they have said that it is not praiseworthy for a person to leave his home on the festival.

C. M'SH B: R. Ila'i' went to R. Eliezer in Lud. He said to him, "Now what's going on, Ila'i'? Are you not among those who observe the festival? Have they not said that it is not praiseworthy for a person to leave his home on a festival? For it is said, *And you will rejoice on your festival* (Deut. 16:14)."

T. 2:1 L p. 260, ls. 1-4

A. *Sick folk and those who serve them are exempt from the requirement of dwelling in a sukkah* [M. 2:4C],

B. And [this is the case] not only of one who is seriously ill,

C. but even if someone has a headache or a pain in the eye.

D. Said Rabban Simeon b. Gamaliel, "M'SH W: I had a pain in the eye in Caesarion, and R. Yosé b. Rabbi permitted me to sleep, along with my servant, outside of the *sukkah*."

E. Said Rabbi, "When we were coming—I and R. Eleazar b. R. Ṣadoq—to visit R. Yoḥanan b. Nuri in Bet She'arim, we would eat figs and grapes outside of the *sukkah*" [cf. M. 2:4D].

F. And so did Rabbi say, "Any *sukkah* which is not four cubits by four cubits is invalid."

G. And sages say, "Even if it holds only one's head and the greater part of one's body alone, it is valid" [cf. M. 2:7].

T. 2:2 L p. 260, ls. 4-10

A. M'SH B: The Jerusalemites would let down their beds through the windows ten handbreadths high and covered them over with a *sukkah*-roofing, and they slept under them.

B. Waste-matter which protrudes from a *sukkah* is judged equivalent to the *sukkah*.

C. City guards by day are exempt from the religious requirement of dwelling in a *sukkah* by day, but they are liable by night.

D. City guards [cf. M. 2:5B] by night are exempt from the religious requirement of dwelling in a *sukkah* by night, but they are liable by day.

E. City guards by day and by night are exempt from the religious requirement of dwelling in a *sukkah* by day and by night.

F. Those who are out on a trip are exempt from the religious requirement of dwelling in a *sukkah* by day, but they are liable by night.

G. Garden-guards and orchard-guards are exempt by night, and liable by day.

H. Said R. Eleazar b. R. Ṣadoq, "When I was studying with

Yohanan b. Hahoranit, I saw him eating a dry piece of bread, for it was a time of famine. So I came and told my father. He said to me, 'Here are some olives for him.' So I brought him some olives. He took them and examined them and saw that they were wet. He said to me, 'I'm just not an olive-eater.' I came home and told my father, and he said to me, 'Go tell him, 'It was from a perforated basket, in accord with the House of Hillel [and so the sap which exuded from them is not deemed to have rendered the olives susceptible to uncleanness], but the lees stopped it up [on which account the liquids collected and dampened the olives, which is of no account].'''

I. Now [this story] tells us that he ate his unconsecrated produce in a state of cultic cleanness.

J. For even though he was one of the disciples of the House of Shammai, he obeyed only the teachings of the House of Hillel.

K. Under all circumstances the law is in accord with the House of Hillel.

L. To be sure, he who wants to impose a more strict rule on himself, to follow the law in accord with the opinion of the House of Shammai and in accord with the House of Hillel—concerning such a one, Scripture says, *The fool walks in darkness* (Qoh. 2:14).

M. He who holds by the lenient rulings of the House of Shammai and the lenient rulings of the House of Hillel is out-and-out wicked.

N. But if it is to be in accord with the teachings of the House of Shammai, then let it be in accord with both their lenient rulings and their strict rulings.

O. And if it is to be in accord with the teachings of the House of Hillel, then let it be in accord with both their lenient rulings and their strict rulings.

T. 2:3 L pp. 260-262, ls. 10-26

T. 2:1, 2A-E, cite and illustrate M. T. 2:2F-G place Rabbi into the House of Shammai. T. 2:3A illustrates the Hillelite view. T. 2:3C-G illustrate M. 2:4B. Because of M. 2:7D's reference to Yohanan, T. then supplies further information about him, none of it relevant in any way to M. or to T.'s antecedent materials.

2:8

A. Women, slaves, and minors are exempt from the religious requirement of dwelling in a *sukkah*.

B. A minor who can take care of himself is liable to the religious requirement of dwelling in a *sukkah*.

C. M'SH W: Shammai the Elder's daughter-in-law gave birth, and he broke away some of the plaster and covered the hole with *sukkah*-roofing over her bed, on account of the infant. M. 2:8

The exemptions, M. 2:4B-D, are augmented. Shammai rejects B; note M. Yoma 8:4.

2:9

A. All seven days a person treats his *sukkah* as his regular dwelling and his house as his sometime dwelling.

B. [If] it began to rain, at what point is it permitted to empty out [the *sukkah*]?

C. From the point at which the porridge will spoil.

D. They made a parable: To what is the matter comparable?

E. To a slave who came to mix a cup of wine for his master, and his master threw the flagon into his face.

M. 2:9

Random meals, M. 2:4D, are not eaten in the *sukkah*; regular meals, M. 2:9A, are.

A. [If] one was eating in a *sukkah*, and it rained, and he went and stood somewhere else [cf. M. 2:9B],

B. even though the rain let up,

C. they do not obligate him to go back, until it completely stops.

D. If he was sleeping in a *sukkah* and it rained and he got up and went away,

E. even though the rain let up,

F. they do not obligate him to go back, until it is dawn.

T. 2:4 L p. 262, ls. 26-29

A. On account of four sorts of bad folk are the lights [of the heaven] eclipsed:

B. because of counterfeiters, perjurers, people who raise small cattle, and people who cut down good trees.

C. And because of four sorts of bad deeds are Israelite householders handed over to the government:

D. because of holding on to writs of indebtedness which have already been paid,

E. because of lending on interest,

F. because of pledging funds to charity but not paying up, and

G. because of having the power to protest and not protesting [wrong-doing].

T. 2:5 L p. 262, ls. 29-33

A. When the lights are in eclipse, it is a bad omen for the whole world.

B. It is to be compared to a mortal king who built a palace and finished it and arranged a banquet, and then brought in the guests. He got mad at them and said to the servant, "Take away the light from them," so all of them turned out to be sitting in the dark.

C. R. Meir did say, "When the lights of heaven are in eclipse, it is a bad omen for Israel, for they are used to blows.

D. "It is to be compared to a teacher who came into the school house and said, 'Bring me the strap.' Now who gets worried? The one who is used to being strapped."

E. When the sun is in eclipse, it is a bad omen for the nations of the world.

F. [When] the moon is in eclipse, it is a bad omen for Israel,

G. since the gentiles reckon their calendar by the sun, and Israel by the moon.

H. When it is in eclipse in the east, it is a bad omen for those who live in the east.

I. When it is in eclipse in the west, it is a bad omen for those who live in the west.

J. When it is in eclipse in-between, it is a bad omen for the whole world.

K. When it turns red, it is a sign that punishment by the sword is coming into the world.

L. When it is like sack-cloth, it is a sign that punishment by pestilence and famine are coming into the world.

M. If they are smitten at its entry [into sunset], the punishment will tarry. [When they are smitten] when they rise, the punishment is coming fast.

N. And some say matters are reversed.

O. You have no nation in the whole world which is smitten, the god of which is not smitten right along with it,

P. as it is said, *And against all the gods of Egypt I will execute judgments* (Ex. 12:12).

Q. When Israel is occupied with Torah, they do not have to worry about all these omens,

R. as it is said, *Thus says the Lord, Do not learn the way of the gentiles, nor be dismayed at the signs of the heavens, for the nations are dismayed at them* (Jer. 10:2).

T. 2:6 L pp. 262-263, ls. 33-47

T. 2:4 augments M. 2:9B. T. 2:5-6 complement M. 2:9D-E, in a very general way, on the matter of bad omens.

CHAPTER TWENTY-TWO

SUKKAH CHAPTER THREE

From the rules for the *sukkah*, the tractate turns to the rite of taking up the *lulab*, with its four species, the palm-branch, myrtle-branch, willow-branch, and the citron (*etrog*), and of waving the *lulab* in the synagogue-service. In its usual, logical way, M. first of all defines the several species and specifies the acceptable and unacceptable sorts: M. 3:1, palm-branch; M. 3:2, myrtle, M. 3:3, willow-branch; then an appendix M. 3:4; and, finally, M. 3:5-7, the citron, with another appendix, M. 3:8. The necessary, second question is the use of the four species during the synagogue-services, which is at the recitation of the *Hallel*-Psalms, 113-118. M. 3:9-11 treat the liturgical function of the *lulab*. Finally, as expected, we shall turn to some special problems, and these invariably involve the Sabbath. So M. 3:12-15 treat using the *lulab* on the first festival day of the Festival of Tabernacles which coincides with the Sabbath.

In the present chapter, the word *lulab* bears two meanings, first, palm-branch, second, the combination of the species all together, that is, the palm-branch, willow-branch, myrtle-branch. When the latter sense is at hand, I give the word as *lulab*; and in the former sense, palm-branch. The shift is at M. 3:8.

3:1-3

I   A. A stolen or dried up palm branch is invalid.
    B. And one deriving from an *asherah* or an apostate town is invalid.
    C. [If] its tip was broken off, or [if] its leaves were split, it is invalid.
    D. [If] its leaves were spread apart, it is valid.
    E. R. Judah says, "Let him tie it up at the end."
    F. Thorn-palms of the Iron Mountain are valid.
    G. A palm branch which is [only] three handbreadths long,
    H. sufficient to shake,
    I. is valid.

M. 3:1

II A. A stolen or dried up myrtle branch is invalid.
    B. And one deriving from an *asherah* or an apostate town is invalid.

C. [If] its tip was broken off, [or if] its leaves were split,
D. or if its berries were more numerous than its leaves,
E. it is invalid.
F. But if one then removed some of them, it is valid.
G. And they do not remove [some of them] on the festival day.

M. 3:2

III A. A stolen or dried up willow branch is invalid.
B. And one deriving from an *asherah* or an apostate town is invalid.
C. [If] its tip was broken off, [if] its leaves split, or [if it was] a mountain-willow,
D. it is invalid.
E. [If] it was shriveled, or [if] some of the leaves dropped off,
F. or [if it came] from a [naturally watered] field [and did not grow by a brook],
G. it is valid.

M. 3:3

The formal traits of the triplets are clear in the repetitions, M. 3:1A-C, M. 3:2A-C, M. 3:3A-D. The additional materials make important points. Judah, M. 3:1E, glosses M. 3:1D by maintaining that if the leaves are spread apart, they must be tied up again. The other points of M. 3:1F-H, M. 3:2D-G, and M. 3:3E-G, are clear as given. The theory of M. 3:2F, that one may improve the condition of the myrtle branch and need not get another which to begin with is acceptable, is the same as Judah's.

3:4

A. R. Ishmael says, "Three myrtle-branches, two willow-branches, one palm-branch, and one citron [are required],
B. "even if two [of the myrtle-branches] have their tips broken off, and only one does not have its tip broken off."
C. R. Ṭarfon says, "Even if all three of them have their tips broken off, [they are valid]."
D. R. 'Aqiba says, "Just as one palm-branch and one citron [are required], so one myrtle-branch and one willow-branch [are required]."

M. 3:4

This appendix to M. 3:1-3 contains two disputes, B *vs.* C, and A *vs.* D. Ṭarfon then concurs with M. 3:1C. The antecedent triplet does not take a position on the other issue.

A. A palm-branch which is shaped like a fan,
B. or one, most of the leaves of which were split, is invalid [*vs.* M. 3:1C].

C. A willow-branch grown in a field, and one grown in the hills, is valid [M. 3:3F].

D. If so, why is it said, *Willows of the brook* (Lev. 23:40)?

E. This is meant to exclude the kind which grows in the mountains.

F. What is the kind which grows in the mountains?

G. One which has teeth like a saw.

H. What is a valid willow-branch? One which has a red stem and an elongated leaf.

I. What is an invalid willow-branch? One which has a white stem and a round leaf.

T. 2:7 L pp. 263-264, ls. 47-51

A. A myrtle branch and a willow-branch, of which the berries which grow on the inner side are removed, are valid [M. 3:2F].

B. The required measure of the length of a myrtle-branch and a willow-branch is three handbreadths [M. 3:1G], and of a palm-branch, four.

C. R. Tarfon says, "This is measured by a cubit divided into five handbreadths."

D. These four species—just as they do not diminish from their number, so too they do not add [other species] to them.

T. 2:8 L p. 264, ls. 51-54

T. complements M. as indicated.

3:5-7

IV A. A stolen or dried up citron is invalid.

B. And one deriving from an *asherah* or from an apostate town is invalid.

C. [If it derived from] *'orlah*-fruit, it is invalid.

D. [If it derived from] unclean heave-offering, it is invalid.

E. [If it derived from] clean heave-offering, one should not carry it. But if he carried it, it is valid.

F. One which is in the status of doubtfully tithed produce—

G. the House of Shammai declare invalid.

H. And the House of Hillel declare valid.

I. And one in the status of second tithe in Jerusalem one should not carry. But if he carried it, it is valid.

M. 3:5

A. (1) [If] scars covered the greater part of it,

B. (2) [if] its nipple was removed,

C. (3) [if] it was pealed, split, had a hole and so lacked any part whatsoever, it is invalid.

D. (1) [If] scars covered the lesser part of it,

E. (2) [if] its stalk was removed,

F. (3) [if] it had a hole but lacked no part whatsoever,

G. it is valid.

I   H. A dark-colored citron is invalid.
    I. And one which is green like a leek—
    J. R. Meir declares it valid.
    K. And R. Judah declares it invalid.

M. 3:6

II A. The measure of the smallest [acceptable] citron—
    B. R. Meir says, "The size of a nut."
    C. R. Judah says, "The size of an egg."
III D. And as to the largest [acceptable size]—
    E. "It must be of such a size that one can hold two in one hand," the words of R. Judah.
    F. R. Yosé says, "Even one in two hands."

M. 3:7

Commencing with the established formal-formulary pattern, M. 3:5A-B, the unit on the citron (*etrog*) proceeds in a quite different direction. It makes the point that the citron must be available for eating, and, it follows, what may not be eaten, M. 3:5C, D, also will not serve. Doubtfully-tithed produce must be properly tithed; since, when taken up, they may not be eaten because they require further preparation, the House of Shammai invalidate them. Since they nonetheless can be made suitable for eating, the House of Hillel validate them. Second tithe in Jerusalem may be eaten, but falls under the rule of E. The triplet of contrast, M. 3:6A-C, D-G, is clear as given. (C3 must match D3.) The three appended disputes deal with problems of definition, which surely should have been settled long before the middle of the second century.

A. [If] one does not have a citron, he should not use a pomegranate, a quince, or any other sort of fruit.

B. [If the four species] were wrinkled, they are valid. [If] they were dried up, they are invalid.

C. R. Judah says, "If [the four species] were dried up, they are valid."

D. Said R. Judah, "M'ŚH B: The townsfolk of the villages would leave their *lulabs* to their children in time of need."

E. They said to him, "A time of need does not yield proof."

T. 2:9 L p. 264, ls. 54-57

B-C augment M. 3:5A, showing that Judah rejects M.'s rule.

3:8

A. "They bind up the *lulab* [now: palm-branch, willow-branch, and myrtle-branch] only with [strands of] its own species," the words of R. Judah.

B. R. Meir says, "Even with a rope [it is permitted to bind up the *lulab*]."

C. Said R. Meir, "M'SH B: The townsfolk of Jerusalem bound up their palm-branches with gold threads."

D. They said to him, "But underneath they [in fact had] tied it up with [strands of] its own species."

M. 3:8

The dispute is clear as given. The consideration, A, is not to add to the species which are to be taken and waved, a minor quibble.

A. A *lulab* [palm-branch, willow-branch, myrtle-branch], whether bound up or not bound up, is valid.

B. R. Judah says, "One which is bound up is valid, and one which is not bound up is invalid."

C. One should not bind it up on the festival day.

D. But one may take a shoot from it and bind it up.

E. *"They bind up the lulab only with that which is its own species,"* the words of R. Judah.

F. *Said R. Meir, "M'SH B: The townsfolk of Jerusalem bound up their lulabs with gold threads."*

G. *They said to him, "Is there proof in that precedent? But underneath they had tied it up with that which is its own species"* [M. 3:8].

H. Said R. Eleazar b. R. Sadoq, "It was the practice of the townsfolk of Jerusalem to do things thus: One would enter the synagogue carrying the *lulab* in his hand.

"He would arise to read the translation [of the Scripture] or to take his place before the ark, with his *lulab* in his hand.

"[If] he arose to read in the Torah or to raise his hands [in the priestly benediction of the congregration], he would put it down on the ground.

"When he went out of the synagogue, his *lulab* was in his hand.

"When he went in to visit the sick and to comfort mourners, his *lulab* was in his hand.

"But when he entered the study-house, he would give it to his son or his messenger and return it to his house."

T. 2:10 L pp. 264-265, ls. 57-66

M. does not take a position on A-B. Perhaps H is relevant to M. 3:9E-H, if only in a general way.

3:9

A. And at what point [in the *Hallel*-Psalms, 113-118] did they shake [the *lulab*]?

B. "At *O give thanks unto the Lord* (Ps. 118), beginning and end;

and at, *Save now, we beseech thee O Lord* (Ps. 118:25)," the words of the House of Hillel.

C. And the House of Shammai say, "Also: At, *O Lord, we beseech, thee, send now prosperity* (Ps. 118:25)."

D. Said R. 'Aqiba, "I was watching Rabban Gamaliel and R. Joshua, for all the people waved their palm-branches, but they waved their palm-branches only at, *Save now, we beseech thee, O Lord* (Ps. 118:25)."

E. He who was on a trip and had no *lulab* to carry—

F. when he reaches home, should carry the *lulab* at his own table.

G. [If] he did not carry his *lulab* in the morning, he should carry it at dusk,

H. for the entire day is a suitable time for the palm-branch.

M. 3:9

The dispute, A-C, has an appendix, D, with yet a third opinion. One must even interrupt his meal to take the *lulab* under certain circumstances, E-H.

3:10

A. He for whom a slave, woman, or minor read answers after them by saying what they say.

B. But it is a curse to him.

C. If an adult-male read for him, he answers after him [only] "Halleluyah."

M. 3:10

The child, slave, or woman cannot serve as an adult male's agent, A, but the adult-male, C, can do so. In the former instance, therefore, the man must repeat the words.

3:11

A. Where they are accustomed to repeat [the last nine verses of Ps. 118], let one repeat.

B. [Where it is the custom] to say them only once, let one say them only once.

C. [Where it is the custom] to say a blessing after it, let one say a blessing after it.

D. Everything follows the custom of the locality.

E. He who buys a *lulab* [palm-branch, myrtle-branch, willow-branch] from his fellow in the Seventh Year—[the seller] gives him a citron as a gift.

F. For one is not permitted to buy [the citron] in the Seventh Year.

M. 3:11

A-D complete the discussion begun at M. 3:9E-F. In the Seventh Year one may not purchase produce grown in that year. The citron, picked that year, alone falls under the rule. Hence the citron is to be given as a gift, while the other items may be bought and sold. The other items are wood, not food, and may be bought and sold (Maimonides, *Comm*.).

3:12

A. At first the *lulab* was carried in the Temple for seven days, and in the provinces, for one day.

B. When the Temple was destroyed, Rabban Yoḥanan b. Zakkai ordained that the *lulab* should be carried in the provinces seven days,

C. as a memorial to the Temple;

D. and that the whole of the day on which the ʿ*omer* is waved should be forbidden [for the use of new produce, which may be used only from the waving of the ʿ*omer* and thereafter; this had formerly been offered at noon].

M. 3:12

The two ordinances take account of the destruction of the Temple. The ʿ*omer* was offered on the fifteenth of Nisan, so from the afternoon onward, it had been permitted to eat produce harvested in the present growing cycle. But Yoḥanan prohibited use of the new produce for the whole of the fifteenth of Nisan, as a memorial to the Temple.

3:13-15

A. [If] the first festival day of the Festival [of Sukkot] coincides with the Sabbath, all the people bring their *lulabs* to the synagogue [on the day before].

B. On the next day they get up and come along. Each one finds his own and takes it.

C. For sages have said, "A person does not fulfill his obligation [to wave the *lulab*] on the first day of the Festival by using the *lulab* of his fellow.

D. "And on all other days of the Festival, one does fulfill his obligation [to wave the *lulab*] by using the *lulab* of his fellow."

M. 3:13

A. R. Yosé says, "[If] the first day of the Festival [of Sukkot] coincides with the Sabbath, [if] one forgot and brought his *lulab* out into the public domain, he is exempt [from the obligation to bring a sin-offering],

B. "because he brought it out [intending to do what is] permitted."

M. 3:14

A. A woman receives the *lulab* from her son or husband and puts it back into water on the Sabbath.

B. R. Judah says, "(1) On the Sabbath they put it back into [the same water], (2) on the festival-day they add water, and (3) on the intermediate days of the festival they change the water."

C. A minor who knows how to wave the *lulab* is liable to the requirement of waving the *lulab*.

M. 3:15

M. 3:12 now is shown to serve as a prologue to the final unit of the chapter, since the taking of the *lulab* all seven days means that the prohibitions of the Sabbath must now be introduced. Taking the *lulab* on the first day of the festival coinciding with the Sabbath overrides the restrictions of the Sabbath (a concept made explicit at M. 4:2). We now provide for that contingency. There is no need to carry the *lulab* to the synagogue; it is left there overnight. What can be done in advance must be (M. Shab. 19:1). The explanation of the detail at B about finding one's own *lulab*, C-D, is the first of several appended rules. Yosé's, which is clear as stated and bears its own gloss, is the second. M. 3:15A permits the woman to handle the *lulab* on the Sabbath, even though she is not obligated to wave it. This triggers the addition of B and C, two further rules relevant to M. 3:15A, first, on changing the water, second, on who else is obligated to take up the *lulab*.

A. *On the first day of the Festival a person does not fulfill his obligation [to wave the lulab] by using the lulab of his fellow* [M. 3:13C],

B. unless he gives it over to him as an unconditional gift.

C. M'SH B: Rabban Gamaliel and elders were traveling in a boat and had no *lulab* with them. Rabban Gamaliel bought a *lulab* for a golden *denar*. Once he had fulfilled his obligation with it, he gave it to his fellow, and his fellow to his fellow, so that all of them fulfilled their obligation. Afterward they returned it to him.

D. R. Yosé says, "On the first festival day of the Festival which coincides with the Sabbath, once one has fulfilled his obligation, it is prohibited to carry [the *lulab*]."

T. 2:11 L p. 265, ls. 66-72

A is illustrated by C. Yosé's point is that one does only what is required, a clarification of M. 3:14.

CHAPTER TWENTY-THREE

SUKKAH CHAPTER FOUR

Chapter Four begins with a simple account of the rites connected with the Festival and the days on which these rites are carried on, in all instances taking account of the restrictions of the Sabbath and, in some, of the festival-day as well. There is a catalogue of seven items in four stichs at M. 4:1. This then is systematically spelled out as follows: *lulab*, M. 4:2; willow-branch, M. 4:3, with secondary developments on the theme of the *lulab* at M. 4:4 and of the willow-branch at M. 4:5-7; *Hallel*, M. 4:8, *sukkah*, M. 4:8, water-libation, M. 4:9-10; and flute-playing, M. 5:1.

4:1-3

A. [The rites of] the *lulab* and the willow-branch [carried by the priests around the altar, M. 5:5] are for six or seven [days].
B. The recitation of the *Hallel*-Psalms and the rejoicing are for eight [days].
C. [The requirement of dwelling in the] *sukkah* and the water-libation are for seven days.
D. And the flute-playing is for five or six.

M. 4:1

A. *The lulab is for seven days*: How so?
B. [If] the first festival day of the Festival coincided with the Sabbath, the *lulab* is for seven days.
C. But [if it coincided] with any other day, it is for six days.

M. 4:2

A. *The willow-branch [rite] is for seven days*: How so?
B. [If] the seventh day of the willow-branch coincided with the Sabbath, the willow-branch [rite] is for seven days.
C. But [if it coincided] with any other day, it is for six days.

M. 4:3

We see that M. 4:2 and M. 4:3 take up the items of M. 4:1A and explain why they may be done either on six or on seven days. Only if the first festival day of the Festival coincides with the Sabbath are these rites carried out on the Sabbath. If the first festival day of the Festival is on any other day, then for the Sabbath which falls in the intermediate days of the festival these rites are suspended (compare

M. 3:12). That is the point repeated at M. 4:2 and M. 4:3. It will not be relevant to M. 4:1B or C, since there is no problem with the Sabbath for these rites, or to M. 4:1D, because there is no basis for permitting the flute-playing to override the restrictions of the Sabbath in any event.

4:4

A. The religious requirement of the *lulab* [on the Sabbath]: How so?
B. [If] the first festival day of the Festival coincided with the Sabbath, they bring their *lulabs* to the Temple mount.
C. And the attendants take them from them and arrange them on the roof of the portico.
D. But old people leave theirs in a special room.
E. They teach them to make the following statement:' "To whomever my *lulab* comes, lo, it is given to him as a gift."
F. On the next day they get up and come along.
G. And the attendants toss them before them.
H. They grab at *lulabs* and hit one another.
I. Now when the court saw that this was leading to a dangerous situation, they ordained that each and every one should take his *lulab* in his own home.

M. 4:4

The supplement to M. 4:2 goes over the ground of M. 3:12-13. The narrative is complete at B-F+G. H-I are jarring, just as the consideration of E is surprising in light of the certainty of M. 3:13 on a quite different theory. In all, this is an odd item, contradicting M. 3:12 at I and M. 3:13 at E-F.

4:5-7

A. The religious requirement of the willow-branch: How so?
B. There was a place below Jerusalem, called Moṣa. [People] go down there and gather young willow-branches. They come and throw them along the sides of the altar, with their heads bent over the altar.
C. They blew on the *shofar* a sustained, a quavering, and a sustained note.
D. Every day they walk around the altar one time and say,"*Save now, we beseech thee, O Lord! We beseech thee, O Lord, send now prosperity* (Ps. 118:25)."
E. R. Judah says, "[They say], '*Ani waho, save us we pray! Ani waho, save us we pray!*' "
F. And on that day [the seventh day of the willow-branch] they walk around the altar seven times.
G. When they leave, what do they say?

H. "Homage to you, O altar! Homage to you, O altar!"
I. R. Eliezer says, "For the Lord and for you, O altar! For the Lord and for you O altar!"

M. 4:5

A. As the rite concerning it [is performed] on an ordinary day, so the rite concerning it [is performed] on the Sabbath.
B. But they would gather [the willow-branches] on Friday and leave them in the gilded troughs [of water], so that they will not wither.
C. R. Yoḥanan b. Beroqah says, "They would bring palm tufts and beat them on the ground at the side of the altar,
D. "and that day was called the 'day of beating palm tufts.'"

M. 4:6

A. Forthwith children throw away their *lulabs* and eat their citrons.

M. 4:7

Parallel to M. 4:4, M. 4:5-7 now take up and explain the reference at M. 4:1A to the willow-branch. When the seventh day of the rite coincides with the Sabbath, it will be carried out, M. 4:5F, complemented by M. 4:6. Yoḥanan b. Beroqah has his own view of the rite of the willow-branches as it was conducted on the seventh day.

A. The rite of the *lulab* overrides the prohibitions of the Sabbath at its [the Festival of Sukkot's] beginning [that is, when the Sabbath coincides with the first festival day of Sukkot],
B. and the rite of the willow-branch at the end [when the rite of the willow-branch for the seventh time is to be done on the Sabbath].
C. M'SH W: The Boethusians piled up big boulders [on the willows which had been lined up around the altar] on the eve of the Sabbath.
D. The common folk discovered them and came and dragged them away and took the [willow-branches] out from underneath the boulders on the Sabbath.
E. For the Boethusians do not concur that beating the willow-branches overrides the prohibitions of the Sabbath [M. 4:6A].
F. The law of the willow-branch is a law revealed to Moses at Sinai [but not referred to in written Scripture].
G. Abba Saul says, "It is a matter of the written Torah,
H. "since it says, *And willow-branches grown by a brook* (Lev. 23:4)—
I. "[the plural, branches, indicates:] a willow-branch for the *lulab*, and a willow-branch for the altar."
J. R. Eliezer b. Jacob says, "Thus did they say, 'For him and to you, O altar! For him and for you, O altar!'"

T. 3:1 L p. 266, ls. 1-6

Eliezer means, "We bow down to You, O Lord, and we praise you O altar," roughly parallel to M. 4:5I. T. 3:1A-B are important clarifications for M. 4:1A.

4:8

A. *The Hallel-Psalms and the rejoicing are for eight days*: How so?
B. This rule teaches that a person is obligated for the *Hallel*-Psalms, for the rejoicing, and for the honoring of the festival day, on the last festival day of the Festival, just as he is on all the other days of the Festival.
C. *The obligation to dwell in the sukkah for seven days*: How so?
D. [If] one has finished eating [the last meal of the festival], he should not untie his *sukkah* right away.
E. But he brings down the utensils [only] from twilight onward—
F. on account of the honor due to the last festival day of the Festival.

M. 4:8

The point of A-B is that the Eighth Day of Assembly requires the rites of *Hallel*-Psalms and rejoicing (offering peace-offerings, eating meat). D-F explain that the *sukkah* is left standing all seven days and not dismantled until after the closing festival.

A. On eighteen days in the year and on one night do they recite the *Hallel*-psalms, and these are they:
B. On the eight days of the Festival [of Tabernacles], on the eight days of Hanukkah, on the first festival day of Passover and on the night preceding it, and on the festival day of Pentecost.

T. 3:2 L p. 266, ls. 6-8

T. complements M. 4:8A.

4:9-10

A. *The water-libation*: How so?
B. A golden flask, holding three *logs* in volume, did one fill with water from Siloam.
C. [When] they reached the Water Gate, they blow a sustained, a quavering, and a sustained blast on the *shofar*.
D. [The priest] went up on the ramp [at the south] and turned to his left [southwest].
E. There were two silver bowls there.
F. R. Judah says, "They were of plaster, but they had darkened because of the wine."
G. They were perforated with holes like a narrow snout,
H. one wide, one narrow,
I. so that both of them would be emptied together [one of its wine, flowing slowly, the other of its water, flowing quickly].

J. The one on the west was for water, the one on the east was for wine.

K. [If] he emptied the flask of water into the bowl for wine, and the flask of wine into the bowl for water, he has nonetheless carried out the rite.

L. R. Judah says, "A *log* [of water] would one pour out as the water libation all eight days."

M. And to the one who pours out the water libation they say, "Lift up your hand [so that we can see the water pouring out]!"

N. For one time one [priest] poured out the water on his feet.

O. And all the people stoned him with their citrons.

M. 4:9

A. As the rite concerning it [was carried out] on an ordinary day, so was the rite [carried out] on the Sabbath.

B. But on the eve of the Sabbath one would fill with water from Siloam a gold jug, which was not sanctified,

C. and he would leave it in a chamber [in the Temple].

D. [If] it was poured out or left uncovered, one would fill the jug from the laver [in the courtyard].

E. For wine and water which have been left uncovered are invalid for the altar.

M. 4:10

The topic of M. 4:1C is worked out, but the proposition, that the water-libation is done even on the Sabbath, is subordinate (M. 4:10A-C, parallel to M. 4:6A-B). The interest is in how the rite is performed, M. 4:9. M. 4:10D-E then gloss M. 4:10C. Judah's gloss of B at L is wildly misplaced, but everything else appears properly located.

A. Why is it called "the Water Gate" [M. 4:9C]?

B. Because through it they bring a flask of water for the water-libation on the Festival.

C. R. Eliezer b. Jacob says, "Through it *the water comes out* [*on the south side*] (Ez. 47:2).

D. "This teaches that they flow outward like the water of a flask.

E. "And they are destined to *flow down from below the south end of the threshhold of the Temple,* [*south of the altar*] (Ez. 47:1)."

F. And so it says, *Going on eastward with a line in his hand, the man measured a thousand cubits, and then led me through the water, and it was ankle deep* (Ez. 47:3).

G. This teaches that a man may go through water up to his ankles [without danger].

H. *Again he measured a thousand and led me through the water, and it was knee-deep* (Ez. 47:4).

I. This teaches that a man may go through water up to his knees [without facing danger of drowning].

T. 3:3 (4) L pp. 266-267, ls. 8-14

A. Another matter: *Water up to his knees* (BRKYM)—that it is continually blessed.

T. 3:5 L p. 267, ls. 14-15

A. *Again he measured a thousand, and led me through the water, and it was up to the loins* (Ez. 47:4).
B. This teaches that a man may go through water up to his loins [without danger].
C. *Again he measured a thousand, and it was a river that I could not pass through, [for the water had risen; it was deep enough to swim in, a river that could not be passed through]* (Ez. 47:5).
D. Is it possible to interpret [the passage to mean] that one might not go through by foot, but one could pass over by swimming? Scripture says, *For the water had risen, it was deep enough to swim in.*
E. Is it possible to interpret that one might not pass over by swimming, but one might cross in a small boat? Scripture says, *A river that could not be passed through*—even in a boat.

T. 3:6 L p. 267, ls. 15-19

A. Is it possible to interpret [the passage to mean] that one might not cross in a small boat, but one might pass over in a large boat?
B. Scripture says, *[But there the Lord in majesty will be for us, a place of broad rivers and streams,] where no galley with oars can go, [nor stately ship can pass]* (Is. 33:21).
C. Is it possible to interpret [the passage to mean] that one might not cross in a large boat, but one might pass in a large ship?
D. Scripture says, *Nor stately ship can pass.*
E. And it says, *On that day water will go forth from Jerusalem* (Zech. 14:8).

T. 3:7(8) L p. 267, ls. 19-22

A. Is it possible that they will be mixed with water from other springs?
B. Scripture says, *On that day there shall be a fountain opened for the house of David and the inhabitants of Jerusalem to cleanse them from sin and uncleanness* (Zech. 13:1).
C. There will be a single source [of water for purification] for sin and for menstrual uncleanness.
D. Whither do they flow?
E. To the Great Sea, and to the Sea at Tiberias, and to the sea at Sodom,
F. so as to heal their water,
G. as it is said, *And he said to me, This water flows toward the eastern region and goes down into the Arabah; and when it enters the stagnant waters of the sea, the water will become fresh* (Ez. 47:8).
H. *This water flows toward the eastern region*—this refers to the sea at Sodom.
I. *And it goes down into the Arabah*—this refers to the sea at Tiberias.

J. *And when it enters the stagnant waters of the sea, the water will become fresh*—this is the Great Sea.

K. And it says, *And wherever the river goes every living creature which swarms will live; and there will be very many fish; for this water goes there, that the waters of the sea may become fresh; so everything will live where the river goes* (Ez. 47:9).

T. 3:9 L pp. 267-268, ls. 22-33

A. And it says, *Fishermen will stand beside the sea; from Engedi to Eneglaim it will be a place for the spreading of the nets; its fish will be of very many kinds, like the fish of the Great Sea* (Ez. 47:10).

B. This teaches that all the waters created at the Creation are destined to go forth from the mouth of this little flask.

T. 3:10 L p. 268, ls. 33-35

A. And so was the well which was with the Israelites in the wilderness a rock of the size of a large round vessel, surging and gurgling upward as from the mouth of this little flask, rising with them up onto the mountains, and going down with them into the valleys.

B. Wherever the Israelites would encamp, it made camp with them,

C. on a high place, opposite the entry of the Tent of Meeting.

D. The princes of Israel come and surround it with their staffs, and they sing a song concerning it: *Spring up, O Well! Sing to it! [the well which the princes dug, which the nobles of the people delved with the scepter and with their staves]* (Num. 21:17-18).

E. And they well upward like a pillar on high, and each one [of the princes] draws water with his staff, each one for his tribe and each one for his family, as it is said: *The well which the princes dug.*

T. 3:11 L pp. 268-269, ls. 36-42

A. *And from Mattanah to Nahaliel, and from Nahaliel to Bamoth, and from Bamoth to the valley lying in the region of Moab by the top of Pisgah, [which looks down upon the desert]* (Num. 21:19-20).

B. This surrounds the entire camp of Israel and provides water for the whole desert, as it is said, *Which looks down upon the desert.*

C. And this is turned into mighty streams, as it is said, *The streams overflow* (Ps. 78:20).

D. They sit in small boats and come together, as it is said, *It flowed through the desert like a river* (Ps. 105:41).

T. 3:12 L p. 269, ls. 43-46

A. He who goes up on the right goes up on the right, and he who goes up on the left, goes up on the left.

B. So the water which flows forth from it is made into a great river and flows into the Great Sea.

C. And they derive from it all necessary goods, as it is said, *For the Lord Your God has blessed you in all the work of your hands; he* knows your going through this great wilderness;] these forty years the Lord your God has been with you; you have lacked nothing (Deut. 2:7).

T. 3:13 L p. 269, ls. 47-50

The exegetical materials take up the theme of the water-offering and come to their climax at T. 3:11B.

A. *There were two silver bowls* on top of the altar [M. 4:9E], one for water, one for wine.
B. *The one on the west was for water* [M. 4:9J].
C. In the normal course of approaching the altar, the *one on the east was for wine* [M. 4:9J] [since the priest would meet up with the one for wine as he approached the altar].
D. *[If] he emptied the flask for water into the bowl for wine, or the bowl for wine into the flask for water, he has nonetheless carried out the rite* [M. 4:9K].
E. *R. Judah says, "They were of plaster, but they had darkened because of the wine"* [M. 4:9F].
F. *They were perforated with holes like a narrow snout,* [M. 4:9G], for through them would the water flow into the channel which the one who built the Sanctuary built.

T. 3:14 L pp. 269-270, ls. 50-54

A. They go down into the pit and they split it and are absorbed into it, as it is said, *In the holy place you shall pour out a drink offering [of strong drink to the Lord]* (Num. 28:7).
B. For one has made for it a place so that it may be absorbed in sanctity.
C. R. Yosé says, "The cavity of the pits descended to the abyss, as it is said, *Let me sing of my well-beloved, a song of my beloved touching his vineyard. My well-beloved had a vineyard on a very fruitful hill. And he digged it and cleared it of stones and planted it with the choicest vine and built a tower in the midst of it and also hewed out a vat therein* (Is. 5:1-2).
D. *"And he built a tower in the midst of it*—this is the sanctuary.
E. *"And* [also] *hewed out a vat therein*—this is the altar.
F. *"And* also *hewed out a vat therein*—this is the pits."
G. R. Eliezer b. R. Ṣadoq says, "There was a small passage-way between the ascent and the altar at the west side of the ramp.
H. "Once every seventy years the young priests would go down there and gather up the congealed wine, which looked like circles of pressed figs, and they burned it in a state of sanctity, as it is said, *In the holy place shall you pour out a drink-offering of strong drink unto the Lord* (Num. 28:7).
I. "Just as the pouring out must be in a state of sanctity, thus the burning of it must be in a state of sanctity."

T. 3:15 L p. 270, ls. 54-62

A. At what time do they pour out the [water-libation]?
B. Along with the offering up of the limbs of the daily whole-offering.
C. For there already was the case of the *Boethusian who poured out the water on his feet, and all the people stoned him with their citrons* [M. 4:9N-O].
D. And the horn of the altar was damaged, so the sacred service was annulled for that day, until they brought a lump of salt and put it on it, so that the altar should not appear to be damaged.
E. For any altar lacking a horn, ramp, or foundation is invalid.
F. R. Yosé b. R. Judah says, "Also the rim."
G. *The water libation is for all seven days* [of the Festival Tabernacles] [M. 4:1C].
H. R. Judah says, "For all eight days."
I. But *R. Judah says, "A log of water did one pour out as the water-libation all eight days"* [M. 4:9L].
J. And sages say, "Three *logs*" [M. 4:9B].
K. You turn out to rule, He who wants more water diminishes the number of days, and he who wants more days diminishes the volume of the water.

T. 3:16 L pp. 270-271, ls. 62-69

A. The water used for the water-libation on the Festival [of Tabernacles]—one is liable on its account by reason of violation of the laws of remnant, refuse, and uncleanness.
B. Therefore if it was kept overnight or contracted uncleanness, it goes forth to the place of burning.
C. But the jug and flask themselves are subject to the laws of sacrilege [if filled from the laver, M. 4:10D],
D. for they themselves are holy [cf. M. 4:10B].

T. 3:17 L p. 271, ls. 69-71

A. Said R. 'Aqiba, "The Torah has required bringing the *'omer* of barley on Passover, because it is the season of barley,
B. "so that the grain-harvest would be blessed on its account.
C. "It required bringing first fruits [of grain] on Pentecost, because it is the season of orchards,
D. "so that on its account the produce of fruit-bearing trees will be blessed.
E. "It required bringing the water-offering on the Festival [of Tabernacles]
F. "so that the rain would be blessed on its account,
G. "and it says, *And if any of the families of the earth do not go up to Jerusalem to worship the King, the Lord of hosts, there will be no rain upon them. And if the family of Egypt do not go up and present themselves, then upon them shall come the plague with which the Lord afflicts the nations that do not go up to keep the festival of Tabernacles* (Zech. 14:17-18)."

T. 3:18 L p. 271, ls. 71-77

T. 3:14-17 complement M., citing its materials and glossing them, and then supplement M.'s theme with further relevant information. T. 3:16I-J corrects M.'s presentation of its dispute. T. 3:18 resumes the homiletical discourse.

CHAPTER TWENTY-FOUR

SUKKAH CHAPTER FIVE

The account of the performance of the rites of the Festival is completed at M. 5:1, which treats the last item of M. 4:1, the playing of the flute. M. 5:1 then alludes to the celebration of *bet hashsho'ebah*, generally assumed to be a celebration of the drawing of the water for the water-libation of M. 4:9-10. This is elaborately described at M. 5:2-4 + 5. The concluding unit, M. 5:6-8, turns to the offerings of the Festival, that is, the bullocks, rams, and goat required by Num. 29:13-16. There are twenty-four priestly courses. All are given a share in the liturgy of the Festival, M. 5:6. M. 5:7 then treats the shares accorded to these same priestly courses on the other festivals, and, of necessity, we conclude with the duties of the priestly courses, incoming and outgoing, on other days of the year, M. 5:7-8.

5:1-4

A. Flute-playing is for five or six days:
B. This refers to the flute-playing on *bet hashsho'ebah*,
C. which overrides the restrictions of neither the Sabbath nor of a festival-day.
D. They said: Anyone who has not seen the rejoicing of *bet hashsho'ebah* in his life has never seen rejoicing.

M. 5:1

A. At the end of the first festival day of the Festival [the priests and Levites] went down to the woman's courtyard.
B. And they made a major enactment [by putting men below and women above].
C. And there were golden candle-holders there, with four gold bowls on their tops, and four ladders for each candle stick.
D. And four young priests with jars of oil containing a hundred and twenty *log*s, [would climb up the ladders and] pour [the oil] into each bowl.

M. 5:2

A. Out of the worn-out undergarments and girdles of the priests they made wicks,
B. and with them they lit the candlesticks.
C. And there was not a courtyard in Jerusalem which was not lit up from the light of *bet hashsho'ebah*.

M. 5:3

A. The pious men and wonder-workers would dance before them with flaming torches in their hand,
B. and they would sing before them songs and praises.
C. And the Levites beyond counting played on harps, lyres, cymbals, trumpets, and [other] musical instruments,
D. [standing, as they played] on the fifteen steps which go down from the Israelites' court to the women's court.
E. corresponding to the fifteen Songs of Ascents which are in the Book of Psalms—
F. on these the Levites stand with their instrument and sing their song.
G. And two priests stood at the upper gate which goes down from the Israelites' court to the women's court, with two trumpets in their hands.
H. [When] the cock crowed, they sounded a sustained, a quavering, and a sustained note on the *shofar*.
I. [When] they got to the tenth step, they sounded a sustained, a quavering, and a sustained blast on the *shofar*.
J. [When] they reached the courtyard, they sounded a sustained, a quavering, and a sustained blast on the *shofar*.
K. They went on sounding the *shofar* in a sustained blast until they reached the gate which leads out to the east.
L. [When] they reached the gate which leads out to the east, they sounded a sustained, a quavering, and a sustained blast on the *shofar*.
M. [When] they reached the gate which goes out toward the east, they turned around toward the west,
N. and they said, "Our fathers who were in this place *turned with their backs toward the Temple of the Lord and their faces toward the east, and they worshipped the sun toward the east* (Ez. 8:16).
O. "But as to us, our eyes are to the Lord."
P. R. Judah says, "They said it a second time, 'We belong to the Lord, our eyes are toward the Lord.' "   M. 5:4

The conclusion of the exposition of M. 4:1 is at M. 5:1A-C. Since the celebration herein referred to does not override the prohibitions of the Sabbath, if the first festival day of the Festival does not coincide with the Sabbath, then the Sabbath comes on an intermediate day of the festival, leaving five days for the flute-playing; but if the first festival day of the Festival coincides with the Sabbath, then there will be six ordinary days on which the celebration may take place, so much for A-C. Then there is a narrative, joined to M. 5:1A-C by D. But it is clear that the celebration herein described has nothing to do with the flute-playing.

A. At first, when people would witness the rejoicing of *bet hashsho'-ebah*, the men would watch inside, and the women would watch outside.

B. But when the court saw that they turned to silliness, they set up three balconies in the courtyard, one on each side, where the women sit and witness the rejoicing of *bet hashsho'ebah*.

C. And [the men and women] did not mix together [cf. M. 5:2].

T. 4:1 L p. 272, ls. 1-4

A. *Pious men and wonder workers would dance before them with flaming torches in their hand, and they would sing before them songs of praise* [M. 5:4A-B].

B. What did they sing?

C. "Happy is he who has not sinned. But all who have sinned will He forgive."

D. And some of them say, "Fortunate is my youth, which did not bring my old age into shame"—these [who say this song] are the wonder-workers.

E. And some of them say, "Fortunate are you, O years of my old age, for you will atone for the years of my youth"—these [who say this song] are the penitents.

T. 4:2 L p. 272, ls. 4-8

A. Hillel the Elder says, "To the place which my heart craves, there do my feet lead me.

B. "If you will come to my house, I shall come to your house.

C. "If you will not come to my house, I shall not come to your house,

D. "as it is said, *In every place where I cause my name to be remembered I will come to you and bless you* (Ex. 20:24)."

T. 4:3 L p. 272, ls. 8-11

A. M'SH B: Rabban Simeon b. Gamaliel danced with eight flaming torches, and not one of them fell to the ground.

B. Now when he would prostrate himself, he would put his finger on the ground, bow low, kiss [the ground], and forthwith straighten up.

T. 4:4 L p. 272, ls. 11-13

A. Said R. Joshua b. Ḥananiah, "In all the celebrations of *bet hashsho'ebah*, we never saw a moment of sleep.

B. "We should get up in time for the morning daily wholeoffering.

C. "From there we should go to the synagogue, from there to the additional offerings [in the Temple], from there to eating and drinking, from there to the study house, from there to the Temple to see the evening daily whole-offering, from there to the celebration of the rejoicing of *bet hashsho'ebah*."

T. 4:5 L p. 273, ls. 14-17

A. Said R. Judah, "Whoever has never seen the double colonnade [the basilica-synagogue] of Alexandria in Egypt has never seen Israel's glory in his entire life.

B. "It was a kind of large basilica, with one colonnade inside another.

C. "Sometimes there were twice as many people there as those who went forth from Egypt.

D. "Now there were seventy-one golden thrones set up there, one for each of the seventy-one elders, each one worth twenty-five talents of gold, with a wooden platform in the middle.

E. "The minister of the synagogue stands on it, with flags in his hand. When one began to read, the other would wave the flags so the people would answer, 'Amen,' for each and every blessing. Then that one would wave the flags, and they would answer, 'Amen.'

F. "They did not sit in a jumble, but the goldsmiths sat by themselves, the silversmiths by themselves, the weavers by themselves, the bronze-workers by themselves, and the blacksmiths by themselves.

G. "All this why? So that when a traveller came along, [he could find his fellow craftsmen], and on that basis he could gain a living."

T. 4:6 L p. 273, ls. 17-25

A. *Levites [played on harps, lyres, cymbals, and all sorts of musical instruments* [M. 5:4C].

B. What did they sing?

C. *A song of ascents. Come, bless the Lord, all you servants of the Lord, who stand by night in the house of the Lord* (Ps. 134:1).

T. 4:7 L p. 274, ls. 26-27

A. Some of them would sing, *Lift up your hands to the holy place and bless the Lord* (Ps. 134:2).

T. 4:8 L p. 274, ls. 27-28

A. And when they departed from one another, what did they say?

B. *May the Lord bless you from Zion, he who made heaven and earth* (Ps. 134:3).

T. 4:9 L p. 274, ls. 28-29

A. [*And two priests stood at the upper gate which goes down from the Israelites' court to the women's court*], *with two trumpets in their hands* [M. 5:4G].

B. *When the cock crowed, they sounded a sustained, a quavering, and a sustained note on the shofar* [M. 5:4I].

C. R. Judah says, "They do not sound fewer than seven nor more than sixteen."

T. 4:10 L p. 274, ls. 29

T. fairly systematically glosses M.'s account of *bet hashsho'ebah*, with some obviously extraneous units.

5:5

A. They sound no fewer than twenty-one notes in the Temple, and they do not sound more than forty-eight.

B. Every day there were there twenty-one blasts on the *shofar*:

C. three at the opening of the gates, nine at the offering of the daily whole-offering of the morning, and nine at the offering of the daily whole-offering of the evening.

D. And on days on which an additional offering is made, they would add nine more.

E. And on the eve of the Sabbath they would add six more:

F. three to make people stop working, and three to mark the border between the holy day and the ordinary day.

G. On an eve of the Sabbath which came during the festival there were forty-eight in all:

H. three for the opening of the gates, three for the upper gate and the three for the lower gate, three for the drawing of the water, three for the pouring of the water on the altar, nine for the offering of the daily whole-offering in the morning, nine for the offering of the daily whole offering of the evening, nine for the additional offerings, three to make the people stop work, and three to mark the border between the holy day and the ordinary day.

M. 5:5

The long account of the *shofar*-blowing now bears an appendix on that subject in general.

D. *Three [sounds of the shofar] at the openings of the gates* [M. 5:5C].

E. He who maintains that they blow the *shofar* when they are opened does not maintain that they blow the *shofar* when they are closed.

F. He who maintains that they blow the *shofar* when they are closed does not maintain that they blow the *shofar* when they are opened.

G. Three before the altar.

H. He who maintains that they blow the *shofar* before the altar does not maintain that they blow the *shofar* on the tenth step.

I. He who maintains that they blow the *shofar* on the tenth step does not maintain that they blow the *shofar* before the altar [cf. M. 5:5].

T. 4:10 L p. 774, ls. 30-33

A. *Three to make the people stop working* [M. 5:5F]—how so?

B. The minister of the synagogue takes a trumpet and goes up to the top of the highest roof in town.

C. He begins to sound the trumpet.

D. Those nearest town stop work, and those near the Sabbath-limit come together and go inside the Sabbath limit.

E. Now they did not go in right away, but they waited until all of them came together. Then all of them came in at one time.

F. When did one go in [at the end, to mark the Sabbath]?

G. Once he had filled a jug of water, roasted a fish, and kindled the Sabbath light.

T. 4:11 L pp. 274-275, ls. 33-38

A. *Three to mark the border between the holy day and the ordinary day* [M. 5:5F]—how so?

B. The minister of the synagogue takes a trumpet and goes up to the top of the highest roof in town.

C. He begins to sound the trumpet.

D. They take the cooked dish off the stove and cover it with a warm pot and light the candle.

E. Once he has completed sounding the *shofar*, even if the warm pot is in one's hand, he may not cover [the cooked dish], but he leaves it on the ground.

F. Even if the candle is in his hand, he may not put it into the candle-holder, but he leaves it on the ground.

G. The minister of the synagogue leaves the trumpet up there on the roof and climbs down and goes his way.

H. R. Yosé says, "If he wanted to light afterward, he may do so."

I. They said to him, "You have placed a limit on your opinion.

J. "But there was a place on the top of the roof, where the minister of the synagogue leaves the trumpet."

T. 4:12 L p. 275, ls. 38-44

A. *On a festival which coincided with Friday, they sound the shofar and they do not say habdalah.*

B. *On a festival which coincided with Sunday, they say habdalah and they do not sound the shofar* [M. Hul. 1:7K-L].

C. How do they sound the *shofar*?

D. One plain one, and one does not sound the *teruʿah*-notes [cf. T. Hul. 1:26C].

T. 4:13 L p. 275, ls. 44-46

A. "Flute-playing overrides the restrictions of the Sabbath," the words of R. Yosé b. R. Judah.

B. And sages say, "It does not override the restrictions even of the festival day."

T. 4:14 L p. 275, ls. 46-47

T.'s glosses of M. are clear. M. 5:1A-C reject Yosé b. R. Judah's opinion.

5:6-8

A. On the first festival day of the Festival there were there thirteen bullocks, two rams, and one goat [Num. 29:13, 16].

B. There remained fourteen lambs for the eight priestly watches.

C. On the first day, six offer two each, and the remaining two, one each.

D. On the second day, five offer two each, and the rest, one each.

E. On the third day, four offer two each, and the rest, one each.

F. On the fourth day, three offer two each, and the rest offer one each.

G. On the fifth day, two offer two each, and the rest offer one each.
H. On the sixth day, one offers two, and the rest offer one each.
I. On the seventh, all of them are equal.
J. On the eighth, they go back to drawing lots, as on the [other] festivals.
K. They ruled: "Whoever offered a bullock one day should not offer one the next day.
L. "But they offer them in rotation."

M. 5:6

A. Three times a year all the priestly watches shared equally in the offerings of the feasts and in the division of the Show Bread.
B. At Pentecost they would say to him, "Here you have unleavened bread, here is leavened bread for you."
C. The priestly watch whose time of service is scheduled [for that week] is the one which offers the daily whole-offerings, the offerings brought by reason of vows and freewill offerings, and the other public offerings.
D. And it offers everything.
E. On a festival day which comes next to a Sabbath, whether before or after it, all of the priestly watches were equal in the division of the Show Bread.

M. 5:7

A. [If] a day intervened [between a festival-day and a Sabbath], the priestly watch which was scheduled for that time took ten loaves, and the one that stayed back [in the Temple] took two.
B. And on all other days of the year, the entering priestly watch took six, and the one going off duty took six.
C. R. Judah says, "The one coming on duty takes seven, and the one going off duty takes five."
D. The ones going on duty divide at the north, and the ones going off duty divide at the south.
E. [The priestly watch of] Bilgah always divided it in the south, and their ring was fixed, and their wall-niche was blocked up.

M. 5:8

At the end we deal with the priests' assignments in offering up the various public offerings for the Festival. There were twenty-four priestly watches, all of them allowed to share in the sacrifices. Sixteen of these were occupied with the sixteen beasts (A). Eight were left over for turns on the remainder of the Festival, B. C-I then spell out the consequences. On the first day six of the eight watches offer two sacrifices a piece, and two watches offer one, and so on down, in line with Num. 29:17-32. The point of K-L is that twenty-two priestly watches offer bullocks three times and two have only two turns. The reference, M. 5:6J, to other festivals, then generates the inclusion of M. 5:7, the shares of the priestly watches on other festivals. The principal interest is in the division of the Show Bread, M. 5:7A-B, E, M. 5:8. We recall (*Holy Things* II, pp. 159-161) that the Show Bread is removed from the table and replaced on the Sabbath. What is taken away is given out to the priests. Now, if all the priests are available, who gets it? All divide it, if all are present, M. 5:7E. But if there is an intervening day, e.g., if the festival fell on Thursday, then the priestly watch in charge for the following Sabbath took ten loaves. What about the watch which served the preceding week but remained in the Temple over the Sabbath, since it came so close to the festival? That watch took two. The dispute of B-C, D+E, provides some further information in line with B and completes the triplet, M. 5:7E, M. 5:8A, and M. 5:8B.

A. All the priestly courses repeat the offering of a bullock during the seven days of the Festival a second and a third time, except for the last two, which repeat but do not do it a third time [cf. M. 5:6 K-L].

B. R. Eleazar b. Parta and R. Eliezer b. Jacob say, "There was no drawing of lots for the offering of the fat parts of the goat.

C. "But whoever brought the limbs up the ramp is the one who brought up the fat parts of the goat" [cf. T. Yoma 1:11].

D. Abba Yosé b. Ḥanan says, "There was a drawing of lots only for the heads of the priestly watches alone.

E. "But the rest of all the watches take their turns."

F. R. Ḥanina b. Antigonos says, "There was a drawing of lots only for the first festival day of the Festival alone.

G. "And on all the other days of the Festival they take turns."

T. 4:15 L pp. 275-276, ls. 47-53

A. How do they draw lots?

B. They enter the hewn-stone chamber and stand round about it in the form of a spiral figure.

C. The supervisor comes and takes the mitre of one of them.

D. And then they know that from him the lot begins.

E. They did not put forth two by two, but one by one.

F. And individuals among them put out two by two.

G. But they did not count the extra [cf. T. Yoma 1:10].

T. 4:16 L p. 276, ls. 53-57

A. Now the last day of the Festival had a drawing of lots unto itself, a time unto itself, a festival unto itself, an offering unto itself, a song unto itself, a blessing unto itself,

B. since it says, *On the eighth day he sent the people away, and they blessed the king [and went to their homes joyful and glad of heart for all the goodness that the Lord had shown to David his servant and to Israel his people*] (I Kings 8:66).

T. 4:17 L p. 276, ls. 57-59

A. Is it possible that they did not require being kept overnight?

B. Scripture says, *On the twenty-third day of the seventh month he sent the people away to their homes,* [*joyful and glad of heart for the goodness that the Lord had shown to David and to Solomon and to Israel his people*] (II Chron. 7:10).

C. How so?

D. They took their leave while it was still day, then they went to sleep, and they went along [thereafter].

T. 4:18 L p. 276, ls. 59-61

A. *Daily whole offerings, the offerings brought by reason of vows and freewill offerings* [*and the other public offerings* (M. 5:8C)],

B. firstlings, tithes of cattle, and additional offerings of the Sabbath, sin-offerings of the community and their burnt-offerings, the obligatory burnt-offering of an individual—

C. the work of offering them up and the eating of them

D. [is to be done] by the scheduled priestly watch.

T. 4:19 L p. 277, ls. 62-63

A. The Two Loaves—the work of offering them and the eating of them are by all the priestly watches,

B. because they are brought as an obligation of the festival [when the priests of all watches are present].

T. 4:20 L p. 277, ls. 64-65

A. The Show Bread—the work of offering it is done by the scheduled priestly watch.

B. But the eating of it is done by all the priestly watches.

T. 4:21 L p. 277, ls. 65

A. What does he do?

B. He gives a half a loaf [of the twelve] to each priestly watches [of the twenty-four].

C. And they divide it up among themselves.

T. 4:22 L p. 277, ls. 66

A. R. Judah says, "This one who divides the Show Bread goes out and stands on the mosaic pavement of the porch.

B. "He divides a loaf and leaves it, and divides another loaf and leaves it, and each one comes and takes his share.

C. "For the priests who have suffered disqualifying blemishes they bring their share outside,

D. "for they are unable to enter the area between the porch and the altar" [T. Men. 11:13].

T. 4:23 L p. 277, ls. 67-70

A. The outgoing priestly watch offers the morning daily whole-offering and the additional offerings.

T. 4:24 L p. 277, ls. 70

A. The incoming [priestly watch] then offers the evening daily whole-offering and the Show Bread.
B. On what account does the incoming priestly watch divide up its share at the north?
C. Because that area is close to the place in which they carry out the liturgy.

T. 4:25 L p. 277, ls. 71-72

A. There were twenty-four rings,
B. one each for the twenty-four priestly watches.

T. 4:26 L p. 277, ls. 72-73

A. There were twenty-four niches there,
B. one for each of the twenty-four Levitical watches.

T. 4:27 L p. 277, ls. 73-74

A. [*The priestly watch of*] *Bilgah always divided it in the south, and their ring was fixed, and their wall niche was blocked up* [M. 5:8E],
B. because of Miriam, daughter of Bilgah, who apostasized.
C. She went off and married an officer of the Greek royal house.
D. And when the gentiles went into the sanctuary, she came along and stamped on the top of the altar, screaming at it, "Wolf, wolf! You have wiped out the fortune of Israel, and you [still] did not then stand up for them in the time of their trouble."
E. And some say it was because [the priestly watch of Bilgah] delayed in observing its priestly watch.
F. So the watch of Yeshebab went in and served in its stead.
G. Therefore Bilgah always appears to be among the outgoing priestly watches [at the south], and Yeshebab always appears to be among the incoming priestly watches [at the north].
H. Neighbors of the wicked normally receive no reward,
I. except for Yeshebab,
J. neighbor to Bilgah, who received a reward.

T. 4:28 L pp. 277-278, ls. 74-80

T. 4:15 goes over the ground of M. 5:6 and indicates that M.'s picture of the Temple procedure is not shared by all authorities. T. 4:24-25 augment M. 5:7E-5:8B, the interest in the work done by the incoming and outgoing priestly watches, over the course of the year.

APPENDIX

CORRECTIONS TO JACOB NEUSNER, *INVITATION TO THE TALMUD*

BY RICHARD S. SARASON
HEBREW UNION COLLEGE-JEWISH INSTITUTE OF RELIGION

p. 3, l. 13, for "though" read "thought"

p. 5, l. 9, for "160-150 B.C." read "160-50 B.C."

p. 17, l. 23, for "seats" read "eats"

p. 22, first line of large print, for "Zakkai as" read "Zakkai was"

p. 22, last line of large print, correct reference is to Avot de- Rabbi Natan, Recension A, Chapter 4 (ed. Schechter, p. 11a)

p. 30, RASHI is acronym for *R. Sh*elomo ben *Y*ishaq

p. 35, ls. 8-9 from bottom, read "*Zera-ʿim*"

p. 36, l. 11, chapter deals not with "blessing food", but with blessing (more correctly, praising) *God* for the gift of food. The food is not blessed, but is the occasion for acknowledging God as the ultimate source of food and sustenance (He is the owner of the Land, and the sender of fructifying rainfall). Same correction is to be made on pp. 42, 44 (cf. footnote there), *et passim*. Hebrew BRK ʿL is to be rendered, "to recite a blessing *over, for, concerning, with reference to*"

p. 39, l. 4 from bottom, omit comma after "inheritance"

pp. 42-43, text of *Birkat haMazon*, "Grace after Meals," is given according to the traditional Ashkenazic (North European) rite. The Mishnah does not know a set text with fixed wording, only fixed subjects or topical rubrics, mention of which must be made (cf. J. Heinemann, *Prayer In the Talmud*).

p. 49, middle paragraph, l. 5, "remaining crumbs will not be spoiled by the water": the issue is susceptibility to uncleanness (impurity). Dry goods are insusceptible to impurity. They become susceptible when moistened by any of the seven liquids enumerated at M. Makhshirin 6:4. A source of uncleanness which touches the moistened food-stuff now will render it unclean.

p. 54, l. 8 from bottom, for "would have been" read "would have seen"

APPENDIX

p. 56, l. 3, for "lands" read "hands"

p. 64, l. 3 from bottom, for "continual" read "regular"

p. 66, T. 5:26, read:

A. The House of Shammai say, "They wash the hands and afterward mix the cup, lest the liquids which are on the outer surface of the cup be made unclean on account of the hands, and *in turn* make the cup unclean."

B. The House of Hillel say, "The outer surface of the cup are *always deemed* clean."

Another explanation: "The washing of the hands *must always take place immediately before* the meal (i.e., must lead into the meal with no interruption between the two activities)."

p. 70, second paragraph, read: "The Hillelites say the scraps which are *susceptible to uncleanness* (they are pieces as large as an olive, *the quantity is considered by the rabbis to be food*) will be picked up by the water *before the washing. .*"

p. 73, T. 5:29, for "sweet oil" read "spiced oil"

p. 77, T. 5:31, insert the following sentence between A and B: "A lantern—even though he had not extinguished it (i.e., it has been burning throughout the Sabbath), he recites a benediction over it."

p. 77, first line after Tosefta text, for "Mishah" read "Mishnah"

p. 78, first line of Tosefta text, for "5:39" read "5:30"

p. 78, middle of page, "But we are not told what blessing is being said": in context, it is the *Habdalah* blessing

p. 79, end of second full paragraph, "Here it looks as though the Tosefta's lengthy sayings have been summarized by the Mishnah's": alternatively, the two formulations are autonomous of each other

p. 79, bottom of first column, read: "And the House of Hillel say, 'One recites a benediction for the *wine*, and afterwards recites a benediction for the *day*."

p. 80, bottom of first column, for "cloth" read "napkin"

p. 81, l. 4 of second column, for "pillow" read "napkin"

p. 82, second paragraph, the issue in M. 8:4/T. 5:28 is not oil, but scraps of food

p. 84, end of paragraph, for "While M. 8:6A looks like . . ." read "Tosefta cites and glosses Mishnah."

p. 84, T. 5:21 should read: "They answer 'Amen' after a blessing with the divine name *recited by a gentile*."

APPENDIX

p. 90, l. 16 from bottom, for "covey" read "convey"

p. 99; pp. 100-101, re: "the House of Hillel according to Meir," this is the version of the Houses' dispute found in Mishnah, which the *gemara'* assigns to Meir (cf. Rashi, *ad loc.*)

p. 102, middle paragraph, the problem is not wine drunk in connection with the Grace after Meals, but wine drunk before Grace

p. 103, middle paragraph, for "the man must bless the wine and say Grace" read "drink the wine and *then* say Grace"

p. 105, middle of page, read simply "We turn to the opinion of the House of Hillel"; what follows is *not* a citation of Tosefta, but the *gemara*'s own reasoning

p. 109, l. 1, for "After wiping his hand with" read "He dries his hand on"

p. 116, bottom of page, for "Isaiah 47:5" read "Isaiah 42:5"; also p. 154

p. 125, l. 6, for "eternal" read "external"

p. 128, middle of page, "The furnace may be blessed at the outset"; cf. Rashi: a benediction may be recited at the end, not at the outset, since the fire is lit for cooking, but afterwards chips are thrown in to give light—so also, p. 129, middle

p. 133, middle of B, for "finishing" read "scenting"

p. 134, line in bold type, read "They do not recite a benediction over the light until it has been used ..."

p. 136, bottom, for "But the Mishnah uses" read "But the *baraita* uses"

p. 137, middle of D, for "Zira" read "Zera"

p. 138, letter A, " 'The dispute ... a person deliberately" should not be italicized: the original is in Hebrew, not Aramaic

p. 140, D, for "Psalm 58:14" read "Psalm 68:14"; also p. 164

p. 145, middle, for "Leviticus 11:44" read "Leviticus 20:7"; also p. 166

p. 151, line in bold type face, "f" in "House *of* Shammai" should be set in bold face

p. 171, l. 9 from bottom, for "in Menstrual Women" read "on Menstrual Women"

p. 172, third bold face line, "f" in "House *of* Hillel" should be set in bold face

p. 177, l. 4 of large type, for "The food takes precedence" read "The day takes precedence"

p. 179, G, cf. p. 205, version of y. 8:8

p. 183, C, read "Levi said, 'Wine, light, Havdalah, sanctification."

p. 183, ls. 4-5 from bottom, the benediction referred to as *Birkat hazeman*—the "occasional" benediction—is *Shehehiyyanu*, "who has given us life, and sustained us, and brought us to this occasion"

p. 186, bottom, read "R. Meir says, 'For hands which are unclean and clean."

p. 187, middle, R. Abbahu . . ., read "This is what he said, '[If the water is] before him [i.e., on his way, in his vicinity, near at hand, he must proceed to find it and wash]. But if it is behind him [i.e., out of his way; he would have to backtrack], they do not trouble him [to obtain it and wash]."

p. 187, D, read "Regarding those who guard gardens and orchards [and who cannot leave their guard-posts], what do you do for them? [i.e., how do we rule in their case? Do we judge them to be] like those [for whom water is] on their way or like those who would have to backtrack?" (cf. Pene Moshe *ad loc.*)

p. 189, l. 10, for "hand may be unclean" read "hand be made unclean"

p. 190, middle, the second unit is not exactly "about the difficulty in finding wine"

p. 199, l. 5 from bottom, for "It remains clean" read "It remains unclean"

p. 201, l. 8 from bottom, for "Hillelites" read "Shammaites"

p. 208, middle of F, for "Job 37:2" read "Job 37:3"

p. 209, middle, read "Who created the fruit of the vine."

p. 212, end of D, read "they may be blessed" (i.e., a benediction may be recited over them)

p. 216, y. 8:7, second bold face line, "f" in "House of Shammai" should be set in bold face

p. 217, middle, y. text should read:

B. *Until when does he recite the benediction?*

R. Hiyya in the name of Samuel says, "Until the food has been digested in his bowels."

And sages say, "So long as he is thirsty on account of that meal."

R. Yohanan says, "Until he becomes hungry again."

INDEX TO BIBLICAL AND TALMUDIC REFERENCES

By Arthur Woodman, Canaan, New Hampshire

BIBLE

Amos
  2:6   123

II Chronicles
  5:9   98
  7:10   174
  36:10   42

Daniel
  1:5   59

Deuteronomy
  2:7   163
  6:18   25
  16:13-15   129
  16:14   144
  21:1-2   77
  21:9   25
  22:9   8

Ecclesiastes
  1:15   143
  2:14   145

Exodus
  12:12   147
  20:24   168
  23:19   57-58
  25:12   96-97
  26:31   56
  26:33   56, 96-97
  30:11-16   3
  30:16   12
  30:20-21   83
  32:31   123
  34:7   86, 122-123

Ezekiel
  3:20   122
  8:16   167
  47:1   160
  47:2   160
  47:3   160
  47:4   160-161
  47:5   161
  47:8   161
  47:9   162
  47:10   162

Ezra
  4:3   12
  36:25   121

Isaiah
  1:18   110
  5:1-2   163
  22:14   121
  33:21   161
  43:7   88

Jeremiah
  3:22   120
  10:2   147
  17:13   121

Job
  33:28-29   123

Joshua
  22:22   25

I Kings
  8:8   42
  8:47   86
  8:66   174
  19:19   73

II Kings
  12:16   44
  20:16-17   42
  21:16   77

Leviticus
  2:10   72
  5:15   44
  5:18   44
  5:19   44
  6:13   51
  6:21   77
  6:23   11
  14:10   39
  14:21   39
  Ch. 16   63, 112
  16:1-34   63
  16:3   68
  16:3-5   65
  16:5   29
  16:6   68, 70, 81

16:7   68
16:9   68, 93
16:11   68
16:12   68
16:13   74
16:14   68
16:15   68
16:18   68, 99
16:20   68, 103, 107
16:21   86
16:24   67, 113
16:26   109
16:26-32   63
16:27-28   104
16:29-34   69
16:30   85-86, 93, 107, 121
19:19   8
21:10   72
23:26-32   112
23:27   122
23:33-34   127-128
23:40   150

Numbers
4:35   59
8:24   59
19:1 ff.   29
21:17-18   162
21:19-20   162
28:7   163
28:23   114
29:7-11   63, 112
29:8   67, 113
29:11   113-114
29:12-38   128

29:13-16   166, 171
29:17-32   172
32:22   24-25, 89

Proverbs
3:4   24-25
10:7   87, 91
16:4   89
25:17   123
26:11   124

Psalms
16:10   122
28:17   122
50:2   98
51:3   124
78:20   162
89:32   121
105:41   162
106:6   86
Chs. 113-118   148, 152
Ch. 118   152
118:25   153, 157
127:1   75
134:1   169
134:2   169
134:3   169

Song of Songs
1:13   98
1:17   88

Zechariah
13:1   161
14:8   161
14:17-18   164

MISHNAH

Bekhorot
9:5   23

Besah
5:2   141

Hullin
1:7   171

Menahot
11:8   43

Shabbat
9:1   155

Shebiʿit
8:1-5   18
9:8   18

Sheqalim
1:1   4, 8-10
1:1-2   4, 8-10
1:1-5   8
1:1-7   4
1:2   4, 8-9
1:2-5   4
1:3   4, 8, 10-12
1:3-4   4, 10-12
1:4   4, 8, 11
1:5   4, 8, 12
1:6   13-15
1:6-7   4, 6, 8, 13-15
1:7   13-15
2:1   4, 16-17
2:1-5   4

2:2   4, 16-19
2:3   19-20
2:3-5 4, 16, 19-22
2:4   19-21
2:5   20-22
3:1   4, 23-24
3:1-4 4-5
3:2   24-25
3:2-3 5, 24-25
3:3   24
3:4   5, 25-27
4:1   5, 28-29
4:1-2 5, 28-30
4:1-5 28
4:1-9 5
4:2   29-30
4:3   5, 28, 30-31
4:4   5, 31
4:5   5, 28, 32
4:6   5, 32-33
4:6-9 28
4:7   34-35
4:7-8 5, 33-35
4:8   34-35
4:9   5, 28, 32, 35-36
5:1   5, 30, 37-39
5:1-2 5, 37
5:1-8:8 5-6
5:2   5, 38
5:3   39-40
5:3-5 5, 37, 39-40
5:3-6 5
5:4   39
5:5   39
5:6   5, 37, 40
5:6-8:8 5-6
6:1   41-43
6:1-3 6, 41-42
6:2   41-42
6:3   42
6:4   6, 41-43
6:5   42-47
6:5-6 6, 41, 43-48
6:6   44-46
7:1   6, 48-49, 51
7:1-8:3 6
7:2   6, 48-50
7:3   6, 48, 50
7:4   48, 51
7:4-7 6, 50-52
7:5   48, 51
7:5-7 51
7:6   51-52

7:6-7 48
7:7   51
8:1   6, 53-54
8:2   6, 53-54
8:3   6-7, 53-55
8:4   53, 55-57
8:4-7 6-7, 53, 55-57
8:4-8 6, 53
8:5   55-56
8:6   55
8:6-7 53, 57
8:7   55, 57
8:8   6, 53, 57-59

Sukkah
1:1   129, 132-133, 137-138, 141
1:1-2:3 129-130
1:1-3:15 129-130
1:2   129, 133, 141
1:2-3 132
1:3   129, 134-135
1:4   129, 135-137, 139
1:4-8 132
1:5   129, 135-136
1:6   130, 136-137
1:7   130, 136-137
1:8   130, 137
1:9   130, 137-138
1:9-10 132
1:10 130, 138
1:11 130, 132, 139
2:1   130, 140-142
2:1-3 140
2:2   130, 141
2:3   130, 140-142
2:4   140, 142-146
2:4-6 130, 142-143
2:4-9 130
2:5   140, 143-144
2:5-6 144
2:6   140, 143
2:7   140, 143-145
2:8   140, 143, 145
2:9   140, 143, 146-147
3:1   130, 148-150
3:1-3 148-149
3:1-15 130
3:2   130, 148-150
3:3   130, 148-150
3:4   130, 148-150
3:5   150-151
3:5-7 130, 148, 150-151
3:6   151

3:7   151
3:8   130, 148, 151-152
3:9   130, 152-154
3:9-11   148
3:10   130, 149, 153
3:11   130, 153-154
3:12   130, 154-155, 157
3:12-15   148
3:13   130, 154-155, 157
3:13-15   154-155
3:14   130, 154-155
3:15   130, 155
4:1   130, 156-160, 164, 166-167
4:1-3   156-157
4:1-5:4   130-131
4:1-5:8   130-131
4:2   131, 155-157
4:3   131, 156-157
4:4   131, 156-158
4:5   158-159
4:5-7   131, 156-159
4:6   158, 160
4:7   158
4:8   131, 156, 159
4:9   160, 163-164
4:9-10   131, 156, 159-166
4:10   160, 164
5:1   131, 156, 166-167, 171
5:1-4   166
5:2   166-167
5:2-4   131, 166
5:3   166
5:4   167-169
5:5   131, 156, 166, 169-171
5:6   166, 172-173, 175
5:6-8   131, 166, 171-175
5:7   166, 172-173, 175
5:7-8   166
5:8   172-175

Tamid
3:1   78
4:2   50

Yoma
1:1   65, 70-71
1:1-3   70-73
1:1-4   76
1:1-7   65
1:1-7:5   65
1:2   65, 70-72
1:3   65, 70-71
1:4   65, 73
1:4-8   73
1:5   65, 73-74
1:6   65, 73-74
1:7   65, 74-75
1:8   65, 74, 76
1:8-2:6   65-66
2:1   76-77
2:1-2   66, 76-77
2:1-4   76
2:2   76-78
2:3   77-80
2:3-4   66, 77-79
2:4   78
2:5   79
2:5-7   66, 76, 79-80
2:5-3:5   66
2:6   79
2:7   79-80
3:1   81-82
3:1-2   66
3:1-4   81-84
3:2   81-82
3:3   82-84, 114
3:3-4   66
3:4   66, 82, 84
3:5   66, 83-84
3:5-7   84-85
3:6   66, 84
3:6-7   68
3:6-8   66
3:7   84
3:8   68, 85-86, 93
3:8-9   81, 85
3:9   66, 68, 81, 85-87
3:9-5:7   66-67
3:10   87
3:10-11   66, 81, 87-91
3:11   87-91
4:1   66, 68, 85, 92-93
4:1-3   92
4:2   66, 93
4:2-3   68, 93-94
4:3   66, 92, 94-96, 98
4:4   94-95
4:4-6   67, 92, 94
4:5   95
4:6   95
5:1   96-97
5:1-2   67-68, 96-98
5:2   97-98
5:3   67-68, 96-100
5:3-4   102
5:4   67-68, 96, 99-102
5:5   67, 100-101

5:5-6   68, 96
5:6   67, 100-101, 103-104
5:7   67, 96, 101-104
6:1   67, 105-107
6:1-8   67
6:2   105, 107-108
6:2-4   67, 107-108
6:2-6   68, 105
6:3   108, 110
6:4   108
6:5   108-109
6:5-6   67, 108-109
6:6   109-111
6:7   105, 109-111, 113
6:7-8   67, 69, 109-111
6:8   67, 110
7:1   67, 110, 112-113
7:1-5   67
7:2   67, 112-113

7:3   112-114
7:3-4   67, 84, 113-115
7:4   112, 114
7:5   67, 112, 114-115
8:1   68, 116-119
8:1-7   68-69
8:1-9   68
8:2   68, 117-118
8:2-6   116
8:3   68, 117-118
8:4   68, 118-119, 145
8:5   119-120
8:5-6   117
8:5-7   68, 119-120
8:6   116, 119-120
8:7   116, 119
8:8   68, 116, 120-121
8:8-9   68
8:9   68, 116, 121-124

TOSEFTA

Ḥullin
  1:26   171

Menaḥot
  11:13   174

Shabbat
  2:14   134

Sheqalim
  1:1   9-10
  1:2   9-10
  1:3   9
  1:4   10
  1:5   10
  1:6   12
  1:7   12
  1:8   15
  1:9   17
  1:10   18
  1:11   19
  1:12   22
  2:1   25
  2:2   25
  2:3   26
  2:3-4   26
  2:4   26
  2:5   27
  2:6   30
  2:7   32
  2:8   31, 33
  2:9   33
  2:10   35

  2:11   36, 40
  2:12   36
  2:13   36
  2:14   38
  2:15   38
  2:16   40
  2:17   42
  2:18   42
  3:1   44
  3:2   45
  3:3   45
  3:4   45
  3:5   46
  3:6   46
  3:7   46
  3:8   46
  3:9   50
  3:10   50
  3:11   52
  3:12   52
  3:13   56
  3:14   56
  3:15   56
  3:16   57
  3:17   57-58
  3:18   58
  3:19   58
  3:20   46
  3:21   47
  3:22   58
  3:22-24   59
  3:23   58

3:24   58
3:25   58
3:26   59
3:27   59

Sukkah
1:1   133
1:2   133
1:3   133
1:4   133, 135
1:5   135-136
1:6   135
1:7   137
1:8   134-135, 138
1:9   135
1:10   139
1:11   142
1:12   142
1:13   142
2:1   144-145
2:2   144-145
2:3   145
2:4   146-147
2:5   146
2:6   147
2:7   150
2:8   150
2:9   151
2:10   152
3:1   158-159
3:2   159
3:3 (4)   160
3:5   161
3:6   161
3:7 (8)   161
3:9   162
3:10   162
3:11   162-163
3:12   162
3:13   163
3:14   163
3:14-17   165
3:15   163
3:16   164-165
3:17   164
3:18   164-165
4:1   168
4:2   168
4:3   168
4:4   168
4:5   168
4:6   169
4:7   169

4:8   169
4:9   169
4:10   169-170
4:11   170
4:12   171
4:13   171
4:14   171
4:15   173
4:16   173
4:17   174
4:18   174
4:19   174
4:20   174
4:21   174
4:22   174
4:23   174
4:24   175
4:24-25   175
4:25   175
4:26   175
4:27   175
4:28   175

Yoma
1:1   71
1:2   71
1:2-3   71
1:3   71
1:4   72
1:5   72
1:6   73
1:7   73
1:8   75
1:9   75
1:10   77, 173
1:11   78, 173
1:12   77
1:13   77, 80
1:14   80
1:15   82
1:16   83-84
1:17   83
1:18   83
1:19   83
1:20   83-84
1:21   84
1:22   85
1:23   85
2:1   86
2:2   86-87
2:3   87
2:4   88
2:5   89

2:6   89
2:7   90
2:8   91
2:9   92
2:10 93
2:11 95
2:12 97
2:13 98
2:14 98
2:15 98
2:16 100
3:1   101
3:2   102
3:3   102, 104
3:4   102, 104
3:5   103
3:5-6 104
3:6   103
3:7   103-104
3:8   104
3:9   106
3:10 106-107
3:11 107
3:12 107
3:13 108

3:14 109
3:15 110-111
3:16 111
3:17 111
3:18 112
3:19 114
3:20 114
4:1   118
4:2   118
4:3   118
4:4   120
4:5   117, 120-121
4:6   120
4:7   121
4:8   121
4:9   122
4:10 122
4:11 122
4:12 122
4:13 123
4:14 124
4:15 124
4:16 124
4:17 124

GENERAL INDEX

Abba Saul, Day of Atonement, conduct of Temple rite, 71; Feast of Tabernacles, rites and offerings, 158; *sheqel*-tax for altar use, 29-30

Abba Yośe b. Ḥanan, Day of Atonement, conduct of Temple rite, 82; Feast of Tabernacles, rites and offerings, 173

ʿAqiba, Day of Atonement: conduct of Temple rite, 77-78, 90, 92, 104, 113-114; laws governing, 118, 121, 123; Feast of Tabernacles: *lulab* and *etrog*, 149, 153; rites and offerings, 164; *sheqel*-tax: for altar use, 30-34; collection of, 12; support of Temple, 55-57

Ben ʿAzzai, Day of Atonement, conduct of Temple rite, 77-78, 90; *sheqel*-tax: for altar use, 23-24, 32-33; collection of, 15; support of Temple, 39

Ben Bukhri, *sheqel*-tax, collection of, 10-11

Ben Zoma, Day of Atonement, conduct of Temple rite, 82

Day of Atonement: conduct of Temple rite, 65-67, 70-115; laws governing, 68, 116-124

Dosa, Feast of Tabernacles, *sukkah* and obligations, 139

Eleazar, Day of Atonement: conduct of Temple rite, 102-104; laws governing, 118, 122; *sheqel*-tax: for altar use, 23-24, 34-35; collection of, 14

Eleazar b. ʿAzariah; Day of Atonement, laws governing, 121

Eleazar b. Parta, Feast of Tabernacles, rites and offerings, 173

Eleazar b. R. Ṣadoq, Feast of Tabernacles: *lulab* and *etrog*, 152; *sukkah* and obligations, 144; rites and offerings, 163

Eleazar b. R. Yośe, Day of Atonement, conduct of Temple rite, 100

Eliezer, Day of Atonement: conduct of Temple rite, 93, 100-101, 103, 109, 113-114; laws governing, 116; Feast of Tabernacles, *sukkah* and obligations, 132, 134-135, 139-140, 143-144; rites and offerings, 158-159; *sheqel*-tax: for altar use, 5, 28, 34-35; support of Temple, 42, 55-57

Eliezer b. Jacob, Day of Atonement: conduct of Temple rite, 78, 88; laws governing, 124; Feast of Tabernacles, rites and offerings, 158, 160, 173; *sheqel*-tax, support of Temple, 41

Eliezer b. Simeon, Day of Atonement: conduct of Temple rite, 83; laws governing, 124

Ezra, *sheqel*-tax, collection of, 12

Feast of Tabernacles: *lulab* and *etrog*, 130-131, 148-155; *sukkah* and obligations, 129-130, 132-147; rites and offerings, 130-131, 156-175

Gamaliel, Feast of Tabernacles: *lulab* and *etrog*, 153, 155; *sukkah* and obligations, 140, 143; *sheqel*-tax: for altar use, 24; support of Temple, 41-42

Ḥananiah, Prefect of Priests, Day of Atonement, conduct of Temple rite, 71-72; *sheqel*-tax: for altar use, 31; support of Temple, 41

Ḥanina b. Antigonos, Feast of Tabernacles, rites and offerings, 173

Ḥanina b. Gamaliel, Day of Atonement, conduct of Temple rite, 73

Heave-offering, *sheqel*-tax for altar use, 4-5, 23-36

Hillel the Elder, Feast of Tabernacles: rites and offerings, 168

Hillel, House of, Feast of Tabernacles; *lulab* and *etrog*, 150-151, 153; *sukkah* and obligations, 132, 136, 140, 143, 145; *sheqel*-tax, support of Temple, 50, 55-57

Ilaʿiʾ, Feast of Tabernacles, *sukkah* and obligations, 144

Ishmael, Day of Atonement, conduct of Temple rite, 92-93, 110; laws governing, 120; Feast of Tabernacles, *lulab* and *etrog*, 149; *sheqel*-tax, for altar use, 24-25, 30-31

Ishmael b. R. Yosé, Feast of Tabernacles, *sukkah* and obligations, 139; *sheqel*-tax, for support of Temple, 52

Jacob, Feast of Tabernacles, *sukkah* and obligations, 142

Jehoida, *sheqel*-tax for support of Temple, 44

Joshua, Day of Atonement, conduct of Temple rite, 77-78; Feast of Tabernacles, *lulab* and *etrog*, 153; *sheqel*-tax, for altar use, 5, 28, 34-35

Joshua b. Ḥananiah, Feast of Tabernacles, rites and offerings, 168

Judah, Day of Atonement: conduct of Temple rite, 70-71, 78, 82-83, 88-89, 93-95, 99-102, 104-108, 110-111, 114; laws governing, 120, 122; Feast of Tabernacles: *lulab* and *etrog*, 148-149, 151, 155; *sukkah* and obligations, 130, 132-133, 135-137, 140-142; rites and offerings, 157, 159-160, 163-164, 167-169, 172, 174; *sheqel*-tax, collection of, 8-10, 19, 21; support of Temple, 38, 42-43, 45, 51, 56-57

Judah b. Laqqish, *sheqel*-tax for support of Temple, 42

Judah b. Paterah, Day of Atonement, conduct of Temple rite, 71; laws governing, 123

Lieberman, Saul, Day of Atonement, conduct of Temple rite, 104; *sheqel*-tax for altar use, 36

Lulab and *etrog*, Feast of Tabernacles, 130-131, 148-155

Maimonides, Feast of Tabernacles, *lulab* and *etrog*, 154

Mattiah b. Ḥarash, Day of Atonement, laws governing, 119

Meir, Day of Atonement: conduct of Temple rite, 72, 84, 86, 95, 101, 108, 110-111; laws governing, 123; Feast of Tabernacles, *lulab* and *etrog*, 151-152; *sukkah* and obligations, 130, 136, 142, 146; *sheqel*-tax: for altar use, 26-27; collection of, 13-15, 20-21; support of Temple, 54

Menaḥem, Day of Atonement, conduct of Temple rite, 94

Nathan, *sheqel*-tax, collection of, 20, 22

Offerings: Feast of Tabernacles, 130-131, 156-175; Heave-offering for altar use, 4-5, 23-26; *sheqel*-tax, collection of, 4, 8-22

Pappyas, *sheqel*-tax, for altar use, 34

Poll tax, collection of *sheqel*-tax, 4, 8-22

Ṣadoq, Day of Atonement, conduct of Temple rite, 77; Feast of Tabernacles, *sukkah* and obligations, 143

Shammai the Elder, Day of Atonement, laws governing, 118

Shammai, House of, Feast of Tabernacles: *lulab* and *etrog*, 150-151, 153; *sukkah* and obligations, 132, 136, 140, 143-145; *sheqel*-tax, collection of, 4, 16, 19; support of Temple, 50, 55-57

Sheqel-tax: for altar use, 4-5, 23-36; collection of, 4, 8-22; support of Temple, 5-7, 37-59

Simeon, Day of Atonement, conduct of Temple rite, 101-104, 107, 109-111; Feast of Tabernacles, *sukkah* and obligations, 140, 142; *sheqel*-tax, collection of, 18-19, 21; support of Temple, 42, 51, 55, 57-58

Simeon b. Eleazar, Day of Atonement, laws governing, 117; Feast of Tabernacles, *sukkah* and obligations, 142; *sheqel*-tax, for altar use, 27

Simeon b. Gamaliel, Day of Atonement, laws governing, 116; Feast of Tabernacles; *sukkah* and obligations, 144, rites and offerings, 168; *sheqel*-tax, support of Temple, 55

Simeon Shezuri, *sheqel*-tax, collection of, 15

Sukkah, Feast of Tabernacles, 129-130, 132-147

Taxation, *sheqel*-tax, collection and use of, 4-7, 8-59

Temple support, *sheqel*-tax for, 5-7, 37-59

Yoḥanan, Feast of Tabernacles, *sukkah* and obligations, 135, 145

Yoḥanan b. Beroqah, Feast of Tabernacles, rites and offerings, 158

Yoḥanan b. Haḥorani, Feast of Tabernacles, *sukkah* and obligations, 143, 145

Yoḥanan b. Nuri, Day of Atonement, conduct of Temple rite, 90

Yoḥanan ben Zakkai, Feast of Tabernacles: *lulab* and *etrog*, 154; *sukkah* and obligations, 143; *sheqel*-tax, collection of, 11

Yosé, Day of Atonement: conduct of Temple rite, 72, 78, 94-98, 103-104, 107-108; laws governing, 117, 122; Feast of Tabernacles: *lulab* and *etrog*, 151, 154-155; *sukkah* and obligations, 138, 142, 144; rites and offerings, 163, 171; *sheqel*-tax: for altar use, 26-27, 29, 35; support of Temple, 50-52, 54, 59

Yosé the Galilean, *sheqel*-tax, collection of, 12

Yosé b. R. Judah, Day of Atonement, laws governing, 116; Feast of Tabernacles: *sukkah* and obligations, 142; rites and offerings, 164, 171; *sheqel*-tax for altar use, 24